Sustainable Development Goals Series

The **Sustainable Development Goals Series** is Springer Nature's inaugural cross-imprint book series that addresses and supports the United Nations' seventeen Sustainable Development Goals. The series fosters comprehensive research focused on these global targets and endeavours to address some of society's greatest grand challenges. The SDGs are inherently multidisciplinary, and they bring people working across different fields together and working towards a common goal. In this spirit, the Sustainable Development Goals series is the first at Springer Nature to publish books under both the Springer and Palgrave Macmillan imprints, bringing the strengths of our imprints together.

The Sustainable Development Goals Series is organized into eighteen subseries: one subseries based around each of the seventeen respective Sustainable Development Goals, and an eighteenth subseries, "Connecting the Goals", which serves as a home for volumes addressing multiple goals or studying the SDGs as a whole. Each subseries is guided by an expert Subseries Advisor with years or decades of experience studying and addressing core components of their respective Goal.

The SDG Series has a remit as broad as the SDGs themselves, and contributions are welcome from scientists, academics, policymakers, and researchers working in fields related to any of the seventeen goals. If you are interested in contributing a monograph or curated volume to the series, please contact the Publishers: Zachary Romano [Springer; zachary.romano@springer.com] and Rachael Ballard [Palgrave Macmillan; rachael.ballard@palgrave.com].

Pinki Mathur Anurag ·
Santwana Dwivedy
Editors

Violence in Intimate Spaces

Law and Beyond

Springer

Editors
Pinki Mathur Anurag
Jindal Global Law School
O. P. Jindal Global University
Sonipat, India

Santwana Dwivedy
Jindal Global Law School
O. P. Jindal Global University
Sonipat, India

ISSN 2523-3084 ISSN 2523-3092 (electronic)
Sustainable Development Goals Series
ISBN 978-981-97-2656-1 ISBN 978-981-97-2657-8 (eBook)
https://doi.org/10.1007/978-981-97-2657-8

This Springer imprint is published by the registered company Springer Nature Singapore Pte Ltd.
The registered company address is: 152 Beach Road, #21-01/04 Gateway East, Singapore 189721, Singapore

In the Hope of Light
Hamsini Marada, Assistant Professor, Jindal Global Law School

Conjuring

There is a conjuring
within us all
a whisper in the air
a call to arms
like an incarnation
or the beginning
of the kind of storm
that brings about
change,
transformation.

Some call it
sisterhood,
Some call it
Feminism
But another word
for this paradigm shift
is simply called
revolution.

Nikita Gill[1]

---

[1]Nikita Gill, Wild Embers—Poems of Rebellion, Fire and Beauty, Trapeze, Orion Publishing Group, London, 2017.

Foreword

Before we even begin to approach this book, we need to define for ourselves what *the intimate* is. We can be in a crowd and yet be intimate; we can have no tactile connection or relationship and yet be intimate. There is no one size fits all, nor is there a singular specific way of being intimate. Now, is there a heterosexual norm which permits intimacy? Why is intimacy so important for us to become the subject matter of a book such as this? It is because intimacy is a human need to live a meaningful life. Viewed from this perspective, it becomes a right—not just a right confined to the bedroom; it goes beyond that to the several spaces and relationships we occupy during our lifetime. Hence, before one begins to look at violence in intimate spaces, we need to look at intimacy as a right and as a human good.

This book presents perspectives on violence that shift our attention to substantive roots of violence by examining institutions not simply as the cause of violence, but as 'spaces' where institutionalized forms of violence thrive, but ought not to, if overall human happiness is the goal of our existence. The foremost point that this book makes is that it is unacceptable to tolerate patriarchy as the governing principle of intimate relationships. It is now accepted that violence subordinates several groups, subgroups, and individuals to the will of the person or a group of persons who wield the power in relationships in a given situation. While historically the focus of private violence has been restricted to violence perpetrated against a married cis-woman by her husband and the marital family, voices on non-binary and transgender persons as victims of violence by their natal families, the community, and the lashing out of religious sensibilities need to get louder. Although marriage and family remain violent spaces in the way these institutions perpetuate patriarchy and reinforce gender norms, they have the approval and sanction of the community, religious institutions, and our courts. The real contribution of non-heterosexual relationships to the advancement of human values is that they compel women in heteronormative relationships to re-examine their tacit acceptance of violence as natural. The socio-cultural conditioning to preserve the relationship at all costs despite the oppression in such intimate dynamics leads to the disregard of the individual right to a violence-free safe relationship. Cis-women thus have a vested interest in liberating the law from patriarchy and therefore redefining the intimate assumes primary importance for them.

Chapters in this volume present instances of significant shifts in the perception of heteronormatively organized families as violent but normal, where individual autonomy and choice have no space. We must however be brave in calling out violence for what it is and not simply as a lack of choice. What is this hegemony of heteronormative family structures which is unquestioningly accepted as a norm and superior to other forms of relationships? Chapter authors have demonstrated that gender-based harm takes several forms and exists in several intimately organized spaces, especially those sanctioned by law and society. Violence comes disguised in different forms depending on circumstances and context to serve the purpose of dominance and as a mode to demolish the victim. And yet, this is not an argument for gender neutrality of anti-violence laws, but rather for a law to address all forms of violence in multiple forms of relations regardless of the sex or gender of those involved in a relationship. The objective is to magnify the hitherto hidden and normalized dynamics of dominance and subordination which sustain such myriad forms of violence.

Violence is not the exclusive preserve of heterosexual men. Are only men violent as is depicted in popular normative discourse? While most violence is perpetuated by men, the reality of family violence well disguised as a tool of discipline is perpetrated by women as much as men. The causes and consequences of violence by women against women, especially in the context of communal violence to safeguard the 'honour', are too numerous to document but are a well-researched subject. However, that it exists cannot be denied; it has also been suggested that sitcoms such as *Kyunki Saas Bhi Kabhi Bahu Thi* have contributed hugely to this trend. Given that Bollywood tends to be the role model for a life of aspiration, what is depicted on sitcoms matters, and is a reflection of society and its tolerance for violence as a mode of control and dominance.

During the drafting of the first civil law on domestic violence in India, the *Protection of Women from Domestic Violence Act, 2005* (PWDVA), utmost care was taken to ensure that the law addresses all types of violence that occur within the four walls of intimate spaces between adults. Mindful that the *domestic* has always been a site for violence, all relationships between persons residing in a *shared household* who have a *domestic relationship* with each other were placed at the centre of the law. However, it was specifically ensured that the beneficiary of protection under the law was the woman in the household or in a domestic relationship with the abuser. The assumption was that men had several other means to approach the law and had the ability to deny women their rights by sheer animal force. Traditionally, conversations on domestic violence have remained confined to violence between married heteronormative partners, even by the women's rights movement. There have been scant conversations about violence inflicted within the institution of family that makes every member of the family vulnerable. In India before the PWDVA, Section 498A of the Indian Penal Code (the substantive criminal code in the country) existed, this provision attempted to address violence directed at a married woman by a member of the marital family *unit*. However, the carceral challenges of this provision prompted the search for a civil remedy which could afford a swift remedy and would be more accessible to women trapped in violent homes.

The civil law widened the idea of the *domestic* and thereby acknowledged the existence of the domestic as an inherent site for violence.

The heterosexual marriage remains at the centre of intergenerational, patrilineal families. The marital rape exception in the Indian Penal Code is one of the most glaring legal inequalities within marriage. The justification for and the insistence by the legislature in retaining the exception is that a husband cannot rape his wife unless she is below fifteen years of age (now 18 years by judicial interpretation). The High Court of Karnataka in 2022 gave a judgement in support of putting the husband on trial for sexually assaulting his wife. While the arguments presented in this judgement lacked rigour, it sparked my imagination and it is now my contention that a husband can be prosecuted for rape of his wife under the law as it stands today and the Indian Supreme Court is looking at the issue currently, to determine the interpretation of the law definitively. The state government has in the meantime refused to quash the rape charges filed by the wife, thereby defying the exception in the Indian Penal Code. The court has called upon law makers to acknowledge 'voices of silence' and 'rape as rape' irrespective of the relationship between the rapist and the victim. The High Court has also held that a husband cannot treat his wife as a 'sex slave'. In court, I contend that it is not the *degree of violence* that matters but whether the sex is 'against her will', that sex by a man with his wife against her will is not sex but sexual violence. This case has revived the conversation on marital rape which can also be seen as a challenge to the so-called 'exception' earlier in the High Court of Delhi leading to a split decision in the Division Bench deciding this case. Reading the two judgments is very enlightening as they demonstrate the emotional hype around the issue of 'an ideal marriage' and the need to preserve the family, once again compelling us to redefine *marriage* and *family* as the collection of chapters in this volume truly does.

The limitations of the judiciary in its interpretation and approach to social issues were evident in the recent same-sex marriage judgement where the Supreme Court of India urged the Parliament to consider a change in laws to accommodate persons of same-sex desirous of marriage in the name of equality and non-discrimination. Once again it was culture and custom that ruled the day, rather than the law of life by which we live. The ideal notion of a family is also observed in the words of the Supreme Court in its recent order while deciding the petition of a 44-year-old single woman seeking permission to become a mother through surrogacy. The Supreme Court opined that, in India, being a mother outside the institution of marriage is not the norm and that the "*woman cannot have everything in life*" reinforcing regressive ideas and norms of ideal motherhood and family, the ramifications of which have been explored in one of the chapters that narrates the violence in motherhood.

The judicial imagination clearly dictates normative scripts on how we must lead our lives in our most private and intimate spaces by ignoring the myriad other ways of interactions in the intimate and choices that must be seen as an essential human right. By privileging the ideal image of a *family* in judicial and legal discourse, there is consistent disregard for alternate ways of intimacies based on care, compassion, and a strong sense of community where individual rights bloom and tolerance for individual choice flourishes. It is my hope that such alternative ways of kinship become the norm. This lens of hope envisions the formulation of the *intimate* as a space which nurtures the autonomy of the individual in relationships by re-negotiating the imbalances of power on the path to an egalitarian society.

Violence in Intimate Spaces—Law and Beyond should be essential reading for all who shy away from facing the widespread existence of violence as well as those who wish to understand the evolution of private forms of violence based on contemporary feminist theory.

New Delhi, India

Indira Jaising
Senior Advocate
Supreme Court of India

Acknowledgements

This book is a labour of love that rests on the strong shoulders of our friends that carry the lessons and the burden of their lived experiences, thoughts, ideas, and beliefs.

Our contributors have been amazing! They are academics, activists, and researchers whose exceptionally brilliant research and writing have found their way into the deeply insightful chapters that enrich the intellectual tapestry of this volume.

Warmest appreciation to our reviewers Albeena Shakil, Aashita Dawer, Saptarshi Mandal, Deblina Dey, Swapnil Dhanraj, Anmol Diwan, and Arijeet Ghosh for providing invaluable in-depth inputs. Your commitment to academic excellence has been instrumental in maintaining the scholarly rigour of this volume.

Immense gratitude to Ms. Indira Jaising for graciously agreeing to write the foreword for the volume.

Our heartfelt gratitude to Prof. (Dr.) C. Raj Kumar, Professor and Founding Vice Chancellor, O. P. Jindal Global University, India, for ensuring an institutional space that promotes academic freedom and exemplary opportunities for intellectual growth conducive to extensive academic research and publishing. We are ever indebted to Prof. (Dr.) S. G. Sreejith, Executive Dean, Jindal Global Law School (JGLS) for his unwavering support, guidance, and encouragement. Prof. Dipika Jain as the Vice Dean, Research, JGLS ensures meaningful collaborations and critical engagement with research and writing. We truly value the thriving research and learning community created by you at JGLS, you inspire us every day!

Thank you Albeena Shakil for your exceptional guidance. Your spirit, laughter, and intellect inspire us every day. Hamsini Marada, thank you for generously offering your beautiful artwork, 'In the Hope of Light', it truly embodies the spirit of this volume.

Student interns Deveshi Chand, Nysa Khandelwal, and Adithi Rajesh provided invaluable research assistance. Our colleagues at the Centre for Human Rights Studies (CHRS), JGLS, for moral support and encouragement through the book's journey.

A warm thank you to Noopur Singh at Springer Nature for her patience and hard work in seeing this volume to its completion.

Our family for being our strength and unwavering support from the moment of conceptualization to the point of completion.

Kasturi, Dillip, Sukanya, Mahesh and Maanya.

Aakriti and Avi.

Thank you Vineet Anurag for keeping us awake with endless coffee and food during the last critical weeks of work on the manuscript.

Pinki Mathur Anurag
Santwana Dwivedy

Contents

Editors and Contributors

About the Editors

Pinki Mathur Anurag is Associate Professor and Director, Centre for Human Rights Studies at Jindal Global Law School, O.P. Jindal Global University, India. Prior to joining academics, she was Technical Director at the Lawyers Collective, India. Pinki co-edited "*Conflict in the Shared Household, Domestic Violence and the Law in India*" (2019, with Indira Jaising). Her research interests include gender, ageism and the law and international human rights law.

Santwana Dwivedy is Assistant Professor and Assistant Director, Centre for Human Rights Studies at Jindal Global Law School, O.P. Jindal Global University, India. Prior to this, she was Assistant Professor at KIIT Law School, KIIT University, Bhubaneswar. She was also Advocate at Supreme Court of India , Legal Consultant at the Women Safety Division in the Ministry of Home Affairs, Government of India and has also served as Legislative Assistant to a Member of Parliament of India (LAMP Fellow). Her areas of teaching and research are human rights and criminal justice, specifically issues of gender violence and the relationship between law and gender equality.

Contributors

Wungreithan Awungshi is a Ph.D. candidate at the Tata Institute of Social Sciences, Mumbai, India. His research interests include culture, identity, gender, folklore, peacebuilding, and social exclusion. He is currently researching "The influence of Korean wave: Articulating culture through the lived experience of Naga youth" which explores the complex relationship between Naga cultural identity and external influences within the Naga community. He holds an M.Phil. in Inclusive Development and Social Justice, and a Master's degree in Peace and Conflict Studies. In 2021, he was selected to participate in the Empower Leadership SDGs and Human Rights (ELSAH) programme for South Asia organized by the Korean Association of Human Rights Studies (KAHRS). He was also selected as the representative from India for the ELSAH Training of Trainers (ToT) programme in Asia. This programme provided comprehensive training on advocacy and policy engagement related to the Sustainable Development Goals (SDGs) using a human rights-based approach at both national and international levels. He was a Team Lead at Grassroot in Shillong, India, contributing to the conception and implementation of the project "*Strengthening Women's Voice in Land Resources Governance*" for the International Indigenous Women Forum (FIMI) under the AYNI project in Imphal, Manipur. He presented a paper titled "Beyond Spirits: Contemporary Narratives of State Atrocities as Modern Folklore" at a conference "Re-Imagining Northeast Writing and Narratives: Literature, Border, Ethnicity, and Cultural Imagination in 2023" organized by the Jamia Millia Islamia, New Delhi, India.

Niharika Banerjea is Professor at Jindal Global Law School (JGLS), O. P. Jindal Global University, Sonipat, India. Niharika completed her Ph.D. in Sociology at University at Buffalo, The State University of New York, in 2007. Her research and teaching interests and commitments are in the areas of gender-sexuality studies, queer studies, social theory, transnational feminisms, queer feminist, and collaborative methodologies. Niharika identifies as an academic-activist, as a way to critically address familiar binaries between academia and activism—in classrooms, activist spaces, and writing practices. Across all these sites, along with her co-thinkers, co-writers, and co-workers, Niharika tries to make 'theory' relevant to interrogate everyday hegemonic relations and self-referential understandings of 'lived experiences'. At the same time, she invests in bringing the complexes of lived experiences to interrogate familiar theoretical endeavours. Niharika also identifies as queer, and this identification includes an assemblage of socio-political histories of varied journeys, rather than as an already arrived moment.

Poushali Basak is Ph.D. scholar at Advanced Centre for Women's Studies, Tata Institute of Social Sciences, Mumbai, India. Poushali's academic research focuses on histories of feminist and queer movements, queer lives and liveabilities, citizenship rights and right to the city, public education, place-making, and urban studies. Her M.Phil. work focuses on the history of sex workers' organizing and negotiating developmental governance, and her doctoral thesis is about the histories of autonomous women's collectives in India. Poushali is part of Forum against Oppression of Women (an autonomous feminist organization working since 1980s) in Bombay, India, Sappho for Equality (a queer feminist LBTQ organization, 1999), and Feminists in Resistance (an autonomous feminist collective, 2019) in Kolkata, India.

Brototi Dutta is an intersectional feminist lawyer currently working as the Advocacy Adviser at the Asia programme in the Centre for Reproductive Rights, Delhi, India. Her research interests revolve around feminist engagements with the law, including how law and its instrumentalities develop narratives of and about women, issues of consent and autonomy, and decolonial analysis of courts and jurisprudence. She holds an LL.M. in Human Rights Law from National Law School of India University (NLSIU), Bengaluru, India, and is currently pursuing her doctoral work at the Tata Institute of Social Sciences, Hyderabad, India. She has worked extensively on gender, violence against women, sexual and reproductive health and rights (SRHR), and law and human rights issues. She has previously worked with Lawyers Collective, The Centre for Law and Policy Research, as a Senior Consultant with the Ministry of Women and Child Development, Government of India, and with UN agencies in India in various capacities. She has co-authored a Handbook for Judges and was a contributing author of the chapter *'Of Keeps' and 'Concubines': Rights of Cohabitees under Domestic Violence Act'* in *Conflict in the Shared Household: The Law and Domestic Violence in India* (OUP 2019, Eds. Indira Jaising, Pinki Mathur Anurag). She has also written policy papers and opinion pieces on women's rights and SRHR issues.

Diditi Mitra is Associate Professor of Sociology at Brookdale Community College, New Jersey, USA. Her research focuses on race and immigration. Diditi has authored "*Punjabi Immigrant Mobility in the United States: Adaptation through Race and Class*" (Palgrave Macmillan 2012). She has also co-edited a collection of essays on race, ethnicity, and age titled "*Race and the Lifecourse: Readings from the Intersection of Race, Ethnicity and Age*" (Palgrave Macmillan 2014) and has also published numerous peer-reviewed academic articles. Most recently, Diditi served on the executive board of Eastern Sociological Society as well as co-chaired the committee on community colleges at the organization. Diditi currently serves on the editorial board of Sikh Research Journal as the book review editor. Diditi is also a Kathak dancer.

Kolika Mitra is a sociologist and queer rights activist who currently identifies as gender-free/agender. Kolika is a member of the West Bengal Transgender Development Board under the Department of Women and Child Development and Social Welfare, Government of West Bengal, India. They are an independent researcher and teach Sociology at Rabindra Bharati University, Kolkata, India. They have completed their Ph.D. in Sociology from Jawaharlal Nehru University (JNU), New Delhi, India. Challenging heteronormative power structures from every possible angle is the biggest boost in their life.

Varsha Mohan is Assistant Professor and Fellow at the Center for Human Rights Studies (CHRS) Jindal Global Law School (JGLS), O. P. Jindal Global University, Sonipat, India. Her research centres around migration and citizenship in the global south, specifically in post-colonial citizenship policies, rights of non-citizens, intersection between technology and migration, and the overlaps between migration and labour law. She graduated with an LL.M. in Global Governance and Human Rights from Tel Aviv University, Israel. She also served as an Assistant Editor in Theoretical Inquiries in Law, a journal by De Gruyter publications at Tel Aviv University, Israel. She teaches Labour Law and Human Rights, Migration, and Citizenship. She was faculty at Nirma University, Ahmedabad, India, and National Law University, Jodhpur, India, where she taught courses on International Humanitarian and Human Rights Law.

Ezinwanne Roseline Raymond is a lawyer with research and teaching experience in socio-legal studies. She is Associate Lecturer at York St. John University, York, UK, and a Policy Officer at Nottingham Women's Centre, UK. Her areas of teaching and research interests span across law and society, gender, human rights, and jurisprudence. She has experience working with international, national, and regional institutions including the European Court of Human Rights, where she conducted research on the court's jurisprudence on human trafficking. She has previously worked with the International Nuremberg Principles Academy, Germany, where she supported the development of the *Sexual Crimes in Conflict Database*. She was a visiting scholar at the University of Toronto, Canada, in 2018. She has conducted several research projects across Canada, Germany, Nigeria, and the UK on a variety of topics and has three forthcoming publications.

Prabha Sridevan (Retd.) is a former judge of the Madras High Court, India (2000–2010), and former Chairperson of the Intellectual Property Appellate Board, India (2011–2013). Her judgments have dealt with pertinent human rights issues such as the right to freedom of speech, protection of heritage buildings, rights of oppressed classes, rights of persons with disabilities, gender equality, the economic worth of a homemaker's work, compulsory licensing of a cancer drug, and challenge by Novartis to India's Patent Act. She was named one of 50 most influential persons in the world of Intellectual property in 2012, 2013, and 2015. She was also named one of World IP Review's Influential Women in Intellectual Property 2020. She writes in English and Tamil on issues of law and life. "*Seeing in the Dark*" (OUP 2015), a collection of short stories by Chudamani, was her first work of translation. Her second work of translation of Chudamani's short stories "*Echoes of the Veena*" (Ratna Books 2018) won the Valley of Words (VOW) Award, 2019, for best translation. Her third book of translation is "*Meeran's Stories*" (Ratna Book 2022). She has translated other writers, like Seeta Ravi, Imayam, Meeran, Ravikumar, and S. Ramakrishnan. Recently, she has translated a collection of short stories by Imayam, titled "*If there is a God and other stories*" (Ratna Books 2022).

Devyani Tewari is Assistant Professor of Legal Practice at Jindal Global Law School (JGLS), O. P. Jindal Global University, Sonipat, India. Her areas of research interest are human rights, gender rights, disability rights, family law, constitutional law, comparative constitutional law, and jurisprudence. She is currently a Ph.D. candidate (Law and Society) at the Faculty of Law, University of Victoria, Canada. She is a recipient of several prestigious fellowships and grants, such as the Margaret McNamara Education Grant, Graduate Fellowship, Law Foundation of British Columbia, Graduate Student Fellowship, Centre for Studies in Religion and Society, and Chevening Scholarship. She completed her LL.M. in International Human Rights Law from London School of Economics and Political Science, UK, and B.A. L.L.B.

(Hons.) from NALSAR University of Law, Hyderabad, India. She studies the interplay and intersections of various marginalities, especially gender and disability, with the politics of desirability, familial structures, popular culture, public health, legal effectiveness, and the disability and gender rights movements in the contemporary world.

Introduction: *"Don't Think Twice, It's Alright"*: Normalizing Intimate Violence

1

Pinki Mathur Anurag

Abstract

The chapter introduces the central idea behind this volume that makes it a unique contribution to literature on intimate violence. The volume reflects complexities of society and its institutions that enmesh interpersonal violence in patriarchal heteronormative ecosystems within which violence operates as a tool for maintaining inequalities in society. This chapter pivots violence as a manifestation of 'entitlements' based on gendered social hierarchies and critical intersectionalities. Ideological conditions created by legal, social, and economic structures allow the normalization of intimate violence. The anecdotal meets feminist theory to understand institutional responses to violence in intimate spaces. The focus remains the ecosystem of violence, the 'space' within which violence is situated. The volume proposes that while cis-men are the primary 'actors' of violence; state, society and its institutions are the 'agents' of violence.

Keywords

Gender · Identity · Intimate relationship · Gendered behaviour · Social construction · Gendered norms · Social norms · Social order · Family · Marriage · Persecution · Third wave feminism · Fourth wave feminism · Gendered ecosystem · Toxic masculinity · Courts · Judgements

As I begin to write this, I am struggling with a rather *banal* decision—given that I have a fast-approaching deadline to meet for the submission of my book manuscript—*should I, or should I not*, cancel the dinner reservations I made a month ago at a fancy restaurant to celebrate my spouse's fifty-third birthday. I am distressed, yet not surprised at myself. The conundrum behind this is: will my decision *to cancel, or not to cancel* impact the way I feel about myself? If I cancel, will my guilt guide the way I behave in my most intimate relationship through the year and culminate, perhaps, in 'guilt'-ridden decision-making for his birthday next year? Will I plan a vacation instead of 'just' a fancy meal? How do I detach myself from the trap of guilt and self-doubt, this tussle with priorities—*mine over*

The line *"Don't think twice, it's alright"* in the title of this chapter is taken from a song written by Bob Dylan in 1962, released in 1963. The lyrics are something you would say to yourself to feel better, normalizing the distressing thoughts and pain you are experiencing. It also represents the general attitude towards life and its experiences…..

P. M. Anurag (✉)
Jindal Global Law School, O.P. Jindal Global University, Sonipat, India
e-mail: pmanurag@jgu.edu.in

P. M. Anurag and S. Dwivedy (eds.), *Violence in Intimate Spaces*, Sustainable Development Goals Series, https://doi.org/10.1007/978-981-97-2657-8_1

others? Most self-limiting constraints appear to germinate from a *space* beyond our control. What is appropriate? What must be the limits of our expectations? Who controls the strings that make us flop and wobble about in our designated places like puppets?

I have struggled, tugged at these strings hard to break free; free my thoughts, actions, emotions, and desires from the constant tussle with 'expected' standards of 'goodness' and 'righteousness'. I know I am not alone. Conversations with fellow humans struggling just like me have helped. Most of these fellow humans are 'women'.[1] They all identify, to a greater or lesser degree with the underlying social conditioning that controls and guides our behaviour, the constant buzz in our brain that emanates from socially constructed gendered norms, roles, and expectations[2]: "this is the way it is *supposed* to be done". Reflections on shared experiences through life, keen observations, reading, absorbing, and listening attentively clearly expose the social conditioning that stage manages us all and constrains us within its complex folds. What complicates the understanding of socially constructed norms of behaviour is that, for the most part, they appear 'self-imposed'. Perhaps they are. This self-imposition of social norms is in itself the result of our cultural conditioning, yet, gendered behaviour appears to be the 'natural' order of things that operates in us all at a subconscious level. Social order is maintained by *faithful performance of prescribed rituals over and over again throughout one's lifetime. Complex networks of cultural reproduction are dedicated to this sole purpose. But the ultimate goal ....is to produce the effect of untouched naturalness.*[3] The most critical social institutions through which social order is maintained in the world of humans are 'family' and 'marriage'. While men also bear the burden of gendered expectations, and in numerous ways face persecution rooted in the deeply patriarchal social order that we are all bound by, patriarchy impacts cis-men and cis-women in disparate ways. While women are regulated and controlled through the imposition of rules of 'good behaviour' to become 'virtuous' 'goddesses', men are trained for 'power'.[4] It is this struggle for power that cis-men have felt entitled to through the ages, while the discrimination and inequality in the way women are treated epitomize the struggles of feminism.[5] To be a feminist has nothing to do with being men or women, but about understanding *the hierarchical ordering of the world around gender as key to maintaining social order.*[6]

This volume is about 'violence' in our 'intimate relationships' and in 'private spaces' that is a result of the way humans are programmed by society. All chapters in the volume interrogate social institutions that control us all, and examine a variety of human relationships and social structures within which inequalities are maintained through violence. In doing so, the chapters critique institutions through which systems of injustice based on discrimination flow. The principal social institutions, family, marriage, community, and courts are examined through the lens of violence that resides and is normalized within these institutions. The chapters in this volume highlight the normalization of violence, beyond disciplinary and topic boundaries from a range of methodologies to understand the complex relationship between perpetrator and victim that legitimize violence in private spaces, exposing the role violence plays in preserving status quo and gendered hierarchies in society and its institutions. The objective of the volume is to look 'beyond' individuals at violence that is generated and often sanctioned by social institutions like family and marriage, the law and

[1] Here I use the term women to principally refer to persons who identify as cis-women.

[2] Judith Butler's understanding of the 'performativity' of our identities, that social reality is not given but created as an illusion through the way: "One is not born, but rather becomes, a woman." Simone de Beauvoir, The Second Sex (1949).

[3] Menon (2012).

[4] Loehnen (2023).

[5] Loehnen (2023).

[6] Menon (2012).

its implementation, and the wider framework of inequality and discrimination that underline social institutions. The volume shines a flashlight in dark corners of society and its institutions to make violence visible in spaces where silence is the norm and invisibility the practice.

Violence operates within an imposing, complex, and rigid 'gendered ecosystem'. Understanding and locating gender violence within this ecology that sustains it is thus critical. The *violent space* examined in this volume encompasses not just acts of violence committed, but also acts of violence tolerated. It is this ecosystem that ensures its survival. Courts are complicit in their tolerance of violence when they place the victim on the stand to question the victim's actions, inaction, or mannerisms as possible incitement for the violence. Institutionalized heterosexuality is designed to perpetrate the social power of cis-men across gender, race, and class; when someone does not conform to such institutionalized heterosexuality, they are subjected to violence. Identity is thus a critical marker in the way we relate to others in society, those we see as belonging to a 'different' identity, and this is critically intertwined with the idea of violence that is manifested as a result of competing or antagonistic identities.

For Amartya Sen, *identity* is a *complex matter*.[7] Almost everyone is a member of a *variety of groups* and we can *belong to all of them*, and this does not necessarily, in fact, almost never, leads to any contradiction between our multiple identities and membership to several groups at the same time. The *solitarist* approach to identity, according to Sen, fallaciously places human beings as members of exactly one group. He provides several examples of coexisting membership to several groups:

> an American citizen of Caribbean origin, with African ancestry, a Christian, a liberal, a woman, a vegetarian, a long distance runner, a historian, a schoolteacher, a novelist, a feminist, a heterosexual, a believer in gay and lesbian rights,[8] a theatre lover, an environmental activist, a tennis fan, a jazz musician, and someone who is deeply committed to the view that there are intelligent beings in outer space with whom it is extremely urgent to talk (preferably in English).[9]

All these provide this 'one' person with a *particular identity*, and no single one of the above can be mistaken as their *only identity or singular membership* to any one group. It is our *inescapable plural identities*, says Sen, that make it imperative for us to decide on the *relative importance of our different associations and affiliations in a particular context*.[10] This sense of the inevitability of a unique, singular, and often *belligerent identity* can promote violence. Sen posits that there appears to be a *perceived absence of choice* that suggests to us that we cannot exercise choice with regard to our identities, and this impedes efforts to *defeat violence* or to overcome identities that demand violence through dominant systems of religion, community, culture, and nation. The idea put forward by Sen essentially points to the perceived sense that we do not have a choice and that it is the neglect of the idea of the existence of choice and not *nasty intentions* that contributes to the violence we see around us. We are significantly influenced by others with whom we 'identify' and that *a fostered sense of identity with one group of people can be made into a powerful weapon to brutalize another*. According to Sen, most violence around the world is *sustained through the illusion of a unique and choiceless identity*. The construction that justifies violence towards one predominant 'identity' or persons belonging to a 'identity' often drowns our other affiliations, and this in turn destroys any sympathy or natural kindness that may have normally existed. This, says Sen, can result in *homespun elemental violence or globally artful violence and terrorism*. The belief that people

---

[7] Sen (2006).

[8] A restrictive terminology, perhaps because this was written in 2005! We can safely assume that he meant persons of all gender identities and sexual orientations.

[9] Ibid.

[10] Ibid.

can be uniquely categorized on the basis of religion or culture is, according to Sen, a principal source of potential conflict in the contemporary world.[11]

The thesis put forth by Sen can be applied to explain the way in which cis-male forms a dominant 'identity', within the patriarchal heteronormative hegemonic structure with the belief that they must imbibe and perform the set norms assigned to all persons who 'identify' with this group. Toxic masculinity and the violence it generates, and may I daresay *misogyny*, operate as *normal* codes of behaviour within this seemingly singular identity, *male*. This 'belonging'*ness* and singular dominant identity normalize violence by men on women and 'others' who are perceived as 'inferior' or outside the socially accepted gender identity of 'male' or 'female'. Toxic masculinity explained through this understanding and the *perceived absence of choice* as belonging to a singular identity is learnt and 'performed' in irrational and aggressive ways towards persons seen as 'other'. In this praxis, women are viewed through the singular identity—gender. Bourdieu says that women as a disadvantaged group have lived an inferior life in society for centuries and have faced immense discrimination, been subjected to abjection, non-recognition, and misrecognition, and treated as mere 'objects' to be exploited by male 'subjects'.[12] Baker et al. similarly opine that society has construed men as the guardians of purity and honour of the family, caste, and the nation.[13] It is unfortunate that, in an effort to respect and protect this honour, they themselves become victims of honour. The notion of honour has been introduced by the patriarchal system of society for preserving male dominance; it acts as a double-edged weapon for women that justifies repressive control measures within the home; consequently, it restricts women's participation outside the home by defining the public sphere as 'male' and off limits for women. Patriarchy requires both men and women to behave in ways subscribed for them as 'appropriate' and 'honourable' through rigid gender roles. Deprived of the right to exercise their will, says Fanon, women go through a process of '*symbolic violence*' every moment of their life. It is this violence that is inflicted daily upon women as the dominated group and as a result they are forced to see themselves through the symbolic schemas of the dominant.[14] This then becomes the perceived singular 'identity' of women.

Courts and their judgements reflect, similarly, the inflexible nature of social institutions and focus singularly on marriage as a heterosexual unit within rigid definitions of family and gender norms, thus establishing law's limitations in addressing intimate relationships beyond normative familial units. The understanding of violence in this volume is contextualized within the idea of gender inequality enforced by gendered hierarchies in society, and toxic masculinity as a tool for perpetuating patriarchal institutions that generally centre around cis-male violence against women. The idea that cis-men are the sole embodiments of violence in both public and private spaces must be viewed in light of rigid gendered roles in society. While most violence is perpetrated by cis-men, who is the 'real' agent of violence, where does this violence emanate from? How, why, and by whom is the violence 'enacted' through cis-men normalized? Through this volume, we assign state, society, and its institutions as the real 'agents' of violence. Though cis-men remain the primary '*actors*' of violence, the recipients are not just cis-women but persons of all gender identities and sexual orientation who are considered '*inferior*' by society or do not belong to the dual heteronormative gender identity. The volume foregrounds violence as a manifestation of 'entitlements' based on gendered social hierarchies and examines its countless forms in a variety of intimate 'circumstances' and 'spaces'.

In 2019, a 36-year-old farm labourer in Nanded, Maharashtra, was charged with

[11] Ibid.

[12] Bourdieu (1991).

[13] Baker et al. (1999).

[14] Fanon (1986).

murdering his wife[15] because *she had not cooked meat properly and she burnt it.* The accused invoked the exception under Section 300 of the Indian Penal Code (IPC)[16] praying for a lesser punishment in view of the exception since the act occurred following *a sudden fight*, while the prosecution alleged *the accused had committed her [sic] murder by assaulting her repeatedly and due to the repeated blows the deceased had sustained in all six injuries as well as internal injuries which resulted in her instantaneous death.* The High Court of Bombay[17] (HC) in its judgement,[18] quoted Sidney Brandon[19]: "*Statistically it is safer to be on streets after dark with a stranger than at home in the bosom of one's family, for it is there that accident, murder and violence are likely to occur.*" Recognizing that *evidence on record sufficiently shows that the death of the deceased was caused in the house of the accused due to the assault by the accused on account of not preparing the food properly*[20]; the decision stated that this was a sudden quarrel and there was no premeditation, the injuries that caused the death were not on the vital parts of her body, *the weapon used was a stick*, the *accused did not act in a cruel manner. When he saw that the deceased had not prepared the food, he abused and assaulted her.* The HC decided that this is a case of culpable homicide not amounting to murder and that the accused *need not undergo imprisonment for life and his sentence be modified to rigorous imprisonment for ten years.*[21] This is not an isolated case where the court normalizes spousal violence, thereby justifying the 'simple' task of not cooking a meal well by the wife as provocation or incitement to violence, in this case, causing death. This approach reeks of patriarchal stereotypes imbued in judicial systems. The word and 'judgement' of the court become the moral compass of society and enhance the strict codes of behaviour demarcated by society for men and for women, especially within the institution of marriage, exposing deep-rooted biases, and gender stereotypes that thrive and are normalized in the haloed halls of justice.

With the principal objective of critiquing institutions for their role in perpetrating violence in private spaces and the failure of the State to address gender-based violence, this volume locates itself and finds resonance with *third and fourth wave feminism*[22] that unabashedly expresses its disdain for the State and remains focused on the identification and the critique of State inaction, principally on sexual violence. The following 'violence' question thus emerges: *What is the belief system that eroticizes, aestheticizes, and legitimizes sexual desire associated with violence?*[23] Issues of violence

[15] Under Section 302 of the Indian Penal Code, 1860 (IPC).

[16] Exception 4 to Section 300 of IPC that culpable homicide is not murder if it is committed without premeditation in a sudden fight in the heat of passion upon a sudden quarrel and without the offender having taken undue advantage or acted in a cruel or unusual manner.

[17] Nagpur Bench.

[18] Suresh Madhukar Shende v State of Maharashtra, 6/12/2022, Criminal Appeal No. 347 of 2019, High Court of Bombay, Nagpur Bench, Nagpur. Access at: https://www.livelaw.in/pdf_upload/bombay-hc-order-448193.pdf.

[19] Para 16.

[20] Para 26.

[21] Para 32, 33.

[22] The fourth wave is believed to have appeared around 2012 while the third wave started in the early 1990s and continues right up to the fourth wave. Since the two happened within less than 40 years of each other, they have a lot in common. There is some debate as to whether there are two separate waves; some call these twin waves; see Basmechi, F. 2017. Third and Fourth Wave of Women's Movements: Are They Twins? https://www.researchgate.net/publication/344150360_Third_and_Fourth_Wave_of_Women%27s_movements_Are_They_Twins.

[23] See Charlotte Kroløkke, Anne Scott Sørensen, Three Waves of Feminism: From Suffragettes to Grrls, in Gender Communication Theories & Analyses: From Silence to Performance, Chapter DOI: https://doi.org/10.4135/9781452233086; *Focus rests on the sustained tension between structure and agency, spelled out as a tension between performance and performativity, in order to overcome the split between society and subject and to situate the possibilities and means of agency and change.*

and harassment have remained critical for third wave feminists in the post-modern world, and the newer fourth wave, considered to be in its nascency, continues the critical work on violence, abuse, and harassment over social media, through viral campaigns, protests, and movements. Focus on sexual harassment, rape culture, body shaming, support for gender diversity, sex positive approaches, body positivity, and inclusivity of transgender persons further nuances the dialogues on violence.[24] The freedom to construct and choose one's gender identity requires non-interference from social, cultural, and religious institutions; instead, the institutions of family and marriage stubbornly ensure the reproduction of gender inequality and exclusion. Third wave feminism constitutes a significant move both in theory and politics towards what has been termed the *performance turn* marking a sharp divergence from thinking and acting within systems, structures, fixed power relations, and thereby 'suppression', focusing instead, on highlighting the complexities, contingencies, and *challenges of power and the diverse means and goals of agency*. Embedded in the scientific paradigm shift from *structuralism* to *post-structuralism*, the *performance turn* is connected to a broader intellectual transformation.[25]

This volume thus addresses violence in intimate spaces within this feminist framework and offers an unequivocal critique of the institutions of family, marriage, community, and courts in their present form as critical spaces and harbingers of violence. Dangers of exclusion in dualistic gender ordering, commonly referred to as heteronormative dominance, is a structure in which not only are the differences between 'genders' highlighted, the recipient of violence is always positioned and occupies a 'space' *lesser than* the other. Violence has historically been conceptualized as a form of gender discrimination; this is an oversimplification. Through the different waves of feminism, values, ideas, and methodologies have differed; the focus of the first wave of feminism primarily was about the political struggle for equal rights as citizens where right to vote and reproductive rights were issues of primacy; resistance to essentialist notions of identity become vital not only with respect to individual autonomy but also with the way social institutions, most critically family and marriage, are understood and constructed only during the third wave. Justice and inclusivity are at the core of third wave feminism aimed at redistribution within the framework of private and public.

Where does the 'private' end, and 'public' begin? The line between public and private appear porous in the way discrimination is approached and addressed under international human rights law. Increasingly, State and its institutions are being held vicariously liable for all forms of violence that takes place in private intimate spaces. State's complicity in private violence is now ascertained by examining the adequacy of steps taken by the State to prevent and redress systemic violence, including gender-based violence. State responsibility extends to creating mechanisms, ensuring due diligence by its agencies and personnel—bureaucracy, police, legislature, and the judiciary act in positive ways towards the prevention and redressal of wrong caused by private actors. The discussions in this volume are located within this context of State responsibility in creating or failing to create systems for prevention and redressal of intimate space violence. Today, a crisis in all social institutions is palpable; a reconfiguration in the way family, marriage, and community are defined has become necessary, if equality for all is the desired goal. The nature and ecosystem of these institutions that represent inequality and sustain violence clearly points us in this direction. This volume is situated in the perpetration of violence within the space of family, marriage, and community, or, as a consequence of laws, policy and its enforcement. Ideological conditions created by the legal, social, and economic

[24] Ibid.; the most significant milestone thus far remains the Me-Too Movement started in the US in 2006: Gender equality and equal pay, equal opportunities, and intersectionality. Challenge to the heterosexual matrix is the most crucial aspect of third wave feminism.

[25] Ibid. at pg. 21.

structures that allow violence to proliferate[26] are at the heart of the analysis presented.

Each chapter in this volume stands on its own footing, examining a specific type or nature of violence within ecosystems of the restrictive understanding of family, marriage, culture, religion, and the law—are all inextricably patriarchal in nature. The objective is not to put forward suggestions or recommendations; instead, we provide clarity and depth of perspective and understanding of the *spaces* within which violence is located. In *Family, Gender and Violence: Images from Life, Literature and Courts*, Justice Sridevan provides simplistic narratives of the ways in which the dynamics of violence and gender hierarchies and stereotypes come alive in everyday life. The author uses examples from everyday interactions in the court room—legal deliberations and judgements and through literature as a window to life. This chapter sets the context for the remaining chapters through the lucid images woven from life, law, and literature.

The next three chapters analyse, from different vantage points, gendered violence within the institution of marriage. In *Documenting Psychological Tactics as Violence in Meena Kandasamy's "When I Hit You Or, a Portrait of the Writer as a Young Wife"*, Santwana Dwivedy focuses on the fallacy of the necessity of producing physical evidence of violence as a benchmark for assessing severity of abuse and violence by society and the legal system. Law focuses on extremities—*a bad marriage* (divorce laws, criminal law on cruelty) or *a good marriage* (where the spouses fulfil their socio-culturally assigned gendered roles in private). In doing so, law invisiblizes violence that lies and shifts between the two extremities. Indifference, pain, and agony are now recognized as emotional violence but are tough to prove in a court of law which demands, in most cases, strict adherence to 'legal jargon' and discounts a person's subjective experiences.[27] Wife battering, domestic violence, and intimate partner violence—every case includes one or more of a series of abuses in the form of manipulation, use of psychological tactics, economic and social control or deprivation, social isolation, and familial estrangement. Psychological abuse is a serious form of violence; in the absence of the exercise of physical force, however, these harms are not perceived or treated as violence, thereby invisibilizing and normalizing the damage caused by psychological tactics as violence in the form of intimidation, coercion, gaslighting, and stone-walling.

The Indian criminal justice system requires the level of mental and/or physical cruelty to be of 'serious gravity'.[28] Legal scholars have criticized the provision's narrow understanding of violence. Kothari argues that 'mental or physical cruelty' does not accurately represent the varied other forms of violence women face in domestic *spaces*—emotional, economic, psychological, and sexual violence and that IPC is silent on other forms of non-marital violence such as natal violence.[29] Though psychological tactics can amount to 'mental cruelty'[30] and may cause a grave degree of harm as envisaged under this provision, courts are hesitant to convict persons solely on claims of psychological

26 Price (2009).

27 Sen (2010).

28 IPC. Section 498A: *Husband or relative of husband of a woman subjecting her to cruelty:*
Whoever, being the husband or the relative of the husband of a woman, subjects such woman to cruelty shall be punished with imprisonment for a term which may extend to 3 years and shall also be liable to fine.
Explanation: For the purpose of this section, 'cruelty' means
(a) any willful conduct which is of such a nature as is likely to drive the woman to commit suicide or to cause grave injury or danger to life, limb, or health (whether mental or physical) of the woman; or
(b) harassment of the woman where such harassment is with a view to coercing her or any person related to her to meet any unlawful demand for any property or valuable security or is on account of failure by her or any person related to her to meet such demand.

29 Kothari (2005).

30 Under Section 498A, IPC.

abuse.[31] The civil law on domestic violence in India, the Protection of Women from Domestic Violence Act, 2005 (PWDVA) recognizes psychological and emotional violence. The law provides the *aggrieved woman* quick remedies through protection orders, residence orders, monetary reliefs, compensation orders, and custody orders.[32] It has been observed that physical or economic abuse co-exists with emotional abuse in cases of domestic violence before the court.[33] Sen emphasizes that 'pure' emotional abuse, unless combined with other forms of overt physical or sexual violence is not generally treated as 'grave' in the judicial imagination.[34] This is also reflected in situations where the domestic violence victim is required to produce evidence showing 'substantive degrees of violation to her personhood'. Is emotional abuse treated as seriously as physical abuse under the PWDVA? There is little evidence to show that in the absence of physical abuse, emotional abuse by itself would constitute a prima facie case of domestic violence.[35] This chapter argues for the

[31] There are cases of mental cruelty before courts; these are generally combined with charges of physical cruelty. Rukmini Sen emphasizes that complaints of physical abuse are often combined with taunts of dowry demand amounting to mental cruelty. In these cases, courts have considered some cases solely under mental cruelty (such as extra-marital relationship of the husband). Judges generally hesitate to convict under Section 498A unless such an extra-marital relationship leads to severe consequences such as driving the spouse to death by suicide. In a case of disagreement between spouses about undercooked food, Bombay High Court held that such normal and ordinary disagreements in marital life do not amount to cruelty. The court observed that *cruelty implies harsh and harmful conduct with certain intensity and persistence. It covers acts causing both physical and mental agony and torture or tyranny and harm as well as unending accusations and recrimination reflecting bitterness putting the victim thereof to intense miscarries.* In the absence of a standard definition of mental cruelty under this section, there is wide judicial discretion with respect to the interpretation of the meaning and scope of mental cruelty. Analysis of the observations of courts regarding mental cruelty under Section 498A indicates that courts recognizes mental cruelty only where it is shown to be *grave enough to reach the level of highest torture with the tendency of driving the victim to death.* This sets a dangerous narrative. In other cases of psychological violence, courts are unlikely to consider psychological abuse as mental cruelty to be 'severe' enough for criminal sanctions. *See* Sen, Rukmini. 2010. Women's subjectivities of suffering and legal rhetoric on Domestic Violence: Fissures in the two discourses. *Indian Journal of Gender Studies* 382: 375–401; Ghusabhai Raisangbhai Chorasiya vs State of Gujarat 2015 SCCOnline SC 137 (Supreme Court); Neeraj Subhash Mehta vs State of Maharashtra 2017 SCCOnline Bom 62 (Bombay High Court).

[32] Protection of Women from Domestic Violence Act, 2005. Sections 18–22, Section 3(a)–(d), Section 3 Explanation I (iii). PWDVA defines domestic abuse as acts or omissions which lead to or threaten to cause physical or mental harm or suffering (may be economic, emotional, verbal, sexual, or physical) and put someone's life or health at risk. It also includes acts and omissions of coercion or threats of coercion for the purpose of dowry demand and also comprises any other act which causes mental or physical suffering to the victim. Section 3 Explanation I (iii) of PWDVA defines 'verbal and emotional' abuse as insults, remarks to ridicule and humiliate a person especially with respect to them having a male child. It also includes within its ambit threats to physically harm a third person who is close to the aggrieved person. In the overarching definition of violence, the inclusion of terms such as 'omissions', 'mental harm', and 'emotional abuse (which includes humiliation)' raises possibilities of the recognition of the adverse harms of psychological violence in a marriage as a form of violence. These immediate reliefs in PWDVA were viewed as a welcome change from criminal sanctions under Section 498A Indian Penal Code which mostly led to the imprisonment of the abusive husband (who is usually the breadwinner) leaving the victim without a source of sustenance. As PWDVA was a civil remedy, the aggrieved woman had a lower burden of proof to prove her case in contrast to the highest burden of proof in criminal law. The broad definition of domestic violence as encompassing physical, sexual, economic, verbal, and emotional abuse was also seen as a welcome change in the legal framework for cognizance of the varied forms of abuse.

[33] Sen (2010).

[34] Sen (2010).

[35] However, there are certain cases where courts have granted legal redress under PWDVA even when they are not combined with allegations of physical abuse. This is observed in Maharashtra in a case where the husband married for the second time and alleged that his first wife's child was not his; it was held that this amounted to emotional abuse and mental violence as it cast doubts on her chastity. Similarly, in another case in Manipur, where the wife was told that she was unworthy of fulfilling her role as a wife and sent to her parents' house,

inclusion of psychological tactics as a serious form of violence providing extensive analysis of this form of violence with Meena Kandasamy's novel as the backdrop.

The next two chapters examine the normalization of sexual violence and rape within marriage from two very distinct settings. In *Blurred Lines: Sexual Abuse (or not) in "Big Little Lies"*, Devyani Tewari interrogates the *blurred lines* between consensual sex and sexual violence in a marriage. She examines the marriage between a heterosexual couple from a privileged background as depicted through a popular television show. Domesticity and marriage create deeply gendered norms of female subordination and loss of body autonomy that blur the distinction between consensual sex and sexual violence. The husband uses manipulation, gaslighting, verbal, and physical abuse to ensure that the wife remains powerless in the marriage, to the extent that she herself normalizes the emotional and sexual abuse suffered by her. Roseline Raymond in *An Examination of the Married Body of a Woman as Reflected through Marital Rape in Nigeria* provides a socio-legal analysis of the institution of marriage through the examination of the practice of bride price in Nigeria and establishes interlinkages between tradition, culture, violence, and the exception of marital rape under the legal system in Nigeria. The chapter discusses theories under which consent is deemed valid simply by the factum of marriage. This legal understanding is not limited to Nigeria; arguments against criminalization of rape within marriage are based essentially on the same principle—objectification and complete lack of freedom and bodily autonomy of the wife and conversely the ownership and privilege of the husband over the wife's body. Sexual violence in a marriage is the most normalized form of violence in the intimate space; law's inability to recognize rape as rape underlines the deep fissures in society and the normalization of gender inequality in its most revered institution—marriage.

Unwanted childbearing, enforced motherhood by the family, husband, or the State, denies women control over their body and life. Why is motherhood idealized, yet mothers subjected to obstetric violence? These have been addressed by Brototi Dutta in her chapter, *The 'Joy' of Motherhood, the Violence in Motherhood: A Decolonial Feminist Analysis of Sexual and Reproductive Rights*. Motherhood is examined as an institution through the lens of violence. Drawing from international human rights framework on the right to health, Dutta exposes discriminatory norms against marginalized bodies of women, examining the violence in law within the context of carceral and punitive biases that exist in laws, including for marginalized bodies of women, prisoners, juveniles, and in same-sex relationships.

The two chapters that examine natal family as a violent *space* shatter the myth of the biological 'family' as a nurturing space for its members. As exemplified by Justice Sridevan in her chapter, a family where violence prevails is already broken, and does not require the initiation of legal proceedings to 'break' the family. This is true equally in the case of the institution of marriage, the preservation of which lies at the core of legal protection and 'imagined' privileges associated with it. This includes the

---

it was held that this was a case of emotional abuse and she was granted compensation and a protection order. Another example of recognition of emotional abuse in the absence of any overt physical abuse is a case where the aggrieved woman's father-in-law secretly watched her changing clothes, asked for massages, and tortured her emotionally when her husband was not present. Here, the court held that such acts posed a serious risk to life and limb of the victim and amounted to mental and physical violence. Although these cases are laudable for recognizing emotional abuse even in the absence of physical violence, it is observed that, within the realm of psychological abuse, all these instances reveal overt acts such as name-calling, insulting, and so on. Thus, viewing covert or passive acts like gaslighting, manipulation, and isolation in a marriage might not reach the severity criteria of violence in the judicial imagination. *See* Women's Rights Initiative (Lawyers Collective), ICRW. 2012. *Staying Alive: 5th Monitoring and Evaluation 2012 on the Protection of Women from Domestic Violence Act, 2005* New Delhi 160: 1-227. https://lawyerscollective.org/wp-content/uploads/2023/04/Staying-Alive-5th-ME.pdf. Accessed on 10 June 2023.

instant disapproval suffered by persons who choose to remain outside of this institution. Niharika Banerjee, Kolika Mitra, and Poushali Basak's Chapter, *Natal Family Violence: Crisis Interventions and Paths to Survival with LBT Persons* is based on an empirical study of crisis intervention for survivors of natal family violence related to their *gender-sexuality intersectional locations*, exposing the urgency of breaking the silence on heteropatriarchal natal family violence in the absence of legal protection from natal family violence inflicted on LBT persons. The chapter explores pathways to survival facilitated with sensitivity and skill of queer and trans persons working at the fore of facilitating survival from natal family violence. The deep sense of loss of trust in natal families is equally evident in the experiences of girls and women who are forced to undergo Female Genital Mutilation/Cutting (FGM/C) by their mothers, grandmothers, and other female members of the family and by the community. This loss of trust has been shown as the foremost trauma suffered by FGM/C survivors. *Navigating Intimate Spaces of Violence: Global Legal Responses on Female Genital Mutilation/Cutting* explores FGM/C as a form of violence against women and girls committed by the natal family supported by the community to control sexuality and sexual desire in girls and women. Experiences from several jurisdictions that have enacted laws criminalizing this serious form of violence in intimate spaces examined in this chapter by Varsha Mohan demonstrates that when the State is willing to protect women and girls from violence perpetrated in the name of culture, tradition, or religion; laws and their strict enforcement can send a powerful message to society and the community that violence under the guise of cultural and religious practices will not be tolerated.

The final two chapters examine 'violent spaces' that are directly attributable to discriminatory and, at times, overzealous legal systems and regimes. For whose benefit are laws enacted? Whose interests do they protect? In "*Family Disruption*" *as* "*Family Violence: Immigrant Sikh Families in the United States*", Diditi Mitra's research on immigrant families exposes the violence perpetrated by immigration laws on migrant families. While laws across the globe claim that the preservation of 'family' is critical to society, immigration laws clearly do not respect this norm. States are unmindful of the human right of migrants to family life. The violence on families inflicted due to strict immigration and work regimes has been examined from a uniquely gender-neutral perspective grounded in 'economics' of intimate relationships. Wungreithan Awungshi examines the violence committed on Naga women within the context of the law that enforced a ban on liquor in the state in the chapter *Violence on Naga Women in the Context of Illegal Liquor Trade: A Study in Kohima, Nagaland*. The legal prohibition of liquor has created an *ecosystem* in which violence on women liquor traders in the form of extortion, threats, and harassment thrives, while the men who buy and consume the liquor, thereby creating a demand for it and the Government Excise officers who extract illegal taxes, humiliate, and threaten women who refuse to pay them bribes, do not face any consequences. Law and its enforcement, far from ensuring the prohibition, promote violence and discrimination. Women liquor traders suffer violence of exclusion, enforced through the orthodox catholic society of Nagaland. This exclusion is spearheaded by the catholic church through its teachings and operates as a form of gender-based ostracization of women traders by encouraging the perception that women engaged in this illegal trade *moonlight* as prostitutes.

This chapter exposes the *ecosystem of violence* evident in all chapters from different vantage points. In this volume, we not only examine acts of commission but also acts of omission that have the effect of perpetrating violence. All such commissions and omissions trigger fear, anxiety, and suffering in all its forms, including immediate and long-term trauma or vulnerability that impact the well-being of the recipient of violence. Intent to cause harm is not necessary, neither are we concerned only with violence caused by individuals. Every act or omission may not necessarily lead to the violation of specific articulated rights directly or indirectly, if the impact demonstrates characteristics of violence; these have been defined as violence in this volume.

The idea of this volume has grown over decades of engagement—personal and professional with violence in intimate relationships and spaces through interactions with domestic violence survivors who came to the Lawyers Collective, Women's Rights Initiative (WRI) for legal advice, and through cases filed on their behalf. The legal process and the outcome of their case was always unpredictable, complex, and operated in an impersonal space. What left a tangible impact on me was the pain and emotional struggles that accompanied the experience of violence, betrayal, and loss of confidence in spaces, institutions, and its relationships that came through the deeply personal stories shared by the survivors. Loss of faith in relationships they had imagined would sustain them—where do these ideas and ideals emerge? Clearly, these are carefully engineered narratives that are religiously (pun intended) and culturally injected into our psyche through fallacious narratives of 'bliss' imparted by people, films, and the media. Idealization of the institution of marriage, primacy of family as a revered unit in society, and the 'rules' within these restrict free thinking and self-preservation. Gender is foundational to the definition of violence inflicted in intimate spaces and relationships. The normalization of this violence is embedded in our socialization; it goes 'beyond' the control of humans, and lies deep within society and its institutions.

References

Baker N, Gregware P, Cassidy M (1999) Family killing fields: honour rationales in the murder of women. Violence against women. N.D

Bourdieu P (1991) Language and symbolic power (Trans Raymrld G, Adamson M). Polity, Cambridge

Fanon F (1986) Black skin, white mask (Trans Markmann CL). Pluto Press, London. First Published in 1968

Jaising I, Mathur Anurag P (eds) (2009) Conflict in the shared household, domestic violence and the law in India. Oxford University Press, Delhi, India

Kothari J (2005) Criminal law on domestic violence. Econ Pol Wkly 4844:4843–4849

Kroløkke C, Sørensen AS (2006) Three waves of feminism: from suffragettes to grrls. In: Gender communication theories & analyses: from silence to performance. https://doi.org/10.4135/9781452233086

Loehnen E (2023) On our best behaviour, the seven sins and the price women pay to be good. The Dial Press, New York, US

Menon N (2012) Seeing like a feminist, Zubaan, India, Penguin Books, UK

Price LS (2009) Feminist frameworks, building a theory of violence against women. Aakar Books for South-East Asia, Delhi, India

Sen R (2010) Women's subjectivities of suffering and legal rhetoric on Domestic Violence: Fissures in the two discourses. Indian J Gend Stud 394:375–401

Sen A (2006) Identity and violence, the illusion of destiny. Allen Lane, Penguin Group, London, UK

Suresh Madhukar Shende v State of Maharashtra, 6/12/2022, Criminal Appeal No. 347 of 2019, High Court of Bombay, Nagpur Bench, Nagpur. https://www.livelaw.in/pdf_upload/bombay-hc-order-448193.pdf

2 Family, Gender, and Violence—Images from Life, Literature, and the Courts

Prabha Sridevan

Abstract

This chapter will focus on ways in which imbalances of power appear in surprising *spaces* where it works to reinforce the status quo. Do courts look at these *spaces*? If they do not, this may not even be a deliberate act of omission on their part; this can be attributed simply to the *normalization* of imbalance in society as the norm. We do not question norms. Recently, in an auditorium stuffed to full capacity with college students, I asked them to mentally design their homes, navigate the spaces, and tell me what they see. Their mental plan did not include the kitchen. After I pointed this out, they added the kitchen. I then asked them who they see in the kitchen and the answer was *the mother*. This is the norm. The woman always occupies the *invisible spaces*. Through this chapter, I share my encounters with the *normative* as it applies to family, marriage, and gender. These norms lie latent, consistent, and unquestioned. I draw from my life as a lawyer and, later, as a judge to reflect on the normative through the lens of life and literature, as I weave images of how this status quo can either be reinforced or it can be questioned and changed.

Keywords

Norms · Gender · Family · Home · Homemaker · Violence · Courts · Women · Invisibilization · Law · Literature · Judgements · Internalization · Equality · Substantive equality · Agency · Empowerment · Protectionism · Domestic · Labour · Unseen work · Compensation · Religion · Guilt · Hierarchy

2.1 Introduction

This chapter takes inspiration from Justice Albie Sachs' book "*The Strange Alchemy of Law and Life*"[1] where Sachs weaves life's reflections and judicial pronouncements into his book. The court struggles with interpreting human suffering in the larger context and offers lessons in exactly the same way as the life stories of ordinary people. Sachs' book weaves a rich tapestry of narratives on human rights and the right to equality for all. Rights are held by ordinary human beings whose lives are touched by those who work towards the ideals of equality for all,

P. Sridevan (✉)
Madras High Court, Chennai, India
e-mail: prabha.sridevan@gmail.com

[1] Sachs (2009).

P. M. Anurag and S. Dwivedy (eds.), *Violence in Intimate Spaces*, Sustainable Development Goals Series, https://doi.org/10.1007/978-981-97-2657-8_2

as did Justice Sachs.[2] In this chapter, I have similarly, attempted to weave narratives from my life as a lawyer, a judge, and a writer. These reflections drawn from my own life experiences include narratives and my thoughts and reflections from my favourite works of literature. All of this encompasses and together constitutes my journey towards questioning the status quo in society. The chapter will trace imbalances of power that I note, appear in surprising spaces and operate to reinforce the status quo in the lives of people and in society. I ask: Do courts look at these spaces? And if they do not, is this a deliberate act of omission or a simple case of internalization of these norms? One such norm that goes *unquestioned* by courts is the *invisible space* occupied by women, especially at home and within the family structure.

The chapter draws attention to these invisible spaces occupied by women to highlight the hidden elements of violence in these spaces. Narratives and examples will be drawn from courts and from literature to contextualize the idea of normalization of violence in society. The chapter does not cite examples of direct violence alone; instead, it draws one's attention to gendered spaces, subtle and silent norms within rigid social structures that produce violence. The line between discrimination and violence—both direct and indirect—is fragile. We need to access spaces that produce and allow violence to be perpetrated by the ones who have been accorded a higher status in society than others. The powerful always occupy spaces that are visible, while the marginalized spaces remain in the dark, as does the violence they suffer.

In a case before me, a college student who did not have the requisite attendance was not allowed to appear for her examinations. The university rules did not permit condonation beyond a specified number of days' absence. The reason for her absence was that she was pregnant. Relying on the Convention on the Elimination of all forms of Discrimination Against Women (CEDAW) and the constitutional principle of equality,[3] I decided that the shortfall in attendance should be condoned. One of my colleagues disagreed with the stand taken by me, stating that if we were to condone the shortfall in attendance on grounds of pregnancy, this could encourage a culture where university rules will be given a go-by, and *any reason* could be cited by students as a valid cause for their absence and shortfall in attendance. In recent years, the debate on menstrual leave has gained momentum.[4] The view that menstruation has to be free of social, cultural, and religious[5] taboos supports menstrual leave, while the argument that as a natural biological function it does not warrant any special treatment for women opposes it. If we are to look at menstruation and pregnancy[6] fair and square in the eye, the discomfort associated with menstruation needs to be made visible, only then will it be possible to view women at work through the lens of equality. Therein lies the central issue—of being equal, yet different. The fellow judge who disagreed with my position on special treatment for pregnancy, was being dismissive of substantive equality for women. In order to avoid

---

[2] Justice Sachs is a renowned former judge of the South African Constitutional Court and anti-apartheid activist. He was one of the forerunners in the struggle for freedom and equality in South Africa during apartheid. During his days as a lawyer, his practice involved defending people who were unjustly "charged under racist statutes and repressive security laws". Later in life, he was a part of the negotiations that made South Africa a constitutional democracy and was appointed by Nelson Mandela to serve in the Constitutional Court. His tenure as a judge was marked by judgements which placed emphasis on the human rights of all and he earned the reputation as the "conscience of the court". His landmark judgments include the recognition of same-sex marriage, making South Africa the fifth nation in the world to do so.

[3] *The Constitution of India*, Articles 14 and 15.

[4] *See* Levitt and Barnack-Tavlaris (2020).

[5] *Indian Young Lawyers Association and ors. vs The State of Kerala and ors.* (The Sabarimala judgement), Supreme Court of India (2019) 11 SCC 1.

[6] Pregnancy and childbirth, also biological functions, are distinct to one gender; it is now established that special treatment and specific provisions to allow woman special treatment under law and policy are not discriminatory or they qualify as positive discrimination.

discrimination against women in both public and private spaces; we must make room for inherent differences between men and women. I recall a lawyer beginning his arguments in an appeal against a specific performance[7] decree in a property matter with an emphasis on the fact that the appellant was a *widow*. In this case, it mattered little who the appellant was since this was a property matter where the facts did not call for a gender perspective. The lawyer perhaps thought that mercy would drop as gentle rain from above as soon as I heard the term *widow* and sympathy would direct the flow of judicial reasoning. In this case, the woman stood on the same footing as everyone else. The *Specific Relief Act*[8] does not differentiate based on gender, and rightly so. While a gendered perspective requires to be imbued, the infusion of gender can become deeply problematic when it is disguised in the language of *protectionism*. Special treatment requires a fine balance in the way equality is sought to be implemented; this is true in life, and in law. The lawyers' attitude here was one that reinforced a sympathetic, as against an empathetic, response to his client's gender. Empathy is necessary; sympathy is selfish, and it disempowers and reinforces subordination. Let us not take away agency in our eagerness to project ourselves as gender-sensitive persons. In the language of equality, agency is critical; without agency, there can be no equality and therefore no empowerment.

2.2 Questioning Norms, Appropriate Behaviour…

It is interesting to note how notions about the appropriateness and acceptable behaviour for women are deeply embedded in an invisible space in the minds of lawyers and judges. In failing to examine this space they render it invisible. They do not think they are denying equality or being judgmental in a deeply gendered manner. This incident dates back to the time when I was the junior judge on a division bench[9] at the Madras High Court. The judge's chambers at the Madras High Court are not always adjacent to the respective court rooms,[10] so we would have to take a *ceremonial walk* along the corridor from our chambers to the court room. On one such day, I met a fellow judge who asked me casually, the purpose of my visit the previous evening to a *coffee shop* near his house, where he had spotted me. My reply was a simple "*I like the coffee there*". He looked at me with a puzzled expression, and we continued the rest of the way to our courtroom in silence. The first case before us that afternoon related to a murder that was committed in a public street during the early morning hours. A woman who had stepped out for coffee the morning of the murder, was the sole witness who had testified in court. The counsel for the appellant[11] began his case thus: "*The eyewitness is unreliable. Will any woman go out of her house to have coffee? She is lying.*" My senior colleague who had, just a few minutes ago expressed amazement at my visit to the coffee shop near his house, looked at me with a snigger in his eyes and asked under his breath, "*Shall I tell him about your visit to the coffee shop?*" The appeal was dismissed by us, not because of the opening remarks by the appellant's counsel, but on grounds that the evidence was strong enough to confirm the conviction for murder. Society's expectation that a woman must constantly be conforming to unwritten codes of conduct was glaringly evident from the conversations in court that day. Women are perhaps completely unmindful of the fact that their testimony in court may fail simply because a judge finds it *odd* that a woman would step

[7] Specific Performance as defined under *The Specific Relief Act*, 1963.

[8] The law is considered a branch of the *Indian Contract Act*, 1872.

[9] Hearing criminal appeals.

[10] Judge's chambers are, as a matter of practice and tradition, situated next to the court room they preside over.

[11] The accused in this was prosecuted; he will be appealing the verdict.

out of her home for coffee, and, if she does, this could be construed as *unacceptable* gender behaviour cemented in our minds. If the bench hearing the appeal had agreed with the counsel that no woman will ever step out of her house to have coffee in the early morning hours, then the verdict could have turned from a life sentence for murder to an acquittal. I am not so sure how relevant the morning hours, when the witness was out for coffee, or the evening, when I chose to visit the coffee shop, are. Did it seem unusual because a woman is expected to be home tending to early morning chores or that I should have rushed home after work, instead of stopping for coffee? To me it appears this might have played in the appellate counsel's mind, though he did not expressly state it. Perhaps he thought it was so obvious that he did not even feel the need to elaborate. Evidently, my fellow judge had not hesitated either before questioning my presence in the coffee shop.

2.3 Making the Invisible, Visible

In a story I translated recently,[12] a scene describes crowds gathered and packed like *sardines in a can* to attend an election meeting. The lure was five hundred rupees, a sari, and a packet of biryani. Is this the price of democracy? Approximately four lakh people had congregated in a huge field, yet there was no facility provided by way of toilets—portable or otherwise, for women's comfort. The women waited for the candidate to arrive while their bladders cramped. Unable to hold on any longer, they spread their saris, careful not to lift the saree above their ankle, squatted on the ground, and relieved themselves. One woman in this crowd remarked that the banners that were put all along the road that led to the field, and the cut-outs of images of the candidate were as long as ten towns, and the stage as big as a village. They had even installed a massive TV screen. People had been dragged and brought here in vans, buses, and some by cars, while others were stacked like cattle and goats on carts and dumped here. Yet, there was not an inch of space that could have been secluded for women to relieve themselves. This is fact, not fiction! It depicts how easily women's needs are invisibilized and appear to be of no consequence at all. In one of Tamil Nadu's oldest District Courts,[13] women's restrooms were finally built in the year 2001, while the court had been in existence since colonial times. I attended a private function there after I became a judge. The women lawyers proudly announced that a women's toilet has been built recently. So I asked them, "*What did you do till now?*" It appears they ran across the campus and jumped over the wall and well…that is one long tale of neglect and indignity. One fail-proof way of ascertaining if an organization or an institution is built on equality is to try and find toilets for women in their premises and study their location, accessibility, and cleanliness.

2.4 Gender, Work, and Violence

In her book "*Flying with Wings of Wax*",[14] famed Swiss writer Eveline Hasler recounts the life story of Emilie Kempin-Spyri,[15] the first Swiss woman to receive a Doctor of Law in Europe.[16] A pioneer in the women's rights movement, her life has been aptly called *a life of triumph and tragedy* by Hasler. Emilie married a progressive-minded German immigrant who supported women's equality. Her father, however, disapproved of her marriage and cut all

[12] Imayam (2023). The author of this chapter translated this book of Imayam from Tamil to English.

[13] District Courts administer justice in India at a district level. There is a district court for every district or for one or more districts together based on the volume of cases and population distribution.

[14] Hasler (1994).

[15] Emilie Kempin-Spyri (1853–1901).

[16] Schelbert (2008). Accessed 5 October 2023. The article narrates the story of several Swiss women who were active in the advocacy of women's equality, yet very little is known about them.

ties with her. In 1883 she enrolled to study law at the University of Zurich. When she earned her doctor of law degree *summa cum laude* in 1887, she was the mother of two daughters. The cantonal authorities in Switzerland denied her the right to practice law, and this decision was supported by the Swiss Supreme Court.[17] She had to be content with the position of a Lecturer at the University of Zurich, after she had re-applied for a second time. In 1886 New York State[18] began admitting women to the bar for the first time on terms identical to those for men. Emilie migrated to the United States with her family to start legal practice in New York State. She established the first law school for women; this was later integrated into the City University of New York. In her personal life, however, she continued to be submerged in unhappiness. Her husband was not happy in the United States so she returned to Zurich with her children in 1892, where she was finally able to open a law office. Following her divorce in 1895, Emilie moved to Berlin. She was engaged with the women's movement for a while but her political views were declared too conservative, and she suffered social isolation. From then on, she was housed in several mental health institutions. Pioneering lawyer, women's rights activist, academic, and author suffered a lonely death in an asylum for the insane.[19] Why did this happen? Is this not a form of invisibilization of a woman's life, success, and calibre by society and its institutions? Does this not qualify as a form of violence against women?

I have felt invisible several times in my life. I attended Law College after marriage and children, subsequently I joined my husband's law practice. The law firm was populated with his juniors who were all male. The clients who came to the office would walk past me and go directly to the junior male lawyers. It took them some time to realize that I was not there to simply while away my time and that I intended to work seriously. I had to work very hard to carve an independent identity for myself as a lawyer in the law office that my husband now shared with me. Yet, my gender, my status as someone's wife, always mattered more than my skills and education. Both men and women pass the same examinations, and study identical curriculums, but women have to work several times harder than men to prove their credentials in most professions, law is no exception. Women's work at home is invisible too. The value of her labour at home is not included in the Gross Domestic Product in most nations. When a married man is asked what work his wife does, the answers range from, "*Nothing. She stays at home*" to "*She is a homemaker.*" *Homemaker* has replaced *housewife* to accord formal dignity and recognize the role of a woman and her contribution at home, but has it achieved its purpose? It does not appear to me like it has. I will discuss this in the context of a case before me as a judge. In principle, because housework is gendered, no matter what nomenclature you use to address it, women's work at home will always be undervalued, like in any professional work traditionally performed by women.

I was part of a two-judge bench at the Madras High Court hearing an appeal[20] filed by the National Insurance Company. The mother and father of a minor died in the same accident. The insurance company submitted that since the minor was already receiving compensation on account of the father's death, the claim for loss arising out of the mother's death will not stand. We were unable to fathom how simply because both parents died in the same accident;

[17] The Bundesgericht or the Federal Supreme Court of Switzerland.

[18] Affected by an amendment to the Civil Law Procedure of New York.

[19] Hasler, Eveline.1994. *Flying with the Wings of Wax: A Biographical Novel*, Trans. Edna MacCown. Fromm International Publishers.

[20] *National Insurance Co. Ltd. vs Minor Deepika*, Madras High Court, Civil Misc. Appeal Nos.3049, 3050 and 3775 of 2004 and 605 of 2007. https://indiankanoon.org/doc/931785/. Accessed 3 October 2023.

> the child should be deprived of the compensation that she is justly and reasonably entitled to on the death of her mother. The tort-feasor cannot take advantage of the fact that both the parents got wipe of [sic] in the same accident and each claim is a separate claim. On that ground, the Insurance Company's liability cannot be reduced. Each claim has to be dealt with independently and on its own merits.[21]

While evidence of a business partnership between the wife and the husband was indeed not available, the claim for the mother was being assessed as one to be awarded to a *housewife*. This case gave me the opportunity to deliberate on the monetary quantification of the work done by women at home. I referred to Recommendation No. 17 of the CEDAW Committee[22] which affirms that State Parties to the CEDAW have a duty to encourage and support research to evaluate the unremunerated domestic activities of women and to quantify and include this in the Gross National Product. This is in recognition of the fact that *most of the unpaid work around the world is performed by women*. Indeed "*unpaid care work is the foundation of human experience*".[23] In evaluating the loss suffered by the child because of her mother's death in the same accident as the father, the bench decided that *we must give a monetary value to the work of a caregiver, for after all, the home is the basic unit on which our civilized society rests.*[24] In light of the especially tragic and unique circumstances in this case, we felt that it would be appropriate to express our view on the quantification of the labour of an unpaid homemaker, who in this case (as in most) was the mother. Valuation of a homemaker's unpaid labour is assessed principally by three methods. The first is the *opportunity cost method* which evaluates her wages by calculating what she would have earned had she not remained at home, implying the *lost opportunity*. The second is the *partnership method* which assumes that a marriage is an equal partnership and values the homemaker's salary as half her husband's salary. The *replacement method* determines how much it would cost to replace the homemaker with paid workers. In the case before us, we decided that the minor is entitled to compensation for the death of her mother and the death of her father separately as two distinct claims. The compensation for the loss of the mother cannot be clubbed with the loss of the father simply because he was the earning member of the family, and the mother was a homemaker; her contribution must be quantified for the purpose of computing compensation. This is one of several cases I have seen in my years as a lawyer and as a judge where women's contribution to the household is sought to be minimized and made insignificant and only the man's loss of salary seems to matter. This needs to change; my heart goes out to women who labour at home and remain invisible in life and death.

Judgments in a majority of cases relating to women overflow with deeply ingrained sexism and attitudinal biases about women's capacities, social roles, and sexuality. As a result, a female litigant's success in court in cases ranging from marital disputes, inheritance, workplace discrimination, domestic violence, maintenance, and rape becomes highly subjective. Judges are predominantly male, and think within the frameworks that characterize the worldview of the class, gender, and community that they identify with. In order to encourage male judges to transcend their socialization, *sensitization training programmes* (in bureaucratic jargon) are conducted by the government which are not enough as they do not address the structural causes of the problem.[25]

[21] *Ibid.* at para 6.

[22] CEDAW Committee. Tenth session, 1991. General Recommendation No. 17. *The measurement and quantification of unremunerated domestic activities of women and their recognition in the Gross National Product* https://www.un.org/womenwatch/daw/cedaw/cedaw-25years/content/english/General_Recommendations_1-25-English.pdf.

[23] UNICEF Technical Note (2000). Accessed 10 October 2023.

[24] *National Insurance Co. Ltd. vs Minor Deepika*, Madras High Court, Civil Misc. Appeal Nos.3049, 3050 and 3775 of 2004 and 605 of 2007. https://indiankanoon.org/doc/931785/. Accessed 3 October 2023 at Para 9.

[25] Sunder Rajan Rajeshwari (2015). Accessed 12 October 2023.

2.5 Family, Violence, and the *Veil of Equality*

Recently I addressed a group at a public sector bank on Women's Day. I had stopped attending these celebrations because I felt it is meaningless to celebrate Women's day when infants and little girls are subjected to violence, and parents *punish* their children for choosing their life partners. When, early this year, I read about a woman driving a huge sand shoveler in Madhya Pradesh, just one example among several, where women are making leaps to walk into traditional male roles despite limited opportunities and choices in their lives, it inspired me to look at the glass (of gender equity) as half full and not as half empty. I was told about ways in which the bank has created spaces of equality, that female employees were nearly the same in number as the male employees, they had a grievance cell, they had creches, and *most importantly* even their remotest branches had restrooms for women. At the event, I alluded to the book I was reading at that time, Nafisi's "*Reading Lolita in Tehran*".[26] The author taught Western literature at the University of Tehran.[27] For over two years her most committed female students met secretly every week as a group, to read forbidden[28] Western classical works of literature at the author's home. The author notes that most of her students would come into class wearing their *burkha* (veil). They would remove it the minute they stepped inside and put it on again before leaving. I asked the audience at the bank if they wore their *robe of equality* only when they entered their workplace, or if they kept it on after they reached home. At work, perhaps*: The Times they are a Changin'*[29] and people are being trained (and also warned!) to treat a colleague through the lens of gender equality, while at home this is not so. The services rendered by women at home are taken for granted. Home is a violent space where gender inequity rules every interaction, yet remains the most invisible.

The *Indian Penal Code*[30] was amended in 1983 to create the offence of cruelty to a married woman under Section 498A, that related principally to dowry harassment by the husband or his relatives. I wrote a note several years ago on whether Section 498A is being misused by women as is commonly asserted. I argued that the grounds for the attack were completely baseless. I will address just one of these grounds. It is alleged that Section 498A *destroys the family* by allowing the married woman to file an FIR[31] against her husband and/or his parents and in some cases his relatives, thereby destroying the *sanctity* of the marriage and the family. What is a family? It is a fundamental social unit where each member of the unit has the right to be safe and free from injury and violence from other members. If one member, be it a parent or a spouse, systematically inflicts cruelty on the other, affecting adversely their physical and mental well-being, then the family has set itself off on a path of self-destruction. The destruction commences at this point, and not when the accused is taken into custody. The offence itself is structured on an already destroyed or in the best-case scenario—a highly dysfunctional family.

Section 498A has an interesting legislative history that deserves to be appreciated in order to understand the criticality of this provision for married women in India. The 1970s saw a spate of deaths by *stove bursts.*[32] In 1986 a new offence of *Dowry Death* was inserted in

---

[26] Nafisi (2008).

[27] She was subsequently expelled from the university for refusing to wear a veil.

[28] Forbidden at the University of Tehran, in the Islamic republic of Tehran.

[29] Bob Dylan's song released in 1964 believed to be an anthem for inspiring change during that time.

[30] Section 498A, *Indian Penal Code*, 1860.

[31] First Information Report (FIR) that initiates a criminal investigation by the police and the filing of charges in court.

[32] A stove for cooking that is fueled by kerosene. Vapourized kerosene fuel is passed under pressure through a nozzle and mixes with air to form a flame. Young brides were set on fire; stove burst was being cited as the reason for the death and that they were burned while they were cooking.

the *Indian Penal Code.*[33] Under this section, if a woman dies an unnatural death within 7 years of marriage and there is prima facie evidence of dowry harassment, the death has to be investigated as a dowry death by the police, making it a cognizable offence. The statement that the family is *destroyed* if a complaint is lodged by the woman under Section 498A is an affront to her dignity and her right to life. It is as if her safety and personal autonomy are nothing but a piffle, and the right of the offender to be free is paramount. Institutions such as the family and marriage that become life-threatening to the woman are better demolished. Women's rights are consistently pushed out of the line of vision while the importance of keeping the home *intact* is foregrounded. Recall Dr. Ambedkar's words, in referring to the significance of the Hindu Code: "*To leave inequality between class and class, between sex and sex, which is the soul of Hindu society untouched, and to go on passing legislation relating to economic problems is to make a farce of our Constitution and to build a palace on a dung heap.*"[34]

I have referred to the perspective of inequality in viewing women's work at home as *unseen work*. Another critical area of invisibility is women's ownership of property since she is not seen as a person when inheritance and succession issues arise. As observed by Devaki Jain:

> And gender inequality is different from other forms of inequality, such as those based on economic, racial, ethnic, religious or colour criteria. Inequality between men and women enters the so-called ultimate unit of social organization, namely the household, the family. There can be inequality between sons and daughters, between a father and a mother. To my mind this is the most sensitive and basic inequality. It pervades class, caste, religion, colour and the usual boundaries of homogeneous formations.[35]

Nafisi's "*Reading Lolita in Tehran*"[36] based in 1980s Iran takes us into the home of the English Literature Professor, and the students gathered there secretly to read and discuss specific American literary texts against the backdrop of the Revolution that attacked everything 'American'. These classes were held to protect, affirm, and celebrate individual, independent voices through literature, in defiance of the tyranny of the State. "*These girls, my girls had both a real history and a fabricated one. Although they came from very different backgrounds, the regime that ruled them had tried to make their personal identities and histories irrelevant.*" The author stands in front of the University Allamah Tabatabaei with one of the female students and looks at the university gate. It was a green gate that opened into a wide street on one side.

> Yet that green gate was closed to…all my girls. Next to the gate there was a small opening with a curtain hanging from it. It was an aberration that attracted attention, because it did not belong there: it gaped with the arrogant authority of an intruder. Through the opening all the students, including my girls, went into a small dark room to be inspected.

The green gate was freely open to men. Visualize the image—a wide gate for men to enter and exit freely as they pleased, no questions asked, and a narrow opening constrained for women to enter, subject to inspection. This image is an evocation of the ubiquitous gender inequality. Let us not comfort ourselves with our inner thoughts and calm our indignity with the voice that echoess— *Oh! That's just the way it is.* That is tantamount to self-delusion. The man who recklessly gambled his wife and brothers away, just had to remove his crown and upper cloth, while the woman, who asked if he was

[33] The punishment for causing this death is imprisonment for a minimum of 7 years and maximum of life imprisonment. The provisions under section 304B, IPC are more stringent than that provided under Section 498A of the Penal Code. The offence is cognizable, non-bailable, and triable by Court of Session. Section 304 B by the *Dowry Prohibition (Amendment) Act*, 1986 (43 of 1986).

[34] Government of India, *Report of the Hindu Law Committee*, 1947.

[35] Jain (2020).

[36] Nafisi, Azar. 2008. Reading Lolita in Tehran, A Memoir in Books. New York: Random House.

a free man when he staked her freedom, was stripped. That story[37] is part of our DNA.[38]

> Any intersex child is entitled to and must stay within the folds of its family. The running away from the family to the margins and beyond is a fatal journey that must be arrested. Time has come when they are brought back from the margins into the mainstream.[39]

I was part of a closed public hearing on Familial Violence on Queer and Transpersons. I heard one testimony after another of families that have refused to accept their child's choice of gender identity, sexual orientation, or the choice of partner. The most unsafe and violence-ridden space was their home. What hurt the speakers most was when their parents and the persons they referred to as their *near and dear* ones revealed their ugly faces. Does this social unit deserve to be revered as a *family*? When an individual belonging to this social unit is not treated with dignity and risks losing their life or limb, the second an individual begins to feel unsafe, this unit ceases to be a *family*. How then would you define *family*? Shall we call it a social unit consisting of more than one person living, eating, and sleeping together in a defined space we call *home*? Even if we were to define it in such practical terms, assigning unnecessary reverence to this unit, the bare minimum to be expected from the members of this social unit would be mutual respect for fundamental rights of each other, namely the right to live safely with dignity. The members may be linked to each other biologically or through marriage, but, more critically, are these the only two ways in which a *family* can be constituted? What identifies it as a family is the intention of individuals to live as one. Subsumed in this intent is an affirmation of safety as a bare minimum condition that one will not be violent towards another. Does the parent have a right to inflict violence on their child? Does the parent have a right to inflict violence on a child who does not fall into what is termed *normal*?

Contraceptive advertisements in India in the 1970s and early 1980s unfailingly depicted the image of the *ideal family*: father, mother, daughter, and son. In these images, they are all shown smiling. Such images are deeply impactful, and they are internalized by individuals as *true* representations of an ideal family. Anything that appears contrary to this commercialized image of the *ideal family* raises individuals', institutions', and society's *porcupine spines*. This became the quintessential *perfect family* image that appeared not just on family planning products; the *perfect family* image found its way into school and college textbooks thereby indoctrinating children and young adults. Advertising agencies and ad campaigns have modernized since, though in our minds: *the mother is happy in the kitchen, father sits in an easy chair and the two children, one female and one male, are either sitting somewhere doing their homework or playing in a garden.* This image is cast in stone. Though rarely visible even to the keen observer—caste, class, and religious rigidities are superimposed on the ideal family image

---

[37] The Epic Mahabharata. These lines refer to the famous scene where in a game of gambling between cousins, the 'Pandvas' lost everything and had nothing left to gamble away; the female protagonist of the epic Draupadi who was married to all five Pandava brothers was put at stake. Draupadi questions Yudhishthira's right on her as he has lost himself first and she was still the queen; Duryodhana, angry with Draupadi's questions, commands his younger brother Dushasana to bring her to the court forcefully. Dushasana drags Draupadi to the court by the hair. After the men have fought over whether a king has the right to bet a woman, Karna declares that when Yudhishthira lost all his possessions, he also lost Draupadi, insults her for being wedded to five men, and orders Dushasana to disrobe Draupadi. Seeing her husbands' passivity, Draupadi prays to Krishna to protect her. A miracle occurs henceforward, which is popularly attributed to Krishna. Dushasana unwraps layers and layers of her sari. As her sari keeps getting extended, everyone looks upon in awe, and Dushasana himself is forced to stop due to exhaustion.

[38] This is specifically in the Indian context, where everyone has heard this part of the story, famously referred to as the scene of 'cheerharan' or 'disrobing'.

[39] *Arun Kumar and Sreeja vs Inspector General of Registration*, Madurai Bench of Madras High Court, WP (MD) No. 4125 of 2019. https://www.livelaw.in/pdf_upload/pdf_upload-360185.pdf. Accessed 5 October 2023.

with such deftness that it appears natural.[40] The assumption of a happy family unit comprising heterosexual married parents is assumed, and a child is never depicted as a person identifying with the LGBTQIA+ community. Anything outside the image of this privileged institution is hidden beneath layers of naturalness.[41]

The criticality of this image permeates our legal system and impacts the rights of individuals; rights are contracted within the rigid parameters where institutions of family and marriage are protected above the rights of individuals. Law does not always protect individual freedoms and rights of anyone who falls outside these revered institutions. In this context inheritance rights become critical. Women rank below men under all personal laws in India, even though there is *de jure* equality that has been established in these areas. In an appeal before the Supreme Court, a Hindu male died intestate.[42] The self-acquired property of the deceased was not in dispute, and it was divided equally between the petitioners. For the purposes of tax benefits,[43] the three women wanted to jointly pay wealth tax as a Hindu Undivided Family (HUF). The Supreme Court had to determine if *a Hindu undivided family can consist of female members only*. The Supreme Court adjudicated as follows:

> The principal question that we are concerned with here is the capacity of Hindu females to form among themselves a Hindu Undivided Family. No authorities to support this are brought to our notice; indeed they cannot be, for the concept appears to us to be alien to the Hindu personal law which requires the presence of a male for the purposes of the constitution of an Hindu Undivided Family.[44]

2.6 Religion and Violence

I have mentioned religion earlier as a critical factor. Interestingly, religion generally does not *see* anyone other than a male, and this applies to all religions without exception. In *Pinniyakkal v District Collector*,[45] the Madras High Court observed:

> It is ironical that when the presiding deity of the temple was an "Amman" in a female form, objections are being raised against a woman in performing poojas in such temples. Even in Vedic times it is recorded that women had performed poojas and rituals. Fortunately the present temple is not trapped under any agama sastras. The sub-cultural deities established in the Southern parts of India are freed from the norms of Manu Smritis and hence the women being subordinated to home making alone was not warranted. As said by a great philosopher the women hold half the sky and for human progress we must walk with our two legs. The altars of the God must be made free from gender bias. Only then the constitutional mandate under Articles 15 and 51A (e) will become a reality.

In this case, Pinniyakkal was fighting for her right to perform *pooja* at a temple in South India. The court held in her favour. In 2020 though, she approached the court to provide her with police protection to ensure that she could perform her duty as *Poosari* to the Arulmighu Sri Durgaiamman Thirukovil.[46] She was still

---

[40] This concept of *natural* is best explained by Nivedita Menon by analogizing it to *nude make-up*. Menon explains that "*Nude make-up looks are all about your skin looking fresh and dewy, without looking like you're even wearing any make-up. All you need is eyeliner, mascara, nude lipstick, and a highlighting blush that will give your skin a natural-looking glow. The whole point of nude make-up, clearly, is to spend hours painting your face in order to make it look like you had not touched it at all.*" Menon likens this to the maintenance of the social order through repeated performance of complex socio-cultural normative rituals during one's life to ultimately reach the goal of *naturalness*. *See* Menon (2012) at page ix.

[41] *Ibid.*

[42] Without leaving behind a valid will, the property of the Hindu will devolve in such a case under the rules of intestate succession under the Hindu Succession Act, 1955.

[43] Under *The Wealth Tax Act, 1957*.

[44] *The Commissioner of Income Tax v Smt. Sandhya Rani Dutta*. Supreme Court of India Case No: Appeal (civil) 5450–5451 of 1997.

[45] *Pinniyakkal v The District Collector*, Madras High Court W.P. (MD) No. 9704 of 2007 and M.P. (MD) Nos. 1 of 2007, 1 of 2008 https://indiankanoon.org/doc/1581819/. Accessed at 23 September 2023.

[46] *Ibid.*

fighting twelve years after her right had been recognized by the court. All institutionalized religions and the structures that support these are patriarchal. It is this inequality in all religions that supports women's invisibilization and creates conditions that condone violence against women and other minority gender identities and persons of non-binary sexual orientation.

2.7 Conclusion

To conclude my thoughts on family, gender, and violence, I am going to refer to a short story from my favourite Tamil writer, Imayam's[47] short stories collection, "*If There is a God*"[48] that I have translated from Tamil to English. In the story, "*No Fear in the Burial Ground*", the author takes us to a conversation between two women at a burial ground. While one woman, the narrator, is here as a construction worker, the other is a grave digger. The narrator is surprised to see a woman digging a burial pit all by herself. This is the first time she has entered a cemetery. The grave digger, Sita, could not understand the narrator's shock at seeing her here doing the work that she was doing. On being quizzed, she initially responds with amusement, saying that she saw nothing wrong with the work she does, and why would she do any other work?

The narrator, at finding a thirty-two-year-old woman working in a place where women are ordinarily not even allowed to visit, has several questions, these draw them into a long and deep conversation. Her initial questions to Sita are: Do you not fear the demons, the evil spirits? Why are you not married? Here is the response she gets:

> I have dug graves for women who have consumed poison or hanged themselves within one or two months of marriage, after a quarrel at home or because they did not like their husbands. I have dug graves for young women who have died because of a love 'problem', and women with a four -or- five-month old foetus inside them. There have been women who gave poison to their children and consumed it themselves after a quarrel with their husband, and women who have set themselves on fire, hugging their children. I have dug graves for young girls. So many graves….. After all that, how can I marry?

The narrator is intrigued and continues to ask Sita about her life. Sita tells her that she has been coming to the burial grounds with her grandfather who adopted her and her sister after they were orphaned. At this point, the conversation takes a serious turn, and the narrator learns that Sita's mother set fire to herself and died following a bitter fight with her husband, Sita's father, who later hanged himself out of remorse. Sita and her sister found themselves wandering the burial grounds looking for their mother's and father's graves. This is how they came to be here. The sister married and moved on while Sita chose to be where her parents are buried, and her grandfather works as a grave digger. She wants no other life than this one. She will not leave her grandparents and will look after them since they have no children. Through the seemingly simple conversation between two women, Sita[49] comes across as a woman with grit and determination facing challenges and hardships bravely. Sita's perception and understanding of people's relationships and society is very astute. What is interesting is that most of her life lessons have been learnt through observations of the *alive* and the *dead*. That is what makes the story and its protagonist unique. She tells the narrator that she has nothing to fear in the burial grounds; she feels safer here than in any other place. She says that men who come here also stare at her because *men will be men* wherever they are. Her observations on those alive are grim—she tells the narrator that her sister's husband wants a son and so her sister, who has four girls, finds herself pregnant every year.

[47] Imayam is the pen name of V. Annamalai, a schoolteacher and writer in Tamil, who has published six novels. He has won several prestigious awards.

[48] Imayam (2022).

[49] Imayam's stories are about the extraordinary lives of ordinary people and often depict strong women.

Now it is the narrator's turn to share her life story:

> Married at nineteen, and immediately made me the mother of two children. Then, as if his job was done, he died. Both the children are girls.
> You have to dig a grave to feed yourself; I have to carry concrete mix. I am like firewood that has to burn in stove every day.

The bonding and honest conversation between two women—complete strangers who meet in the most unusual circumstances and *space*, a graveyard, tells us so much about the lives of women, their position in society, and family. This is the life that I have seen every day in court and in the world outside, hierarchies that prompt violent thoughts and violent acts that lace every aspect of our private lives.

References

Arun Kumar and Sreeja vs Inspector General of Registration, Madurai Bench of Madras High Court, WP (MD) No. 4125 of 2019. https://www.livelaw.in/pdf_upload/pdf_upload-360185.pdf

CEDAW Committee. Tenth session, 1991. General Recommendation No. 17. The measurement and quantification of unremunerated domestic activities of women and their recognition in the Gross National Product. https://www.un.org/womenwatch/daw/cedaw/cedaw25years/content/english/General_Recommendations_1-25-English.pdf

Government of India, Report of the Hindu Law Committee, 1947

Hasler E (1994) Flying with the wings of wax: a biographical novel (Trans MacCown E). Fromm International Publishers

Imayam (2022) If there is a god and other stories (Trans (from Tamil) Sridevan JP (retd.)). Ratna Books

Imayam (2023) Vazhga Vazhga (Trans Sridevan JP (retd.)). Penguin Ebury Press

Indian Young Lawyers Association and ors. vs The State of Kerala and ors. (The Sabarimala judgement), Supreme Court of India (2019) 11 SCC 1

Jain D (2020) The journey of a southern feminist. Sage, New Delhi

Levitt RB, Barnack-Tavlaris JL (2020) Addressing menstruation in the workplace: the menstrual leave debate. In: Bobel C, Winkler IT, Fahs B, Hasson KA, Kissling EA, Roberts T-A (eds) The Palgrave handbook of critical menstruation studies. Palgrave Macmillan, Singapore

Menon N (2012) Seeing like a feminist. Zubaan, New Delhi

Nafisi A (2008) Reading Lolita in Tehran, a memoir in books. Random House, New York

National Insurance Co. Ltd. vs Minor Deepika, Madras High Court, Civil Misc. Appeal Nos.3049, 3050 and 3775 of 2004 and 605 of 2007. https://indiankanoon.org/doc/931785/

Pinniyakkal v The District Collector, Madras High Court W.P. (MD) No. 9704 of 2007 and M.P. (MD) Nos. 1 of 2007, 1 of 2008 https://indiankanoon.org/doc/1581819/

Sachs JA (2009) The strange alchemy of life and law. Oxford University Press, Oxford

Schelbert L (2008). Sisters in battle: five portraits. Swiss Am Hist Soc Rev 44(2):49–63. https://scholarsarchive.byu.edu/sahs_review/vol44/iss2/8

Sunder Rajan Rajeshwari (22 May 2015) A woman's worth. Granta. https://granta.com/womans-worth/

The Commissioner of Income Tax v Smt. Sandhya Rani Dutta, Supreme Court of India Case No: Appeal (civil) 5450–5451 of 1997

The Constitution of India, 1950

The Indian Contract Act, 1872

The Indian Penal Code, 1860

The Specific Relief Act, 1963

The Wealth Tax Act, 1957 (India)

UNICEF Technical Note (2000) Women Work: UNICEF approach to women paid and unpaid work. https://www.unicef.org/media/66136/file/Women

3 Documenting Psychological Tactics as Violence in Meena Kandasamy's '*When I Hit You Or, a Portrait of the Writer as a Young Wife*'

Santwana Dwivedy

Abstract

Conversations on intimate partner violence focus on visible acts of physical, sexual, and mental abuse. The chapter explores psychological tactics such as gaslighting, isolation, intimidation, humiliation, and control as a distinct category of violence against the backdrop of Meena Kandasamy's '*When I Hit You Or, a Portrait of the Writer as a Young Wife*'. The narrator in the novel recounts her life after marriage to reveal to the reader the covert psychological tactics used by her husband that irrigate intimate spaces for more overt forms of violence to thrive. In doing so, the narrator draws our attention to the criticality and complexity of the true dimensions of intimate partner violence. The chapter analyses psychological tactics as emotional and psychological violence through the lens of the narrator's experience as a victim to fill critical gaps in the sociological understanding of intimate partner violence. The chapter draws on themes that emerge from the novel to demonstrate the role of gender imbalances within the institution of marriage that are critical in sustaining violence. The overarching objective of the analysis is to deepen and widen the 'intimate violence framework' to include psychological tactics as a serious form of violence.

Keywords

Psychological tactics · Emotional abuse · Manipulation · Intimate violence · Conditioning · Fear · Control · Gaslighting · Isolation · Gender hierarchy · Marriage · Family · Law · Institutional violence · Coping mechanisms · Hidden violence

3.1 Introduction

> Violence is not something that advertises itself. It is not written on my face – he is too careful of that, of course, aiming his fists at my body. As long as a woman cannot speak, as long as those to whom she speaks do not listen, the violence is unending.[1]

The current discourse on intimate violence in marital relationships is focused on the gravity and redressal of physical, sexual, verbal, emotional, and economic abuse.[2] The academic and

S. Dwivedy (✉)
Jindal Global Law School, O.P. Jindal Global University, Sonipat, India
e-mail: sdwivedy@jgu.edu.in

[1] Kandasamy (2017) 197.

[2] *See* Section 3, Definition of Domestic Violence, *Protection of Women from Domestic Violence Act*, 2005 (PWDVA).

P. M. Anurag and S. Dwivedy (eds.), *Violence in Intimate Spaces*, Sustainable Development Goals Series, https://doi.org/10.1007/978-981-97-2657-8_3

legal discourse has been limited in its engagement with violence that is tangible and immediately identifiable as abuse. Research on invisible modes of violence in intimate spaces, specifically between intimate partners and the ways in which this manifests, is in its nascent stages. The chapter brings to the fore psychological tactics used by abusers that lie latent beneath overt forms of violence; namely, physical, sexual, verbal abuse. Tactics of control such as isolation, gaslighting, manipulation, and humiliation deeply impact the victim and gradually erode their sense of self-worth, individuality, and dignity. The criticality of psychological tactics as a form of violence has not received adequate focus since it is not immediately identifiable as violence even by the victim. These acts are obscured by gendered power dynamics and are naturalized within patriarchal relationships. In elucidating and illustrating the insidious ways in which this type of violence operates, the chapter grounds its analysis within the framework of *family* and *marriage* as rigid institutions which enable and encourage both overt and covert forms of violence. In doing so, the chapter seeks to highlight the deeply harmful ways in which psychological violence operates.

At the heart of this chapter lies Meena Kandasamy's exceptionally lyrical novel, '*When I Hit You Or, A Portrait of the Writer as a Young Wife*' (*When I Hit You*).[3] The protagonist narrator in the novel is a writer and a feminist, married to a college lecturer whom she loves for his *idealism* and she is *enchanted* by his *communist credentials*. Despite his open contempt for her feminist leanings, she marries him following a hurried courtship. The novel depicts the saga of the narrator's violent marriage, in which she sees herself as an actor performing the role of an obedient, *dutiful wife*.[4] Through her words and actions, she must express her eagerness to impress him to escape punishment. The marriage that lasted four months was marked by physical, sexual, and psychological abuse. The narrator chronicles her journey and perception of self-identity—before, during, and after the abuse—which corresponds with her life before, during, and after leaving the marriage. Despite her education, awareness, and self-confidence before her marriage, the violence that is unleashed by the husband in the form of psychological tactics of gaslighting, isolation, control, humiliation, and threats, in addition to physical and sexual abuse, leaves her bereft of her sense of self.

In this chapter, the novel '*When I Hit You*' is read as a work of fiction inspired by the author Meena Kandasamy's life and not as her *memoir*. This understanding is based on her claim,[5] "*One of the more troubling aspects of the novel's success, says Kandasamy, was the way in which some readers treated it as autobiography: a Polish publisher wanted to buy the rights so as to repackage the novel as narrative non-fiction.*" She refused to do so and has consistently maintained that it is a work of fiction inspired by her life. In an interview with NDTV,[6] Kandasamy said that initially she had planned on writing this novel in the third person, to distance the author from the protagonist narrator in the novel. She eventually incorporated *the raw material from the experience of her own marriage* and decided to write it in a first-person narration. A review of literature[7] on her novel reveals, that Kandasamy herself faced domestic violence in her marriage

[3] Kandasamy (2017).

[4] Kandasamy (2017) 20.

[5] She states, "*Although there was not a line of falsehood in that book, it was not a memoir. A memoir for me means a person's life story; if I was going to write my actual life story, I would condense this entire marriage into a footnote. By treating it as memoir, people were overlooking the artistry. The idea was: 'I'm going to tell you a story about what happened to me.' For me, the artistic enterprise is: 'I'm going to tell you a story', a narrative that has been shaped. It's not therapy.*" See Self (2019). Accessed 15 September 2023.

[6] NDTV. Aired on June 2017. Meena Kandasamy tells all about her abusive marriage. https://www.ndtv.com/video/news/the-buck-stops-here/meena-kandasamy-s-tell-all-about-her-abusive-marriage-458883. Accessed 28 October 2023.

[7] Das (2022); Rangkuti and Christomy (2017); *See also* Kandasamy (2022). Accessed 28 October 2023.

and it is safe to assume that this would permeate into her work at some level. In this sense, the analysis of the novel in this chapter is structured with the awareness of Kandasamy's personal engagement with the life of the protagonist narrator.

The overarching objective behind the chapter is to contribute to the nascent discourse on *psychological tactics as violence* on three levels: *first*, it unpacks the hidden harms of *hidden* tactics as violence; *second,* it highlights that despite the narrator's acute awareness of her abusive situation, she endures his violent behaviour, voicing her innermost thoughts, including those of fear, to him only towards the end; *third,* it identifies the silence in society and family that fuels the inherent limitations and often unwillingness of the State in recognizing covert acts as violence and thus contributing to the gender imbalances in marriage that condone such behaviour. The novel presents a story that is immediately relatable to the reader because of the simplicity of narration and the direct, lucid style used by Kandasamy in her *chronicle of an abusive marriage* between partners in a *modern love marriage*.[8] The protagonist narrator and her husband are educated and liberal.[9] Through the narrator's unfiltered thoughts, the reader is introduced to violence in a seemingly 'normal' marriage. The normalization of patriarchal gendered roles and behaviour patterns that trivialize this violence as a regular part of marriage is evident. The themes of marriage, family, individual choices, inflexible gender roles and the insignificance of the wife's dignity within marriage are subtly reflected through the narrative that reshapes our understanding of family and marriage as unequal institutions. Kandasamy's '*When I Hit You*' thus presents an apt literary piece for analyzing psychological violence.

The scope of this chapter is limited to the examination of violence in cis-heteropatriarchal marriages.[10] Further, while acknowledging that psychological tactics can be used as violence by either spouse in intimate relationships, this chapter confines itself to understanding the dynamics of such violence where the wife is at the receiving end and the husband is the perpetrator. It is now adequately established that physical and sexual violence, in addition to bodily injury, never exist without causing emotional and mental trauma to the victim.[11] This indicates that the impact of violence is varied and cannot be compartmentalized.[12] The fact that Kandasamy creates a protagonist who is a writer in this story is interesting. This could be interpreted as Kandasamy's personal connection with domestic abuse. The protagonist narrator's engagement with her writing in the novel, forms a major part of her narrative of the violence endured by her. Is her writing a form of coping mechanism? Or has Kandasamy used her skills as a writer to express the deep anguish of a *writer as a young wife* in an abusive marriage? It is this quality of the novel that makes it impossible to disengage oneself from the connection between the protagonist narrator and the author of the novel (Kandasamy). The protagonist narrator's relationship with her writing is also intertwined with the abuse, where she uses her writing as a tool of defiance against her abusive husband.

> Being a writer is now a matter of self-respect. It is the job title that I give myself. I realize that my husband does not hate anything in this universe as much as the idea of a writer (a petit bourgeois woman writer, at that), so I forge a sense of reverence towards the job of being a writer.
> But it's not just about antagonizing him. There is a distasteful air of the outlaw that accompanies the idea of a writer in my husband's mind.

---

[8] Kandasamy (2017).

[9] Additionally, the characters in the novel provide a fresh perspective that dispels the myth that domestic violence only occurs in poor and underprivileged households. See Vranda (2013).

[10] Although intimate violence is also observed in other queer relationships and natal violence, these are beyond the scope of this chapter.

[11] Lammers et al. (2005).

[12] SafeLives (Ending Domestic Abuse) (2019). Accessed 1 July 2023.

> A self-centeredness about writing that doesn't fit with his image of a revolutionary. It has the one – word job description: defiance. I've never felt such a dangerous attraction towards anything else in my life.[13]

The second section of this chapter documents psychological violence seen through the voice of the protagonist narrator in '*When I Hit You*'; theoretical perspectives on psychological violence are discussed in the third section; the fourth section tracks the long-term impact of psychological and emotional violence and juxtaposes it against the narrator's coping mechanisms through her writing. The final section situates the violence within the institutions of family, marriage, and society to highlight the blind spots that hide psychological and emotional violence from our line of vision.

3.2 *Portrait* of Psychological Violence in '*When I Hit You*'

The vivid images drawn by the narrator of her four-month-long marriage portray her sense of isolation within the physical space she calls home. The narrator and her husband move to Mangalore soon after their marriage. The city, the locality, the neighbours, and the language are all 'foreign' to her. Adding to the strangeness of her unfamiliar surroundings is her confinement to the marital home she shares with her husband. She feels trapped in the house—within *the three rooms and verandah*—"*This is the space within which I must move*."[14] The house has a beautiful garden, but it is surrounded by well-defined walls, keeping the house *small and self-contained,* away from people.[15] This spatial confinement frightens her. To escape the reality of the confinement enforced by the husband within the domestic walls, she imagines this space as a *film set* where she is playing the part of a *dutiful wife*.[16]

The narrator takes us to their courtship days and recounts the subtle and gradual control exerted by her husband that takes dangerous forms post-marriage. She met him at an online campaign against the death penalty and fell in love with his staunch leftist ideals for overcoming capitalism. Before marriage, he had *solemnly informed* her that she would have to give up her middle-class lifestyle to become a 'true' communist. The narrator tells the reader that she was *willing to learn* his ways and see the world through his eyes.[17] Then, they get married.

> Marriage became a Re-education camp. He transformed into a teacher, and I became the wife-student learning from this Communist crusader…I must learn, and I must change. There is no other way.[18]

Her willingness to learn the true ideals of communism before her marriage changes. Her husband's communism now transforms itself into a volatile space where he uses it as a tool of control. He makes every attempt to ensure that she is forced to align her political beliefs and ideologies with his. He uses communism as a pretext for disciplining and controlling her ideologically through violence. He tells her:

> Your violence is the violence of the Indian state… My violence is the counter-violence of the insurgents who are fighting for the rights of people… I am not ashamed of my violence. I am proud of it. I am not a liberal, or a democrat. **My violence is a reaction to your violence.** Your violence is your effort to emasculate me, to live the life of middle-class luxury, to go on talking about your feminism…[19]

His control of her thoughts and beliefs includes the tactic of *isolation*. He ensures that she remains disconnected from her world (and ideology) in every possible way. He restricts her online activities and communication. The narrator describes an instance where he convinces her to deactivate her Facebook account:

[13] Kandasamy (2017) 80.

[14] *Ibid* at 13, 15.

[15] *Ibid.*

[16] *Ibid.*

[17] Kandasamy (2017) at 30.

[18] *Ibid* at 32, 33.

[19] *Ibid* at 150.

> There is no reason why you should be on Facebook. It's narcissism. It's exhibitionism... It's merely you voluntarily feeding information straight to the CIA, to the RAW, to the IB, to everyone who is hounding my life. Every fucking thing is being monitored. Your life may be a peep show, but I'm a revolutionary. I cannot let you endanger me...[20]

Facebook is her only means of contact with the world outside her marital home and to stay connected with her professional world as a writer. To enforce his will and ensure she deactivates her Facebook account, he lights one matchstick after the other and *extinguishes them against his skin.*[21] When she asks him to stop, he says, "*If you loved me, this is the quickest way to make up your mind.*" He further restricts her online usage to three hours a week (30 min a day) and only in his presence.[22] He manipulates her into sharing all her passwords, including the one to her email. On one occasion, he deletes all her 25,600 odd e-mails—which included her written work emails from her friends and mother—rendering her bereft of all the memories from her past.[23] Following this, he changes the password of her Gmail ID so she would not be able to retrieve the emails deleted by him or access her account in his absence.[24] She realizes that this is a pattern of abuse as he slowly begins to cut off all her communication with the outside world.

He regularly humiliates the narrator in private. She muses to herself, "*...a communist woman is treated equally and respectfully by comrades in public but can be slapped and called a whore behind closed doors. This is dialectics.*"[25] The husband slut-shames[26] her for applying lipstick; according to him, lipstick is anti-communism.[27] Through sharp words and humiliating insults, he starts controlling everything about her. When she lets out an involuntary moan while having sex, this angers him as he considers this the worst form of sexual behaviour from a communist as it was the treatment of *sex as a public spectacle* and was disgusting in his opinion.[28] She learns to *be still and silent* when in bed with him. The husband exercises this element of control in numerous ways. With time the reader learns that because of this control and ownership of her entire being, she starts self-policing her appearance, behaviour, and language according to his preferences,

> ...I begin by wearing my hair the way he wants it: gathered and tamed into a ponytail, oiled, sleek, with no sign of disobedience. I skip the kohl around my eyes because he believes that it is worn only by screen-sirens and seductresses. I wear a dull T-shirt and pajama-bottoms because he approves of dowdiness...Some days, when I am especially eager to impress and to escape punishment, I slip into the shapeless monstrosity that is: *the nightie*... This is the plainness that makes him pleased. This plainness that has peeled away all my essence, a plainness that can be controlled and moulded to his will...[29]

In addition to these psychological tactics, the narrator also describes several instances of physical and sexual violence.[30] She lives in constant anxiety and fear. She fears that if she does not follow his rules regarding a 'proper' home, a 'real' Communist, and a 'good' wife, she will be the recipient of his disapproval, anger, and violence.

> The smallest thing could start a major fight: the level of salt in the pumpkin *sambar*, the excess oil in the groundnut chutney, the green chilli in the chicken curry, the headline in the newspaper, the suspicion that I went to the shop without wearing a *dupatta*, the agenda for the day, the shopping list I

[20] Kandasamy (2017) at 50.

[21] *Ibid* at 51.

[22] *Ibid* at 59.

[23] *Ibid* at139.

[24] *Ibid.*

[25] *Ibid* at 34.

[26] 'Slut shaming' is defined as "the stigmatization of an individual based on his or her appearance, sexual availability, and actual or perceived sexual behaviour and is primarily aimed at women and girls. This stigmatization is reflected in social and relational sanctions, such as rumours, ostracism, or insults" as defined in Armstrong et al. (2014).

[27] Kandasamy (2017) at 132.

[28] Kandasamy (2017) at 152.

[29] *Ibid* at 15, 16.

[30] Sexual and physical violence always incorporates some elements of psychological and emotional violence, by harming the mental psyche of the victim, leaving them feeling humiliated, ashamed, and confused.

> have forgotten to prepare, the laundry piling up, the failure to bring back the clothes left to dry in the porch the night before, which are now rain-soaked and mud-splattered and have to be washed again, the sticky kitchen floor, the slow speed at which I clear the dishes, his shirt and trousers that I have not ironed. He can be kind, I know he can, I've seen how tender he is with the homeless boys in town, but with me I know he will always choose to be cruel.[31]

These invisible tactics and the manipulation in the form of psychological and emotional abuse and his strictures on her appearance, behaviour and cleanliness are enforced by him not always by physical force but instead through the use of verbal and psychological tactics that border on bullying. It is this psychological manipulation in ensuring obedience of his wife that characterizes the narrator's life through the novel.

3.3 Theoretical Analysis of Psychological Violence: Gaslighting, Isolation and Control, Humiliation and Fear

Violence against women encompasses a broad range of behaviours, including psychological and emotional harm within the family that is often condoned by the State.[32] In the context of intimate relationships '*psychological violence*' *is believed to impact cognitive aspects, hampering the victim's rational thinking and judgement skills and 'emotional abuse' adversely affects the victim's feelings and emotional behaviours and impacts the victim's self-worth and dignity.*[33] The chapter makes an argument that psychological tactics (through words, acts, and omissions) work on the principle of dominance of the abuser over the victim and that such dominance in intimate relationships need not always be overt, as reflected in the novel. Sebastian explains that intimate knowledge that partners have about each other is often used to weaponize the others' weaknesses and vulnerabilities under the guise of love. He explains this by citing examples of covert psychological tactics such as: "*Honey, your assertiveness keeps causing problems for you*" or "*People won't like you because you scare them.*"[34] The message hidden in these words, often not pre-meditated, yet insidious, impacts the victim's perception of 'self' and her relationships adversely. Not only do these tactics bear heavily on the victim's cognitive behaviour ('psychological') by altering their *sense of reality*, but they also have a devastating effect on the victim's self-worth and feelings ('emotional').

Psychological tactics of violence in intimate relationships manifest in numerous forms and are practiced in varied ways such as, *inter alia*, criticizing, blaming, controlling or insulting, that are *acted out* through *emotional maltreatment, verbal battering, social humiliation, extreme controlling behaviour*'[35] Psychological literature speaks of several modes of measurement to assess harms of psychological tactics.[36]

---

[31] Kandasamy (2017) 138.

[32] UNGA (20 December 1993); Similar definition of 'violence against women' also found in Coomaraswamy (1996)

[33] SafeLives (Ending Domestic Abuse) (2019). Accessed 1 July 2023.

[34] Sebastian (1983).

[35] Karakurt and Kristin (2013).

[36] For example, the Conflict Tactics Scale (Straus 1979 and Straus et al 1996) is a self-reporting assessing the nature and frequency of tactics such as sexual coercion, psychological aggression, physical injury, negotiation used to deal with conflict in intimate relationship to understand perpetration and victimization. However, it is criticized by a lot of scholars as it fails to look at the context of the abuse. A more favourable method of analysing psychological violence is through the Psychological Maltreatment of Women Inventory (PMWI) developed by (Tolman 1999) and the Multidimensional Measure of Emotional Abuse (MMEA) by Murphy and Hoover 1999). The PMWI characterizes two domains: emotional-verbal abuse and domination-isolation in a 5-point scale ranging from 'never' to 'very frequently' validated across culture groups. The MMEA considers 4 kinds of behaviours, namely, Restrictive engulfment, Denigration, Hostile Withdrawal and Dominance-Intimidation in a 7-point scale (from 'never' to '20 or more times') within past six, four, or three months. The Measure of Psychologically Abusive Behaviours (MPAB) scale has been developed in the United States measuring milder, moderate, and severe forms of psychological violence. *See* Straus (1979); Straus et al. (1996), Tolman (1999); Murphy and Hoover (1999).

Although there are multiple ways of measuring the scope of psychological tactics, most scholars of Psychology agree that violence includes behaviours that are non-physical in nature to exercise dominance through emotional abuse and controlling behaviour.[37] The United Nations (UN) Guidelines for Producing Statistics on Violence against Women has conceptualized psychological violence as emotional abuse and controlling behaviour. 'Emotional abuse' includes *insulting a woman or making her feel bad about herself, belittling or humiliating her in front of other people, deliberately scaring or intimidating her, threatening to hurt her or others she cares about.*[38] Examples of 'controlling behaviour' could include *isolating a woman by preventing her from seeing family or friends, monitoring her whereabouts and social interactions, ignoring her or treating her indifferently, getting angry if she speaks with other men, making unwarranted accusations of infidelity, controlling her access to health care, education or labour market.*[39] In addition to these psychological tactics, another category of psychological abuse which often goes unnoticed, is the tactic of gaslighting as a form of manipulation.

Through the story of the protagonist narrator's abusive marriage as seen in the novel, this section sets down working definitions for: manipulative behaviour such as gaslighting; controlling behaviour such as social isolation and control of access to health care and employment and finally, emotional abuse in the form of humiliation and fear instilled through direct and indirect threats. These tactics are often employed together, and they overlap to produce the resultant psychological and emotional violence. These forms of psychological and emotional violence have been discussed as separate 'types' simply to facilitate a clear idea of the distinct features that characterize the way these manifest in intimate relationships.

Gaslighting In psychological literature, gaslighting has recently garnered significant attention especially within social media.[40] This term is used to describe behaviour constituting a set of attempts to create a *surreal*[41] social environment by making the victim appear *crazy*. The victim over time begins to believe that they are indeed crazy, and this in turn *distorts their sense of reality, identity and autonomy*.[42] Gaslighting is trivialized and not treated as a serious form of violence. The abuser convinces the victim that they exaggerate the violence, and that the violence is the victim's fault. This is done by attributing the victim's perception of the violence to something that was said or done by the victim themselves and not the words or actions of the abuser.[43] Eventually, gaslighting operates in a way that over a period, results in the victim believing the stories and justifications for the violence that the abuser tells the victim. Moments of introspection laced with confused thoughts have a high probability of leading the victim to impute *craziness* to themselves. In most cases of gaslighting it takes a while before the victim recognizes this as violence attributable to the abuser and not them.

The movie '*Gaslight*' released in 1940 popularized this term,[44] and it chronicles how Gregory intentionally uses manipulative techniques over a period of time to alter his wife Paula's sense of reality and her environment with the objective of relegating her to a hospital for the insane. He sneakily puts his watch in her purse claiming that she has stolen it, and then recovers it from her purse in front of their friends, to whom he has already declared that she is mentally unstable. This leaves Paula confused and unsure of herself, especially when this is

[37] Aizpurua and O'Connell (2020), O'Leary (1991).

[38] United Nations (2014). Accessed 3 November 2023.

[39] *Ibid.*

[40] The term became so popular that Merriam Webster reported that searches for gaslighting increased by 1740%, making it the Word of the Year in 2022. *See* Klein et al. (2023).

[41] Ferraro (2006).

[42] Sweet (2019)

[43] Dobash and Dobash (1979) 105.

[44] Corfield and Dickinson (1940).

corroborated in her friends' presence. In another scene from the movie, Gregory goes to the attic to look for Paula's jewels and when he switches on the light there, the *gaslights* everywhere else in the house get dimmed. When Paula questions this dimming and flickering of the lights, he tells her that she is imagining it, and points to her mental illness, asking her to take rest as she is unable to comprehend reality. Incidents such as these, incited and instigated by Gregory make Paula question her sanity all the time. Paula is completely oblivious that she is the victim of manipulative tactics in the form of gaslighting by her husband. This movie unravels the array of strategies that can be employed by gas-lighters to achieve their objective. Sweet theorizes that gaslighting is often gendered especially in intimate relationships as it builds on the gender stereotypes of women being crazy. The stereotype of 'crazy women' is based on the normative masculine discourse that women are irrational, too emotional and unable to control their emotions.[45] Gaslighting tactics often involve manipulation by the abuser by flipping stories, hacking of victim's social media accounts, by repeatedly insinuating that they are *crazy* or *mad*, confusing and lying about details, blaming them, denying events, financial control, extreme regulation of femininity, and creating perceptions of this madness outside the marriage.

Such gaslighting is evident in '*When I Hit You*':

> If I stand up to him, if I shout back at him, he calls me mad. When I dismiss such a glib label, he says that it is the nature of mad people to claim to be sane.
> *I see, it is no longer fashionable to be mad. Depression is the word, isn't it? Three inches of cleavage, two books of poetry, plenty of sex and depression- that's all it takes to make a woman a famous writer.*[46]

He claims that depression is *a privileged woman's sole ticket to victimhood,*[47] thereby rationalizing that the wife's actions and ways of life force him to be abusive towards her. He uses manipulative tactics to absolve himself of all responsibility for his abusive behaviour, at the same time, he gaslights his wife into believing that she is responsible for this abuse. He portrays himself as the victim in the relationship in the presences of others. The narrator tells us—"*I have watched him play all the roles. The doting husband in the presence of his colleagues, the harassed victim of a suspicious wife to his male friends, the pleading son-in-law to my parents.*"[48] Psychologists opine that the degree of covertness and ambiguity in controlling behaviour by the abuser is directly proportional to the degree of loss of the victim's self-esteem.[49] In the case of gaslighting which is usually ambiguous and covert, the chances of aggravated forms of self-degradation are very high. Such gaslighting is commonly observed in relationships of power inequalities, clearly pointing that in the context of intimate partner violence, these power inequalities are evident in the patriarchal structure of the family and marriage and other institutions. Within a marriage, such psychological abuse is usually perpetrated by the husband, directed at the wife due to gendered hierarchies, also evident from '*When I Hit You*'.[50] The social conditioning of victims *colours* their view of marriage as the embodiment of love and care making it easier for the abuser to gaslight them.[51] These harms manifest as a continuum of violence over time, while the victim's resentment due to the corroding of her sense of self, confidence and independence keeps building over time.

Isolation and Control cement the power hierarchies in intimate relationships. Psychologists view isolation as a tool of controlling behaviour where social isolation is used to assert

[45] Sweet (2019).

[46] Kandasamy (2017) 150.

[47] *Ibid* at 151.

[48] *Ibid* at 185.

[49] Lammers et al. (2005).

[50] Karlekar (1998).

[51] Abramson (2014).

dominance of the abuser over the victim by ensuring that she has no space to seek redress for abuse.[52] Isolation can be defined using Stark's theorization of instances of *coercive control*. Stark equates control and isolation in intimate relationships to *kidnapping and harassment* where the victim is denied access to food, transportation, money, completely cutting them off from their family, friends who might *rescue them from such deprivation*.[53] The goal is intimidation and complete domination, where the victim is left with no recourse but complete and singular dependence on the abuser for their survival. Stark notes that unlike general *capture crimes*, in intimate relationships such isolation and control is personal and gendered since it relies on the *exploitation of a woman's vulnerability* due to their *marginalized role in the patriarchal society* especially in relationships such as marriage, where gender imbalances are pronounced. Such control is exercised almost always by men as a means of domination over women through calculated measures.[54] Acts of emotional isolation within confined spaces are often invisibilized.[55]

In '*When I Hit You*' isolation become the principal weapon of control. The narrator is a writer who procures her writing assignments primarily through online networking and communication. The resultant isolation, consciously enforced by the husband, slowly erodes her agency and choice to live and work on her own terms. She realizes how this *amounts to career suicide*.[56] Isolation combined with controlling behaviour such as rigid directives to the victim on ways to dress, talk, cook, clean, socialize or express their sexuality constricts the victim in a web of abuse and coercive circumstances. It is often easier to passively follow the abuser's rules and directives rather than face physical violence that inevitably follows non-compliance. This form of isolation and control impacts the narrator's ability to navigate the cycle of control, this is evident in the novel.

Humiliation and Inducement of Fear are psychological tactics that work by consistent criticism of the victim's appearance, behaviour, demeanour, sexuality, which is a recurrent theme in the novel. The narrator is invited to write an essay by the editors of *Outlook* magazine for their annual issue on *sex surveys*. The husband humiliates and shames her by saying that she is *a slave of corporate media and that this is elite prostitution because she is selling her body and men masturbate to the image of the woman she represents. He further says that this is vulgar imperialist culture and alleges that she must have had sex with the entire editorial team at Outlook*.[57] This excessive policing and control of the victim's actions, inactions, words, and behaviour through shaming and humiliation impacts their mental health.[58] Due to such continuous humiliation, the victim places herself in a position where she starts believing that she is unworthy of respect and fair treatment, which in turn leads her to question her own behaviour to make sense of the abuser's words.[59]

The narrator elucidates how the excessive control by her husband kept her in a state of constant fear and anxiety. She alters her behaviour, her attire, and demeanour, to gain the husband's approval as against displeasure, since his displeasure incites further infliction of violence. Fear underlines her efforts at *plainness*, so that her *communist* husband could not insinuate that she was dressing to seduce men and goes on to slut-shame her, possibly leading to physical and sexual violence. She begins to lean towards *ugliness* to please her husband and avoid this humiliation and shame. She even goes so far as to entertain thoughts of *disfiguring* herself to remove all doubts from her husband's

[52] Gondolf et al. (2002), Tolman (1989).

[53] Stark (2009)

[54] *Ibid.*

[55] Mitra (2013)

[56] *Ibid* at 52.

[57] Kandasamy (2017) 75, 76.

[58] O'Leary (1991).

[59] *Ibid.*

mind about her unbridled sexuality.[60] The reader watches as the protagonist narrator's sense of self-worth erodes to such a degree that in order to avoid shame and humiliation, she is willing to go to any length to secure approval from the one person who has snatched it away from her. This mental and physical dependency is created through both, overt and covert psychological tactics that sustain and aggravate her emotional vulnerability resulting in an altered sense of reality for the victim and changes the way she attaches meaning to her experience of abuse.[61] Psychological literature documents that victims eventually start blaming themselves for the violence.

O'Leary explains that long term consequences of psychological abuse on sense of self-worth can be even more serious than those caused by physical abuse.[62] Interviews with survivors of psychological violence display loss of confidence, lowered self-esteem coupled with attempts at securing their husband's acknowledgement and approval.[63] The resultant vulnerability and loss of a sense of self further cement the control and dominance of the abuser over the victim.[64]

Social and Cultural Conditioning of the protagonist narrator to *save the marriage* despite intense physical, sexual, psychological and emotional abuse is evident in her hope that it will get better.[65] She fears disapproval as a woman who was unable to be the *perfect wife* in the eyes of the world, and thus endures violence. She engages diligently in the expected role of a wife as a homemaker who cooks, cleans, listens to his stories after he gets back from work with rapture and keeps up the pretence of a 'happy married couple' to *dodge his anger* since *her life depends on it.*[66] The isolation tactics employed by her husband add to her helplessness, since *she has nowhere to run, nowhere to hide, nowhere to evade his presence.*[67] Though circumstances and coping capacities of victims can be individualized, the foundational cause for staying in abusive relationships has been traced to conditioning of the victim which prevents her from recognizing these tactics as violence. Even where the victim is able to identify psychological tactics as violence, there is a tendency to trivialize which is attributable to conditioning that normalizes abuse in a marriage. The gendered conditioning of the narrator in '*When I Hit You*' shaped her actions and inactions that prevents her from immediately exiting her abusive marriage.[68]

3.4 Psychological Violence and Trauma: A Search for Glimmer of Hope Through Writing

By writing in the first-person, Kandasamy amplifies for the reader the erstwhile silenced violence suffered by the narrator and delivers the message that her voice and her story cannot be left unheard.[69] This section of the chapter analyses the impact of violence embedded deep inside the narrator, long after she escapes from her abusive marriage. In addition to focusing on long term impact of violence and the way it continues to control victims, the significance of writing about her abuse seen through the novel, that gives the narrator hope and helps her cope with the abuse, is highlighted in this section. The

[60] Kandasamy (2017) 16, 17.

[61] Queen and Brackley (2009).

[62] O'Leary (1991).

[63] Mitra (2013), Lammers et al. (2005).

[64] Chang (1995), Kirkwood (1993), Loring (1994).

[65] Kandasamy (2017) 182.

[66] *Ibid* at 20.

[67] *Ibid* at 21.

[68] Although she ultimately walks away from the marriage, the end comes only after a long period of time of such psychological and emotional violence. She waits till she is physically threatened with death and an act is carried out in addition to the threat to finally pack her bags and leave the marriage.

[69] Kandasamy (2017) 9.

effects of intimate partner abuse last way beyond the actual period of abuse. The psychological tactics employed by the husband impact the narrator's cognitive and emotional sense of self. On leaving her husband and marriage, the narrator finds her way back to the familiar comfort and warmth of her parents' home. The impressions of the violence suffered by her are perceptible not only in the way she observes and narrates her story, long after she has left the abusive relationship, but it is also evident in the way she acknowledges and narrates the reaction of her parents on her return home. The violence suffered by the narrator continues to control her. A simple reading of the first chapter of the novel[70] presents the reader with a view into her parents' mind and her criticism of their way of coping with the violence suffered by their daughter.

The reader learns that the narrator's mother speaks non-stop to her friends and neighbours about the extent of abuse faced by her daughter which left her *brittle and empty like a shell.*[71] She explains that indignities and stress led to her physical degradation. The mother laments about the daughter's hair infested with lice and how she laboured to get rid of the lice, and nursed her hair back to health, her *feet were scarred and cracked and there was a thick layer of dirt in her toenails.*[72] The mother tells her friends and neighbours that the narrator's father scrubbed, cleaned and applied oil to her feet and he cried afterwards as he imagined the intensity of the violence inflicted on her, just by looking at her feet.[73]

However, the narrator notes that in these conversations about feet and lice, the emphasis is always on the parents' overwhelming love and care as the reason she has healed. In the way she responds to this appropriation of her abuse by her parents, she is effectively expressing her need to re-own the *misadventures in her marriage* when she says:

> This is how my story of Young Woman as a Runaway Daughter became, in effect, the great battle of My Mother versus the Head Lice. And because my mother won this battle, the story was told endlessly... and even those who forgot the original context of the story or the bad-marriage setting always remembered it as a fable about one mother's unending, unconditional, over-conditioned love.[74]

The overwhelming response of her parents to her escape from her violent marriage and the excessive focus on physical signs of abuse, invisiblizes the excessive non-physical harm endured by the narrator. The love and care evident at this point must be seen in view of the fact that it is only when he almost carries out the death threat by inflicting aggravated physical assault, that her cry for help to her parents is heard by them. At this point they ask her to leave. Through the four months of suffering excruciating psychological and physical abuse, every time she spoke to her parents their advice was: "*Your husband is doing this for your own good*".[75] It took the fear that she could be killed, for her parents to react in her favour. Furthermore, the mother's stories do not speak about the harsh impact of psychological trauma.

To take back her voice and the *authorship* of her story by writing about it, the narrator then proceeds to detail the impact of the abuse 'during' the marriage. To further understand the narrator and her relationship with her *writing* that is deeply personal and cathartic, she takes us back to the time of abuse when her only companion was her *writing*. Her ability to pen her feelings and express her emotions of anguish, grief and fear through her writing makes the protagonist narrator unique to the reader.

She describes how her marriage had a debilitating effect on her individual identity. She

[70] The first chapter of the novel begins at the end. It has been five years since the narrator left the violent marital home and returned to her parents. The organization is interesting - it tells the reader that the narrator survives the violence and leaves the abusive husband.

[71] Kandasamy (2017) 6.

[72] Kandasamy (2017) 7.

[73] *Ibid* at 4.

[74] *Ibid* at 8.

[75] *Ibid* at 60.

narrates that the *plainness peeled her of her essence and she was controlled and moulded to her husband's will.*[76] Early in the marriage, the husband tells her that they should exchange their e-mail passwords. She realizes that he has been responding to her mails and signing off with both their names. This breach of her privacy exasperates her, and she feels *her identity has been robbed.*[77] The husband responds nonchalantly that he did this because he wants the *whole world to know that they are a couple and accept them as a unit.*[78] This normative understanding of marriage submerges the rights of individuals in a marriage. He continues to isolate her—virtually, telephonically, and physically. This *rendered her a blank state* bereft of her own memories and individual choices.[79] Her identity as a feminist is constantly belittled by him and is portrayed as the *raison d'etre* for the violence. He mocks her as being too caught up in her idealistic middle-class feminist ideals to know about the real issues affecting people.

> That's how the once-upon-a-time fiery feminist becomes a battered wife. By observing, but not doing anything.[80]

To please him, she fuses her identity with his—reading communist literature, adopting the intellectual style of conversations like her husband. She tells the reader that she plays the *mock role of an intellectual to save her marriage*[81] revealing the deep social conditioning of a married woman. This loss of identity disturbs her constantly. She is regularly shamed for her work as a writer. When she is commissioned to write a piece on sexuality by *Outlook,* despite being slut-shamed, humiliated and forbidden to write by her husband, she secretly completes the assignment by typing on the phone when her husband is away at work and hurriedly mails the editor. She stealthily takes the data-powered SIM card from the USB dongle that the husband keeps hidden. She inserts the SIM in her phone and uses it while she is in the bathroom to send the article to the editor. Achieving this feat is risky since she is forbidden to use the internet without the husband's permission. She feels a sense of achievement when she receives an acknowledgement from the editor.

This narrator's dedication to her writing is evident and she fights for it despite everything in her life during her abusive marriage working against it. The uniqueness of the novel lies in the protagonist narrator's personality as a writer. Here she is not depicted simply as a victim. Her identity as a writer shapes the way she views the abuse and deals with it. Her writing is one of the ways in which she copes with the violence. Her identity as a writer—*the job title that she gives herself,* is her source of self-respect. When she faces despair, it is the thought of the novel she is planning on writing that gives her hope during these trying times.

> Writer. Just that, just to myself, just in front of the mirror. I play wife, but the minute my husband walks out, I'm screaming *yes yes yes yes yes yes* in my head, and I obsess about what I need to be writing. Domestic chores do not allow me to work with deadlines. What propels me forward is my restless urge to tell a story. It's a novel about militant resistance to feudalism and caste. The characters in my book – still half-formed, as yet unnamed - stand up against the brute force of the state machinery, against the menacing threat of landlords. They march across me... The theme is resistance and defiance.[82]

She imagines that her writing will change the narrative of her life. In her mind, she reclaims her agency by flipping the script and re-imagining communism through her individual lens and not the one bracketed by her husband. This writing is in defiance of the violent husband and his ideals.

For her, writing is synonymous to hope. When she is stopped from writing poetry by her

[76] Kandasamy (2017) 16.

[77] *Ibid* at 55.

[78] *Ibid.*

[79] *Ibid* at 139.

[80] *Ibid* at 144.

[81] *Ibid* at 23, 34, 142.

[82] Kandasamy (2017) 81.

husband,[83] she writes letters to imaginary lovers expressing her life's desires, dreams, abuse suffered, and she re-imagines an alternate life with this imaginary lover. This gives her hope. She deletes these letters because she fears being discovered. She *reclaims her space* during the moments that she is writing, charting the authorship of her own life and repossessing her identity.[84] She also dreams of finally penning down the painful ordeal in her marriage after she ends it—this dream keeps hope alive—that one day she will escape and survive. On her return to her parents' home, she finally writes it all down and publishes it. She finally reclaims authorship of her story, un-smothered by her parents' exaggerated claims of love and healing her. The trauma of her abuse does not end here. Instead of empathizing with her on reading her story, she is put on trial by society.[85] Her friends ask if there was no *redeeming* quality in her husband, she is thus forced to humanize her abuser in her mind and try and dig out the good times spent with him, if any, to rationalize that he was after all *not a monster*.[86] This way she re-lives the trauma of her abuse and the nightmare of the treatment she has endured, long after she leaves and decides to put it to rest through the penning of her story in the form of her novel. Will she ever be free of the trauma and violence suffered by her?

> Sharing stories might be catharsis, but to her it is the second, more sophisticated punishment.[87]

3.5 Family, Marriage and Violence—*The Blind Spots*

In India the head of the household in the family is always a male. The men are the principal decision-makers in patriarchal societies while women occupy a subordinate position as homemakers and caregivers in the family. The 'public' and the 'private' are clearly demarcated as spaces to be occupied by men and women respectively. Interestingly, women are only expected to provide labour and not participate in decision-making even in the 'private'. It is this institutional framework of family and marriage in society that normalizes the dominance, control and violence that is observed in '*When I Hit You*'. The narrator muses about her marriage, indicating how she feels trapped in the *three rooms and verandah* that make up her marital home. She performs her *role as a dutiful wife*.[88] She continues with the drudgery of chores silently without voicing her dissatisfaction to her husband which reflects the internalization of gendered roles by the narrator. The normalization of gendered roles is the reason the wife's efforts in the household go unacknowledged. In the protagonist narrator's case, this goes a step further—non-compliance to her wifely duties acts as a trigger for the violence inflicted by her husband.

The dichotomy of the public and private spheres is an excellent example to understand the role it plays in the existing gender inequalities and unequal distribution of power in society.[89] Here, the gender roles are fixed—the 'private' domestic work is strictly for women and the 'public' marketplace for men only. The novel highlights a recurring pattern, where the wife repeatedly asks her husband to help her secure a teaching job in the same college where he works, but he consistently refuses her request. As Chakravarti states, the free labour of women reproduces and sustains a patriarchal household, and such patriarchy is sustained by violence.[90] Hence, the control, isolation and manipulative tactics which cause harm to the victim arise out of structural realities of gendered burdens of domesticity.

The unequal power hierarchies in marriage leads to a situation where the man uses his

[83] He asks her to stop writing poetry because he feels that materializing their miseries on paper will make it permanent and then there would be no chances for resolution of their conflict. *See* Kandasamy (2017) 82.

[84] *Ibid* at 81.

[85] Banerjee et al. (2022) 83.

[86] Kandasamy (2017) 225.

[87] *Ibid* at 248.

[88] *Ibid* at 13.

[89] García-Del Moral and Dersnah (2014) at 662.

[90] Chakravarti (2019).

position of power to control the bodily autonomy of the woman. In this context, gender violence is used as a method to establish such structural power domination and male privilege in the private sphere. Historically, such power hierarchy and gender inequality has been the result of the treatment of women as property by the husbands. According to Christian theology, domestic violence was seen as a way of exercising the legitimate power of the husband to restrain his wife.[91] These values perpetuated with time and have led to the trivialization of gender-based violence especially in the private sphere. It further provides a foundation for the powerholder in the marriage to exercise control over the powerless.[92] This power exercised by the husband is expansive in nature, it does not remain confined to simply commanding obedience within the marriage and family—it extends itself to the expectation that the wife's thoughts, aspirations and politics must be submerged in domesticity or be fused with the husband's politics and way of life. This play of control in a hetero-patriarchal marriage is aptly explained by Stark. In his monograph, Stark states that battering in domestic spaces reflects the domination of men on individual women through *intimidation, isolation and control* which is not an episodic event but is a *malafide* calculated form of control. This form of coercive control is *not just personal but also political* as it strips the victim of her personhood and citizenship rights.[93]

The failure of natal families to support victims of violence leads to its perpetuation through complicity. According to social norms, a woman is expected to tolerate moderate to severe forms of mistreatment by her husband. The woman's compliance with harsh treatment or abuse by the husband often goes unnoticed by society as this is the 'expected' behaviour in marriage. In this context, such normalization and trivialization of violence is itself a form of violence.[94] In the novel, the narrator talks to her parents about the abuse suffered by her, explaining instances where the husband demands that she share her passwords with him, covertly answers her emails, and asks her to deactivate her Facebook account. In response her mother says:

> ...Suspicion is the nature of men; it is in the nature of love. He revolves around one question: What if she loves somebody else?...[95]

The mother suggests that *her world should revolve around him* and to let go of her privacy so that he is not suspicious.[96] The mother normalizes this intrusion—complete control over her daughter's social, professional, and personal life. This reflects inherent and internalized patriarchy. In the garb of love, the wife is expected to compromise her individual rights to pander to the demands of the husband which are often legitimized by the victim's own family. They inherit and normalize the unequal gender hierarchies themselves.[97] Later, when the violence by her husband aggravates, she once again informs her parents that she wants to leave. Her parents convince her to stay.

> If you break off your marriage, everyone in town will mock me. They will say his daughter ran away in less than six months. It will reflect on your upbringing. This is not what I intended for my daughter. You have no idea what a father goes through. A father of a daughter – that is a special kind of punishment. We pay the price. Please. Think about us this once.[98]

She is asked not to raise her voice and ensure peace in her marriage by taking it all in silently, learn to survive the sadness and not talk back.[99] *Silence is golden*—this deters the victim from narrating and owning her story. Solnit terms this *living death*[100]—the victim is unable to seek

[91] Rhode (1989) at 238.

[92] Bunch (1990) at 491.

[93] Stark (2009).

[94] Sapra et al. (2014).

[95] Kandasamy (2017) 56.

[96] *Ibid.*

[97] Kandiyoti (1988)

[98] Kandasamy (2017) 159.

[99] *Ibid* at 157–161.

[100] Solnit (2017) 19.

assistance as no one believes her cries for help, she loses her voice, and this further emboldens such violence.[101] In the novel, the protagonist narrator justifies her experience of abuse by stating that she has had enough of being the victim and telling her story was a way of controlling her own narrative. Thus, such institutional silence takes away from the victim her ability to recognize her violence, speak about it, seek redress for her trauma and she is thus powerless. The silence of the immediate family is compounded by the silence of society; preservation of marriage takes precedence over the protection of individual rights. The narrator's decision to leave her abusive marriage is subjected to intense scrutiny by society. Even her close friends are hesitant to rely on her version of the intense abuse and control suffered by her. Society chains a woman to her marriage; an exception is made only in the case of imminent death. After four months of violence and isolation, the narrator runs away from her abusive marriage. In the last verbal exchange before she leaves, she stands up to him, and says,

> Don't tell me how brave you are. A brave man doesn't run. A brave man doesn't rape and hit his wife. You, my husband, are not a brave man.[102]

Her defiant words incite him, and he beats her up violently and threatens to kill her. She then collects her *passport, ATM card, laptop and phone (which he never lets her use)* in a bag and leaves the house. She writes that she had decided to wait for this threat of death before she would finally leave.[103] Her self-awareness about the abuse and its effect on her is evident throughout the novel, yet she waits for this extreme threat before ending the marriage such that she could then, unambiguously attribute her leaving, on this act of threat to her life.

Before this episode, when she had communicated her fear of being killed by the husband to her parents. Their response was:

> ...Next time he talks of murder, come home,' my mother implores. 'If he does it again, run for your life without even turning to look back,' my father ordered. 'We are here', they say, finally, far too late, but in unison. Until then, I stay. I stay because I have no other choice until I am within touching distance of a permitted resolution. **In the eyes of the world, a woman who runs away from death is more dignified than a woman who runs away from her man. She does not face society's stone-throwing when she comes away free.** In the quest to control the narrative, I still have to endanger my own life.[104]

These words brutally depict the family and society's normative understanding of violence as overt physical or sexual abuse which may lead to death. Only physical violence which can potentially lead to death is viewed as a legitimate reason to end a marriage. The narrator understood this. Any abuse which does not fulfil the criteria of proximity to death is overlooked and normalized. The family, community and the law do not look close enough at the visible forms of violence to unearth the psychological tactics which fuel such violence.

3.6 Conclusion

The critical impact of covert psychological violence highlighted in the chapter is that it impacts the mental health and psyche of the victim. In India, the mental health framework is not adequately equipped to treat mental health issues, including the impact of trauma. As a result, mental health is either neglected or stigmatized.[105] Additionally, psychological abuse and its impact are not discussed and therefore not addressed with the required seriousness. The damaging effect of gaslighting, manipulation, isolation and control in a marriage often go unnoticed or trivialized and the focus remains

[101] *Ibid* at 21.

[102] Kandasamy (2017) 212.

[103] *Ibid* at 213.

[104] Kandasamy (2017) 209.

[105] Uma (2020)

on tangible evidence of violence. An example of this is the undue emphasis on bodily injuries in medico-legal evidence in rape trials, despite verbal testimony to the contrary by the victim.[106] While physical injury is typically considered the most acceptable form of evidence in domestic violence cases, instances of psychological violence like the ones highlighted in the chapter through the analysis of the novel, are often not treated as serious forms of violence[107] and only physical injury is treated as serious.

Allegations of false complaints in domestic violence cases is common. Where there is evidence of physical injury, these allegations are usually not present. However, in the absence of physical injury, where women file cases of psychological and emotional abuse, the allegations of false complaints get louder.[108] This stereotypical narrative of false cases by *vengeful wives* on *poor, unsuspecting husbands* forms a dominant discourse[109] and is sometimes endorsed by courts that then lay down additional criteria to evaluate the veracity of domestic violence cases.[110] These criteria further act as procedural hurdles since psychological abuse is invisibilized by society. The chapter through its analysis draws focus on the prevalence of invisible forms of psychological tactics as violence that has remained limited in the social and legal imagination.

The disproportionate attention on 'grave' forms of overt violence in a marriage leads to a blind spot where law and its enforcement do not always take cognizance of the role of social institutions—marriage and family that perpetuate psychological violence in insidious ways.[111] When a family fails to acknowledge the power imbalances and gender inequalities in a marriage, it allows psychological abuse to continue without consequences from the law.[112] Therefore, such violence is not an individual act, but a product of gender imbalances within families and marriages. In addressing psychological tactics as violence, understanding and reforming patriarchal nature of family and marriage is critical.[113] The objective of such intimate partner violence is to strip the woman of her agency, to domesticate her and subjugate her into obedience and leave her socio-economically and psychologically dependent on her husband who holds the power in the relationship, the marriage and the family.

The astute observations on psychological tactics in Kandasamy's '*When I Hit You*' present a unique turf to understand the intricacies and complexities of the ways in which these operate as hidden yet powerful forms of violence. The empowering act of writing and describing her ordeal by the protagonist narrator with such simplicity paves a path for a holistic discourse on intimate partner violence that includes within its ambit the vocabulary of psychological tactics as a stand-alone serious form of violence that must no longer be overlooked. The protagonist narrator stands out as a feminist writer, her life through the novel shatters the stereotypical image of the domestic violence victim. It is interesting that Kandasamy creates a mirror image of herself through the protagonist who writes her story of violence. The parallel between Kandasamy, a writer and the protagonist, also a writer, elevates the stature of the novel, '*When I Hit You*' to a distinctive genre in literature.

[106] Baxi (2013).

[107] Lammers et al. (2005)

[108] Sen (2010).

[109] Kothari (2005)

[110] *Arnesh Kumar vs State of Bihar* (2014) 8 SCC 273 (Supreme Court); *Rajesh Sharma vs State of Uttar Pradesh* 2017 SCCOnline SC 821 (Supreme Court); *Manav Adhikar vs Union of India* (2018) SCCOnline SC 1501 (Supreme Court).

[111] Tobin (1992).

[112] Solnit (2017) 23.

[113] Mandal (2023).

References

Abramson K (2014) Turning up the lights on Gaslighting. Philos Perspect 28:1–30

Armstrong EA, Hamilton LT, Armstrong EM, Seeley JL (2014) "Good girls": gender, social class, and slut discourse on campus. Soc Psychol Q 77:100–122

Arnesh Kumar vs State of Bihar (2014) 8 SCC 273 (Supreme Court)
Aizpurua E, O'Connell C (2020). Men's Psychological violence against women. In Shackelford TK (ed) The SAGE handbook of domestic violence. Sage, London, pp 98–112
Banerjee S, Ghosh N, Mukhopadhyay M, Goswami R (2022) The violent domestic: law, its practice and strategies of survival. Zubaan Academic, New Delhi
Baxi P (2013) Medicalization of consent and falsity—the figure of the habitué in indian rape law. In: Public secrets of law: rape trials in India. OUP, New Delhi, pp 61–116
Bunch C (1990) Women's rights as human rights: toward a re-vision of human rights. Hum Rights Q 12:486
Chang VN (1995) Interaction patterns that threaten the self. Trans Anal J 25(2):133–140
Chakravarti U (2019) Some thoughts on domestic violence: using violence to regulate a patriarchal family. In: Jaising I, Anurag PM (eds) Conflict in the shared household. OUP, New Delhi, pp 26–39
Corfield J, Dickinson T (1940). Gaslight [motion picture]. British National Films
Coomaraswamy R (1996) UN Framework for Model Legislation on Domestic Violence, report of the Special Rapporteur on Violence against Women, Its Causes and Consequences submitted in accordance with Commission on Human Rights Resolution 1995/85 E/CN 4/1996/53/Add 2
Das J (2022). Reclaiming the body: marital rape and self-sustainability in Meena Kandasamy's When I Hit You. Contemp Voice Dalit, 1–14
Dobash RE, Dobash R (1979) Violence against wives: a case against the patriarchy. Free Press, New York
Ferraro KJ (2006) Neither angels nor demons: women, crime, and victimization. Northeastern University Press, Boston
García-Del Moral P, Dersnah MA (2014) A feminist to the gendered politics of the public/private divide: on due diligence, domestic violence, and citizenship. Citizsh Stud 18:661
Gondolf EW, Alex Heckert D, Kimmel CM (2002) Nonphysical abuse among batterer program participants. J Fam Violence 17:293–314
Kandasamy M (2017) When I hit you or, a portrait of the writer as a young wife. Juggernaut Books, New Delhi
Kandasamy M (2022) I singe the body electric. Outlook. https://www.outlookindia.com/magazine/story/i-singe-the-body-electric/280179
Kandiyoti D (1988) Bargaining with patriarchy. Gend Soc 2(3):274–290
Karlekar M (1998) Domestic violence. Econ Pol Wkly 33:1741–1751
Karakurt G, Kristin E (2013) Silver Emotional abuse in intimate relationships: the role of gender and age. Violence Vict 28(5):804–821
Kirkwood C (1993) Leaving abusive partners. Sage Publications, London
Klein W, Li S, Wood S (2023) A qualitative account of gaslighting in romantic relationships. Pers Relat, 1–25https://doi.org/10.1111/pere.12510
Kothari J (2005) Criminal law on domestic violence. Econ Pol Wkly 40:4843–4849
Lammers M, Ritchie J, Robertson N (2005) Women's experience of emotional abuse in intimate relationships. J Emot Abus 5:29–64. https://doi.org/10.1300/J135v05n01_02
Loring MT (1994) Emotional abuse. Macmillan Inc., New York
Mandal S (2023) Bringing governance home: feminists, domestic violence, and the paradoxes of rights in India. Feminist Legal Stud. https://doi.org/10.1007/s10691-023-09532-x
Manav Adhikar vs Union of India (2018) SCCOnline SC 1501(Supreme Court)
Mitra N (2013) Intimate violence, family, and femininity: women's narratives on their construction of violence and self. Violence Women 20:1–20
Murphy CM, Hoover SA (1999) Measuring emotional abuse in dating relationships as a multifactorial construct. Violence Vict 14:39–53
NDTV. Aired on June 2017. Meena Kandasamy tells all about her abusive marriage. https://www.ndtv.com/video/news/the-buck-stops-here/meena-kandasamy-s-tell-all-about-her-abusive-marriage-458883
O'Leary KD (1991) Psychological abuse: a variable deserving critical attention in domestic violence. Viol Victims 14:3–23
Queen J, Brackley MH (2009) Being emotionally abused: a phenomenological study of adult women's experiences of emotionally abusive intimate partner relationships. Issues Ment Health Nurs 30:237–245. https://doi.org/10.1080/01612840802701257
Rajesh Sharma vs State of Uttar Pradesh 2017 SCCOnline SC 821 (Supreme Court)
Rangkuti RT, Christomy T (2017) Protest against misogyny as portrayed in Meena Kandasamy's When I Hit You or, a portrait of the writer as a young wife. In: Proceedings of the international conference on education, language and society (ICELS 2019), pp 392–401
Rhode DL (1989) Justice and gender. Harvard University Press
SafeLives (Ending Domestic Abuse) (2019) Report on psychological violence. Oak Foundation, London. https://safelives.org.uk/psychological-abuse
Sapra KJ, Jubinski SM, Tnaka MF, Gershon RR (2014) Family and partner interpersonal violence among American Indians/Alaska natives. Inj Epidemiol 1(1):7. https://doi.org/10.1186/2197-1714-1-7
Sebastian RJ (1983) Social psychological determinants. In: Finkelhor D, Gelles RJ, Hotaling GT, Straus MA (eds) The darker side of families: current family violence research. Sage, Newbury Park, CA, pp 182–192
Self J (2019) Interview of Meena Kandasamy: 'If I was going to write my life story, I would condense that marriage to a footnote'. The Guardian.

https://www.theguardian.com/books/2019/nov/25/meena-kandasamy-interview-exquisite-cadavers

Sen R (2010) Women's subjectivities of suffering and legal rhetoric on domestic violence: fissures in the two discourses. Indian J Gend Stud 17:375–401. https://doi.org/10.1177/097152151001700304

Solnit R (2017) Silence is broken. In: The mother of all questions: further feminisms. Granta Publications, London

Stark E (2009) Coercive control: how men entrap women in personal life (Interpersonal Violence). OUP, USA

Straus MA (1979) Measuring intra-family conflict and violence: the conflict tactics (CT) scales. J Marr Fam 41:75–88

Straus MA, Hamby SL, Boney-McCoy S, Sugarman DB (1996) The revised conflict tactics scale (CTS2): Development and preliminary psychometric data. J Fam Issues 7:283–316

Sweet PL (2019) The sociology of gaslighting. Am Sociol Rev 84:851–875

Tobin J (1992) Family violence: opening up the silence. Melb Univ Law Rev 18:851–866

Tolman R (1989) The development of a measure of psychological maltreatment of women by their male partners. Violence Vict 4:159–178

Tolman RM (1999) The validation of the psychological maltreatment of women inventory. Violence Vict 14(1):25–37

Uma S (2020) Female criminality, mental health and the law. In: Anand M (ed) Gender and mental health: combining theory and practice. Springer, New Delhi, pp 143–156

United Nations (2014) Guidelines for producing statistics on violence against women. Department of Economic and Social Affairs, Statistics Division. ST/ESA/STAT/SER.F/110. https://unstats.un.org/unsd/gender/docs/guidelines_statistics_vaw.pdf

UNGA (20 December 1993). UN declaration on the elimination of violence against women. U.N. Doc. A/RES/48/104

Vranda MN (2013) Exploring domestic violence in an indian setting. Indian J Gend Stud 20:135–146

Blurred Lines: Sexual Abuse (or not) in *'Big Little Lies'* 4

Devyani Tewari

Abstract

Big Little Lies, a television show, has been applauded for its deft depiction of domestic violence, infidelity, and childrearing, which helps the viewers in obtaining an insight into the societal conception of gender roles *vis a vis* the familial structure. However, it was reported that many viewers perceived the sex scenes between the two characters of the show, Celeste and Perry Wright, as sexy rather than as abusive, demonstrating a lack of clarity as to which sexual encounters constitute consensual sex and which, if at all, constitute sexual abuse. This chapter explores the blurred lines between consensual sex and sexual abuse in the abusive marriage of Celeste and Perry Wright. Additionally, this chapter demonstrates the intricate relationship between cinema, law, society, and domestic violence. I draw upon feminist and post-structuralist scholarship on the construction of familial structures, patriarchy, consent, domesticity, and sexual violence. This enables me to propose three distinct interpretations of the sexual relationship between Celeste and Perry Wright.

Keywords

Sex · Law · Society and cinema · Domestic violence · Consent · Sexual abuse · Pleasure · Domesticity · Marriage · Dominance · Rape · Subordination · Norm · Love · Discipline · Desire · Consensual · Power · Coercion

4.1 Introduction

> Both law and film are dominant players in the construction of concepts such as subject, community, personal and collective identity, memory, gender roles, justice, and truth; they each offer major sociocultural arenas in which collective hopes, dreams, beliefs, anxieties, and frustrations are publicly portrayed, evaluated, and enacted.[1]

Big Little Lies, a television show which premiered in 2017 and aired for two seasons, has been applauded for its direction, storytelling, and acting. It is based on the lives of five women living in Monterey, California. Through the nuanced manner in which the show depicts domestic violence, infidelity, and childrearing, it

D. Tewari (✉)
Faculty of Law, University of Victoria, Victoria, Canada
e-mail: devyanitewari@uvic.ca

D. Tewari
Jindal Global Law School, OP Jindal Global University, Sonipat, India

[1] Kamir (2006), at 2.

P. M. Anurag and S. Dwivedy (eds.), *Violence in Intimate Spaces*, Sustainable Development Goals Series, https://doi.org/10.1007/978-981-97-2657-8_4

helps the viewers in obtaining an insight into the societal conception of gender roles *vis a vis* the familial structure. Though the show has earned accolades, including an Emmy award for Nicole Kidman who essays the role of the battered traumatized Celeste Wright, several viewers, including, many of the show's devoted fans perceive the sex scenes in the abusive relationship between Celeste and her husband, Perry Wright, played by Alexander Skarsgård as extremely sexy rather than as abusive.[2]

Against the backdrop of domestic violence in their marriage, this chapter discusses: which sexual encounters between Perry and Celeste constitute consensual sex and which, if at all, constitute sexual abuse of Celeste? In this chapter, I explore the sexual relationship between Celeste and Perry Wright by drawing upon feminist and post-structuralist scholarship on the construction of gender, familial structures, patriarchy, consent, domesticity, and sexual violence. Additionally, I aspire that my chapter will demonstrate the intricate relationship between cinema, law, sexual interactions, gender, society, and domestic violence.

These objectives are addressed in two sections. In Section I, I give a synopsis of the show, inasmuch as it pertains to the marriage of Celeste and Perry Wright. In Section II, I critically analyse the sexual interaction in their marriage as it unfolds on the screen from the viewpoint of select feminist theories on gender, domesticity, and patriarchy while also drawing upon scholarship from the field of post-structuralism.

4.2 Synopsis of the 'Not-So Ideal Marriage'

Big Little Lies presents the viewers with many aspects of Celeste Wright—the successful intelligent lawyer, the intelligent woman who questions her therapist on the therapist's assumptions and observations, the domesticated wife, the wonderful mother, the abused wife who defends her abusive husband and conceals the abuse, the abused wife who finally decides to leave her abusive husband, the widow with one-night stands, and the mother who in the capacity of a lawyer for herself questions her mother-in-law, Mary-Louise, in the custody battle between Mary-Louise and herself.

In the pilot of *Big Little Lies,* the viewers are first introduced to the white upper-class Wrights through the eyes of individuals inhabiting the public sphere and having some interaction with Celeste, their children's nanny, and staff at their children's school. Perry, Celeste's much younger husband tenderly kisses his children and beautiful wife goodbye. He goes off on a business trip. The outsiders see the family with rose-rimmed glasses perceiving them as a wealthy happy ideal family which knows nothing but love. Viewers then see Celeste as a dutiful mother dropping her twin sons on their first day at the school and then sitting with her best friend, Madeline Mackenzie who introduces her to a new entrant in Monterey, Jane Chapman. Jane is much younger than Celeste. She is a single parent who lives in a one-room apartment which is very different from the ocean-facing mansions Celeste and Madeline reside in. Through their conversations, we learn that before marriage Celeste was a successful attorney in another city in California. In this scene, the viewers see Celeste through the eyes of Jane who cannot take her eyes off Celeste because she is so beautiful.

The city of Monterey considers the forty-nine-year-old Celeste to be the epitome of perfection—extremely wealthy, gifted with age-defying beauty, married to a handsome man, having wonderful twin sons, owning the perfect house, and intelligent. Later in the same episode, viewers see Perry physically and verbally abusing Celeste in the private confines of their bedroom. It appears that he is about to choke her before she can free herself and tell him angrily that she will leave him. He responds by telling her that she was lucky she survived. It is then that the viewers learn that their perfect marriage is one big lie. Strangely, in the same episode, a

[2] Bernstein (2019).

verbal altercation stemming from Celeste's decisions on childrearing results in a physical fight[3] which leads to sex. But it seems that she is a silent passive object in the sexual act while he looks like an active agent. He grabs hold of her violently before and during sex while she never touches nor tries to touch him. In the majority of the sex scenes, after sex, she flees from him like a rape survivor while he walks triumphantly with a feeling of conquest over his survivor. They never discuss consent.

In the first season of the show, Celeste tells her best friend Madeline and the couple's therapist (whom she later starts visiting alone frequently) Dr. Reisman that she and Perry have a complicated sex life wherein sex is preceded by physical violence. However, in her view, they have great sex. Later, in the second season, she tells her mother-in-law, Mary-Louise, the same.

There are only two out of the many sex scenes in the entire show in which sex is not preceded by violence. In those scenes, they 'make love' to each other. She caresses him and he does likewise. They look at each other lovingly. Those scenes unambiguously present them as two people in love. In the second season, after his death Celeste re-watches scenes of this loving Perry. That is how she wants to remember him as, not as the violent Perry. However, could these lovemaking scenes be interpreted as sexual abuse? In Section II, I engage with this question in greater detail.

The first season of the show is a lot about Celeste coming to terms with domestic abuse, especially emotional abuse. When she first visits Dr. Reisman with Perry, the Wrights show a strong united front, signifying that they are complicit in violence. However, when she visits Dr. Reisman alone, after several denials, she finally admits to being frightened of Perry. Despite being severely bruised by Perry, she defends him against Dr. Reisman's accusations of emotional, financial, verbal, physical, and sexual abuse. Dr. Reisman assesses the reasoning behind Celeste's defence of Perry to be Perry's emotional manipulation of Celeste into believing that violence and love are inextricable. After some sessions, Celeste realizes that Dr. Reisman is correct. The reality she had long believed in was not the reality, it was a reality that Perry had conjured, to keep her in the marriage. She realizes that due to his desire to control her, he had forced her to leave her career, her family, and friends and move to Monterey with him. He brushed away her minutest desire to work in the name of domesticity and if she tried to protest, he used manipulation, gaslighting, and verbal and physical abuse to ensure she submits to his wishes. This way, he remains in control of financial resources. She realizes that until now, she had normalized emotional abuse.

Once Celeste unlearns abuse, she finally tells Dr. Reisman that she had thought of leaving Perry several times, especially when he had threatened to kill her. However, she had stayed back because of her children. From this moment onwards, whenever he makes sexual advances, she withdraws from him, sometimes even using his tennis racquets as a shield to protect herself from his advances. She secretly meets a real estate agent and decides to move into an apartment with her sons. However, until now only Celeste and Dr. Reisman are aware of the domestic violence. She tells Dr. Reisman that she had not told anyone else because her self-esteem depended on what others thought of her. The big lie, or 'their dirty secret' as Celeste calls it, is out in the public eye in the finale of the first season when Perry finally learns of her plans to leave him and assaults her. Her friends and other female characters are finally able to rescue her. It is then that the viewers discover that Perry had raped Jane a few years back. Perry dies in the finale of the first season.

In the second season, when Mary-Louise questions Jane several times in ways that normalize rape as violent sex by arguing that maybe

[3] In fights, Celeste hits Perry only in self-defence. In this specific scene, Perry detests the decision she makes regarding who their children should or should not play with. He also claims that Celeste is trying to overstep him by making many decisions independently and taking the children alone to the opening night of a musical in his absence. Celeste claims she only did so because he was away on business abroad.

Perry assumed Jane liked violent sex or maybe Jane was drunk at that time, Jane counters her by telling her that she screamed 'no' and tried to pull away to no avail. Perry was too physically strong for her. She is also left bruised—emotionally, sexually, and physically.

In the initial episodes of the second season, it is apparent to the viewers that Celeste is emotionally abused and traumatized to an extent that even after Perry's death, she questions the extent of the various types of abuse inflicted upon her. In these episodes, she tells her therapist that she blames herself for his death. When Dr. Reisman tells her that she had no part to play in his death, Celeste asks her if Perry was 'that bad of a man'. Surely, her marriage could not have been that abusive. Dr. Reisman asks Celeste to imagine Madeline in place of her, being 'abused' by Perry. When Celeste visualizes Madeline in her position, she starts screaming, "No, no, no", stomps her foot, and stretches out her hands to rescue Madeline. In that moment she realizes the extent of domestic violence inflicted upon her.

In the last episodes of the second season, especially, its finale viewers witness the engagement of the American law with questions of sexual, emotional, and physical abuse in the fictional courtroom. In the finale of the second season, viewers observe Celeste accusing Perry of domestic violence. To rebut Mary-Louise's claims that she was not a good mother owing to her alleged collusion with Perry in the alleged sexual and physical abuse and her one-night stands with strangers after Perry's death, Celeste produces a clip of severe sexual and physical abuse inflicted upon her by Perry[4] as evidence to appeal to the judge, that "*she protected her children and kept herself alive despite formidable odds when she was abused by Perry in every manner possible*".[5] Celeste pleads to the judge that she will raise her sons to be good men, in contrast to Mary-Louise who abused her sons and raised an abuser. The judge rules in favour of Celeste giving her sole custody of her sons.

4.3 A Theoretical Analysis of the Sexual Abuse in the Wrights' Intimate Relationship

Big Little Lies depicts distinct yet interrelated perspectives of Madeline, Dr. Reisman, Jane, and Mary-Louise, mainly on Celeste, her marriage with Perry, and their sexual relationship. Similarly, I present three interpretations of their marital relationship, especially, their sexual relationship by drawing upon three distinct core philosophical analyses discussing concepts of gender, domesticity, consent, and sexual violence. The first sub-section critically examines their sexual relationship from the perspective of Catharine MacKinnon's *Dominance Approach*. In the second sub-section, I build upon MacKinnon's analyses by drawing upon the notion of 'domesticity' as discussed by Joan Williams and Rebecca Johnson. This sub-section dissects their sexual interactions from the vantage point of domesticity. The third sub-section engages with their relationship by delving into Janet Halley's objections to *dominance feminism* and her theoretical contributions to the field of sexuality.

4.3.1 First Interpretation: Dominance Approach

According to Catharine MacKinnon, gender is a matter of dominance, instead of difference.[6] Men and women are *equally different but not equally powerful*.[7] Eroticisation of male dominance and female submission "creates gender, creates woman and man in the social form in which we know them".[8] The hierarchy of male supremacy and female subordination is also

[4] In the video recorded by her sons, a naked severely bruised Celeste is dragged by Perry. Celeste is cryingly saying "No, no, no".

[5] Celeste's dialogue in the finale of Season 2.

[6] MacKinnon (1987), at 51.

[7] *Ibid.*

[8] *Ibid* at 50.

eroticised.[9] Broadly speaking, it is the hierarchy in our social relations which renders women socially subordinate to men, thus resulting in violence against women, including sexual abuse in patriarchal homes.[10] Generally speaking, this hierarchy and sex difference renders women powerless.[11] Powerlessness breeds silence.[12] Her dominance approach recognizes sex difference, or rather subordination of women to men as political.[13] Therefore, she understands violence against women as systemic, ideological, and political.[14]

She aims to change the nature of social relations between men and women by redefining rape from the standpoint of women.[15] To her, "politically, it is rape whenever a woman has sex and feels violated".[16] Rape is defined, she says, "according to what men think violates woman, and that is the same as what they think of as the *sine qua non* of sex. What women experience as degrading and defiling when they are raped, includes as much that is distinctive to us as is our experience of sex".[17] According to MacKinnon, rape survivors tend to relive the rape the minute they start to have sexual feelings for any man or initiate sex with any man.[18] In *Big Little Lies*, this is shown as true for Jane who finds it very difficult to even have sexual feelings for any man without reliving the horrific rape. However, this is untrue for Celeste. After Dr. Reisman, it is Jane who uses the words 'sexual abuse and rape' to label Celeste's sex life with Perry. Jane expresses her surprise to Celeste on hearing from Celeste that she and Perry had a lot of sex with each other throughout their abusive marriage. This could be because during her marriage Celeste viewed sex as sex and not sexual abuse. Her view could be informed from the legal position where rape victims must prove that the sex was not intercourse, implying, that there was "more force than usual during the preliminaries and that she resisted".[19] The level of force is defined from the male perspective rather than from the women's point of violation.[20]

MacKinnon argues that many women believe that they have never been raped because they were "not raped in a way that is legally provable".[21] "The law of rape presents consent as [a] free exercise of sexual choice under conditions of equality of power without exposing the underlying structure of constraint and disparity".[22] MacKinnon's critique of male supremacy aids in the understanding of the *blurred lines between consensual sex and sexual abuse* in the Wrights' conjugal relationship. Under male supremacy, consent tends to be presumed in the private sphere unless coercion is shown.[23] However, showing coercion may not prove rape as the rape law, specifically the rape law in the USA (because the cinematic context is the USA) assumes that intercourse with force can be

[9] *Ibid* at 53.

[10] *Ibid* at 41.

[11] *Ibid* at 39.

[12] *Ibid.*

[13] *Ibid* at 41.

[14] See especially MacKinnon (1987) and MacKinnon, Catharine. 1989. *Toward a Feminist Theory of the State.* Cambridge: Harvard University Press. *See also* Munro (2013), at 237.

[15] MacKinnon, *supra* note 6 at 82.

[16] *Ibid.*

[17] *Ibid* at 87.

[18] *Ibid.*

[19] *Ibid* at 88.

[20] MacKinnon, Catharine. 1989. *Toward a Feminist Theory of the State.* Cambridge: Harvard University Press at 173.

[21] MacKinnon, *supra* note 6 at 88 (MacKinnon points out that physical violence is not the sole form of coercion used in rape. Financial dependence or love are equally effective forms of coercion. She views that usage of love and economics as coercion leads women into believing that they have never been raped).

[22] MacKinnon, *supra* note 20 at 175.

[23] *Ibid* (rape laws tell men that they can legally have all kinds of sex with their wives as wives are assumed to consent, their actual non-consent is irrelevant, therefore forcible sex is sex, not rape); MacKinnon, *supra* note 6 at 100.

consensual.[24] In marital rape cases, the standard of coercion is even higher because the assumption, even in the most atrocious sexual abuse cases, is that the wife desired and consented to violent sex.[25]

The socio-legal problem lies in recognizing the presence of coercion in the domestic settings because if an experience is coercive, an underlying assumption is that the battered woman, like Celeste, would just leave her husband.[26] This is visible in the second season of *Big Little Lies*, wherein, after getting to know about Celeste's ordeal with domestic violence, several characters repeatedly, ask her, "Why did you not leave?". Towards the end of the second season, in the fictional courtroom, the counsel for Mary-Louise asks Celeste the same question thrice. Mary-Louise's counsel also asks Celeste several malicious questions about her sex life which paint her as a woman who found sadomasochistic and all kinds of forcible sex pleasurable and was portraying herself as an innocent victim of sexual abuse with the sole aim to obtain custody of her children. Further, the judge also asks Celeste why she, an intelligent woman who had formerly enjoyed a successful legal career, chose to stay with Perry. What these characters in the show overlook or choose to overlook is that "*so much force may have been used that the woman never risked saying no. Force may be used, yet the woman may prefer the sex-to avoid more force or, because she, too, eroticizes dominance.....When sex is violent, women may have lost control over what is done to them...*".[27]

Despite Celeste's race and class privilege, many, including those not in the audience, can identify with the line of questioning she faces in the courtroom and in society, with respect to the subject of sexual abuse. Some movies in the past, like *Disclosure* and *Adam's Rib* which presented themselves as premised on the dominance approach, employed an Eve-Lilith distinction to differentiate the righteous 'wife' from the 'other woman'.[28] Unfortunately, cinema has long denied giving voice to victimized female characters by the adoption of a patriarchal masculinist lens—through the usage of patriarchal pigeonholes and 'mythological feminine archetypes' films rule women by dividing them into: "*deadly, sexually brazen Lilith women; timid, domesticated, nurturing, good, sexually subjugated, self-sacrificing Eves*".[29] Similarly, the victimized women in the above-mentioned seemingly feminist movies are pitted against each other: the Lilith protypes, that is, the career-oriented unmarried women characterized by their dangerously unbridled sexuality versus the Eve prototypes, that is, the domesticated, family-oriented, sexually submissive wives and mothers. However, *Big Little Lies* distinguishes itself from these movies by presenting Jane as well as Celeste as sexual beings and allies. Upon learning that Perry raped Jane while still being married to Celeste and is the father of Jane's son, Celeste offers Jane a significant share in Perry's assets. She never looks at Jane as the 'other woman' who lured Perry. Additionally, Celeste organizes group activities where the three children can bond with each other. But most importantly, she believes Jane. She deftly employs *dominance feminism* to defend Jane and herself from Mary-Louise's accusations in the fictional courtroom as well as outside the courtroom, by redefining rape and sexual abuse from the viewpoint of women.

It takes Celeste the end of the second season to realize, identify, and name her sexual abuse before everyone, including the judge, her children, and friends. For the longest duration, she is emotionally abused to an extent that she defends her abuser before her therapist. When her best friend Madeline finds something odd and unnatural with Celeste's sex life, namely,

[24] MacKinnon, *supra* note 20 at 172.

[25] *Ibid* at 176 (this shows that men and women are unequally socially situated with respect to rape).

[26] See MacKinnon, *supra* note 6 at 100.

[27] MacKinnon, *supra* note 20 at 177–178.

[28] Kamir, *supra* note 1 at 146, 155.

[29] *Ibid* at 34.

violent sex preceded by other forms of physical violence and conflict, she yet again defends Perry, calling him a great husband with whom she has amazing sex. She defends Perry with as much grace and ease as she applies makeup and strategically wears apparel to conceal her bruises and wounds. Love and passion, or rather, the illusion of love and passion that Perry has concocted through intense and constant emotional abuse throughout their marriage makes her feel that she has never been sexually abused. Ironically, the eroticisation of dominance and the use of passionate love, at many times, violating, as coercion underpin her belief. Many viewers, especially, survivors of domestic violence can relate to Celeste's journey of employing dominance feminism to identify and unlearn her 'new normal'—the trauma of domestic violence.

Notably, during their marriage, Perry had established and maintained his position as the ruler of the house and Celeste's position as his inferior subject through a systematic use of violence. He had emotionally manipulated her into leaving her job and prohibited her from working. In the first season, viewers see how much she enjoyed working as a lawyer. In a rush of emotions, she cries and confesses to Madeline how much she misses her work. When she is enthusiastically dressing up for a business meeting, Perry assaults and disrobes her. As he is unzipping himself, he is interrupted by the children's cries and rushes to zip himself up. Viewers see Celeste frightened, fallen on the ground, severely bruised. I would call this scene sexual abuse because it was an attempt to rape her.

Similarly, using MacKinnon's theory I call the scenes of 'violent sex' which followed brutal conflicts (amounting to Celeste's verbal and emotional abuse) as well as the scenes of 'loving, tender sex' as sexual abuse. This is because I believe that there is a clear domination and subordination axis in their marriage which renders the question of consent immaterial. Like MacKinnon says, "*If sexuality is relational, specifically if it is a power relation of gender, consent is a communication under conditions of inequality...Rape.. is an act of subordination of women to men*".[30] In addition, when the law itself is framed from the perspective of male supremacy, it is banal to state that women's experiences are neither recognized nor perceived as rape, instead, they are recognized and perceived as sex.[31] Therefore, Celeste's consent or *non-consent* was meaningless because she had been placed into 'a category', that is, of being a wife where Perry was legally allowed to have sex with her[32] howsoever he liked, because a *sexist law* construes rape as sex and sex is not an injury, "*sex is what women are for*".[33]

To rely upon MacKinnon's analyses, I observe that in a marriage as emotionally, economically, verbally, and physically abusive as theirs, all sex (as depicted on screen) is sexual abuse. I assert that the 'tender loving' sex scenes are also abusive because love or rather the mirage of love as constructed by Perry amounts to coercion. It is love, love, love alone or rather the mirage of it which has helped Perry in emotionally abusing her to an extent that he imposes complete control over her mind, inducing her to respond in the way he desires. In the next subsection, I continue my inquiry into components of sexual abuse from the standpoint of battered women, specifically Celeste, and discuss how domesticity and its implications tend to produce female subordination in conjugal relationships.

4.3.2 Second Interpretation: Domesticity as a Discipline Enforcing Female Subordination as the Norm

In this sub-section, drawing upon MacKinnon's critique of Marxism, that is, housework results

[30] MacKinnon, *supra* note 20 at 182.

[31] In the second season, Mary-Louise and her lawyer argue that neither Jane Chapman nor Celeste Wright was raped by Perry, instead, it was just violent sex.

[32] MacKinnon, *supra* note 20 at 175–176 (consent of wives to sex is always inferred rendering them powerless).

[33] *Ibid* at 181.

in female subjugation in the 'private',[34] I argue that domesticity as a discipline creates the gendered norm of female subordination to her husband in all spheres, including the intimate sphere. Deviance from the norm is punished. When Celeste does not adhere to the discipline nor the norm, she is punished by the one in power, her husband. Besides the scenes already discussed, I examine a few more.

When Perry first discovers Celeste's business suit in the closet, he verbally and physically abuses her, controllingly telling her that they had decided before marriage that she would leave her successful career forever and he expected her to deliver on her promise. As she tears up, he *has sex with her*. In the second scene, the children have spread all their toys, including large ones in the sitting room. The nanny is absent. Perry loudly, egoistically, tells Celeste to ask their sons to clean up the mess. Celeste tells him that she will clean up and not to worry otherwise he will miss his flight. As she languidly picks up a toy, Perry rapidly starts cleaning up. Celeste cryingly implores him to stop but he ignores her pleas and after he is finished, he pours all the toys on her head, assaults her, and has sex with her. She is silent, frigid, and bruised. The last sex scene in the first season stems from a housekeeping issue and ends in Perry battering her. For him, sex is simply an aspect of this battering and therefore, clearly, sexual abuse. After this scene, she is in Dr. Reisman's office, narrating her excruciatingly brutal ordeal, and then in the new apartment—which she hopes will be her new home, after she leaves Perry furtively, taking her sons to her new home.

In the middle of the first season, she wants to tell Perry that she longs to return to her career but fears the repercussions she may face. She therefore asks Dr. Reisman's advice on how she should tell him, so he accepts her request and does not act harshly. It is then that Dr. Reisman asks Celeste if she is frightened of her husband. Celeste is at a loss of words. She again asks Celeste if Perry abuses her. Celeste defends Perry then but from the next session onwards we see her slowly coming to terms with her abusive marriage and realizing that "abuse is not simply a 'down' in a difficult marriage".[35] I examine the aforementioned scenes in the context of domesticity, as a discipline producing the gendered norm of woman's submissiveness to her husband or intimate partner and its ramifications.

According to Joan Williams, domesticity entails three components—first, the entitlement of employers to demand an ideal worker who is immune from familial obligations, second, the male entitlement and duty to live up to this work ideal, and last, the obligations of the woman whose life should be framed around nurturing, childrearing, and housekeeping.[36] Initially, masculinity was associated with patriarchy and male supremacy, but later, masculinity was seen as economic success which is ensured by domesticity.[37] Domesticity is a constraint which many women, including Celeste, face and internalize.[38] Choosing to be a stay-at-home mother is a choice she makes within the constraints imposed by domesticity. The constraints of domesticity are inconsistent with gender equality and result in her marginalization.[39] Johnson recognizes domesticity as a discipline in the Foucauldian sense[40] which produces gendered norms, such as women being pushed away from the public sphere to the private sphere to fulfil their familial duties as the caregiver of their children.[41] Drawing upon the work of Williams, MacKinnon, and Johnson, I propose that one such gendered norm that domesticity produces is wifely submission to husband's domination. In my view, domesticity results in affecting

[34] See MacKinnon, *supra* note 20.

[35] In her therapy session, with respect to Perry's abusive actions, Celeste asks Dr Reisman You must have seen many difficult marriages having their 'ups' and 'downs', what if this is a moment of 'down'?.

[36] Williams (2000), 20.

[37] *Ibid* at 25.

[38] *Ibid* at 37.

[39] *Ibid.*

[40] Johnson (2005), at 183.

[41] *Ibid* at 186, 195.

"women's voice… and equal participation in everyday life"[42] which creates "a vicious circle of cultural and economic subordination".[43] In Williams' opinion, domesticity may have replaced patriarchy as the basis of the organization of the familial structure,[44] but I propose that the implications, namely, submission to the husband, remain the same.

Adherence to domesticity implies Perry controls all the economic resources of the family. As per his directions, Celeste left her job and has been a housewife for over four years. Feeling ashamed, Celeste has never spoken about experiencing domestic violence to anyone. Rather she has painted Perry as the perfect father and husband to everyone. Dr. Reisman tells Celeste that being a lawyer she must be aware, that in such circumstances, if she were to divorce Perry, the judges will grant custody of the children to Perry and that the decision of the courts will be influenced by Perry's financial position. Celeste herself had told Dr. Reisman in the first season and the judge in the second season that she had stayed in the abusive marriage only for her children and the shame she would feel if others got to know her secret—that hers was a marriage fraught with violence. She knows she cannot meet the work ideal because she has immense familial responsibilities. Domesticity is also responsible for constructing the *blurred lines* between consensual sex and sexual abuse in her marriage because compliance with the discipline creates female submission to the husband's desires as the norm. There would be no *blurred lines* if Perry and Celeste were not in a conjugal relationship, and he were having 'sex' with her in the public sphere. All *blurred lines* would be construed as rape. Sex would be rape.

However, the gendered norm of obedience creates the *blurred lines*—making some viewers think that Celeste reciprocates his desire for *all kinds* of sex. Viewers do not ask *does she truly desire him; does she enjoy violent sex?* Viewers know that marriage had significantly affected her autonomy. Marriage gave her limited rights but gave her more obligations than Perry, resulting in her silent subordination.[45] Silent subordination as the norm is furthered due to the discipline of domesticity because domesticity ensures the family's financial dependence on the man. *When you are dependent on someone, you cannot be his equal, or even try to be his equal.* He can dominate you in whatever manner he deems fit, and you cannot protest.

Behaviour is regulated according to the norm, which is why sexual abuse and/or rape are normalized as sex in Celeste's mind. Women deviating from the norm are punished. Celeste is one such woman. Until she was 'normal', that is, conformed to domesticity and appeased her husband's demands, forgetting her autonomy, there were no *blurred lines*. All sex was sex. She was a woman in love, "a retired attorney wiping noses of her children".[46]

However, if all power were repressive who would obey it?[47] Therefore, Perry spoils Celeste with lavish gifts until she adheres to the norm of silent subordination to him. Power induces pleasure,[48] including erotic pleasure, and aids obedience to the norm. When she decides to deviate, when she desires to work and chooses to not obey her husband, to assert her authority against an abusive husband, power is used. Whenever a positive conception of power, such as Perry gifting her expensive jewellery, is unable to regulate her, then a more violent form of power is used to punish her, like choking and almost killing her.

For Celeste, her family is the site of oppressive subordination.[49] Like the colonial subject,

[42] Fraser (1995), at 79.

[43] *Ibid* (cultural subordination is best visible in the cultural devaluation of women which is manifest in the form of domestic violence). See UN Women (2020). Henriques (2020).

[44] Williams, *supra* note 36 at 23.

[45] De Beauvoir (1953), at 451, 479.

[46] Celeste says this about herself in Season 1 of *Big Little Lies*.

[47] Foucault (1984), at 61.

[48] *Ibid*.

[49] Williams, *supra* note 36 at 156–7.

she has been "coiled and robbed, taught to remain in [her] place and not overstep [her] limits".[50] When she oversteps her limits, she is violated. I propose that it is not only patriarchy or sex inequality or eroticisation of male domination but also domesticity that defines her limits as subordination. Following MacKinnon's theoretical analyses, I argue that in a state of subordination, the wife cannot be sexually autonomous. Relying upon Johnson and Williams, I propose that domesticity contributes to her socio-economic marginalization and lack of mobility in the public sphere. This ultimately creates a sexist society wherein subordination to the husband in all matters is normalized. This is most visible in Celeste's sexual subordination to Perry. She internalizes and normalizes sexual abuse as violent sex. It is only when she attempts deviance in its most extreme form by accepting and acknowledging that she was caught in an abusive marriage and thus, choosing to leave Perry, that she construes sex as sexual abuse. The next sub-section distinguishes itself from the above discussion on Celeste's subordination by offering a uniquely distinct interpretation of Celeste's sexual relationship with Perry.

4.3.3 Third Interpretation: Actively Seeking Violent Sex

Janet Halley objects to dominance/subordination feminism by arguing that it omits to consider the powers held by women, the vulnerabilities of men, and the possibility that women also have the agency, will, or capacity to harm.[51] According to her, this kind of feminism not only harms men but also women because it objectifies women and takes away their agency in narratives of sexual violence.[52] Feminism unintentionally intensifies female injury.[53] Halley notes that contributors to *Pleasure and Danger: Exploring Female Sexuality* tended to state that danger is essential to physical and emotional intimacy, "and at least potentially part of what one seeks in them. Of what *women* seek in them".[54] Halley also observes that contributors to *Pleasure and Danger: Exploring Female Sexuality* affirm that "sex has a dark side, is a domain of experience in which passion, power, shame, loss of boundary, violent vitality assume erotic dimensions and can give pleasure".[55]

Does Celeste also seek this element of danger which is intrinsic to sex? Does experiencing the dark side of sex, that is, Perry's power, and her shame at loss of her boundaries, give her pleasure? By erasing Celeste's agency, is feminism victimizing Celeste? Could it be that all sex in their relationship is consensual sex? Since Celeste has repeatedly told Madeline, Dr. Reisman, and Mary-Louise that she and Perry had great sex, it can be interpreted that she is as active an agent in sex as Perry is. She desires such dominance; she finds this dark side of sex pleasurable. Maybe feminism ignores that as a powerful actor, Celeste sought danger. After Perry's death, she is seen engaging in sex at the local bar with men she is not acquainted with. When questioned in court, Celeste testifies that in a state of intoxication she had one-night stands with most of the men who she did not know in the restroom of the bar. Perhaps, she also desires violent sex, finds it pleasurable, and later uses feminism deceptively in the custody case to depict herself as a fit mother and Mary-Louise as an unfit mother. Or maybe, Dr. Reisman and later Jane and Madeline convince Celeste that she is sexually abused when in fact, at the time she had sex with Perry, she did not feel so.[56]

[50] Fanon (2007, at 15.

[51] Halley (2006), at 333.

[52] *Ibid* at 343–346.

[53] *Ibid* at 346.

[54] *Ibid* at 117 (Contributors to *Pleasure and Danger: Exploring Female Sexuality* tended to state that danger is bad because it prevents "women from being sexually adventurous, from seeking and finding pleasure.").

[55] *Ibid.*

[56] See Halley (2016), at 272 (Halley argues that many complainants of sexual assault did not feel that they were being assaulted at the time of the encounter but have been led to believe so later).

It is a given that she is intensely drawn to Perry. In the second season, she looks at shirtless videos of Perry while in bed and touches herself intimately. However, he is morally or socially prohibited for her.[57] This is because Perry subjects Celeste to domestic violence, consequently, society, in this case, her friends and therapist, consider him as a forbidden undesirable sexual partner. Violent sex and conflict preceding sex, making the sex as well as the abuser, forbidden. In light of Halley's analyses,[58] it can be interpreted that the 'forbiddenness' of Celeste's desire for Perry intensifies her sexual attraction to him and induces her to have sex with him. After having sex, Celeste is horrified at what she has done—she has disappointed her therapist and friends who expected her to restrain herself from having sex with Perry and consequently, she blames Perry for her conduct.

Contrary to MacKinnon, Halley argues that a monogamous marriage should be viewed as a socio-legal arrangement where husbands and wives have almost identical instead of hierarchical bargaining power.[59] Halley relies on a Foucauldian approach[60] to claim that:

> sometimes power is not domination but micro-relations; sometimes power is not puissance but pouvoir, the capacity to produce effects, not bad or good but just there; freedom might be not a state of release of repression or de-subordination but a practice of active engagement in power; power might combine with knowledge to produce, as an effect of power, intelligibility; sexuality might be one such effect; sexuality might be organized by technologies like the psychiatrization of perversions; gender might be peripheral, not central, to it.[61]

Celeste tells Dr. Reisman that power is always changing hands in her marriage. After Perry assaults her, she has power. She loses that power to him once peace is forged. On applying the post-structuralist philosophies on 'power', one can determine that rather than viewing Perry as the dominator and Celeste as his submissive, the power in their relationship could be viewed as indeterminate.[62] Perry is the perverse sexually violent man who has raped Jane and must live out his deeply sexually violent true self while Celeste is the abused traumatized wife who must live out her deep disturbed self.[63] Perry is the classic subject of the psychiatrization of sexual deviance.[64] In an interpretation relying upon power and not feminism, it can be concluded that maybe it is this violent sex, 'their dirty secret' which follows brutal altercations that send them into a state of sensual pleasure.[65] Their sexual encounters can be construed to imply consensual sex, a sort of sex that they both desire and consent to, sex which enables them to live out their inner selves, sex which they find pleasurable, so pleasurable that without it they would both be lonely.

However, I cannot *take a break from feminism* and accept this interpretation of their sexual relationship. I need feminism to discern and decipher all wrongs, including the presence or absence of sexual abuse in their marriage. In all their vicious conflicts which stem from issues regarding the upbringing of children, her desire to work and spend time with her friends, he tries to control her and dictate to her that she

---

57 *Ibid* at 266–7 (this social and moral prohibition of a potential sexual partner results in a woman intensely desiring that specific partner and wanting to have sex with that partner).

58 Halley, *supra* note 51(Halley believes that we must take a break from feminism as feminism does more harm than good. We should turn to other theories, especially post-structuralist philosophies in order to understand any concept, including sexual violence); Halley, *supra* note 56 at 266–7 (this social and moral prohibition of a potential sexual partner makes the partner more desirable potentially resulting in a sexual encounter. However, to comply with this prohibition, several women who have had consensual sex with the prohibited sexual partner shift the blame of their transgression to the prohibited partner).

59 Cossman et al. (2003), at 616.

60 See Foucault (1990).

61 Cossman, et al., *supra* note 59 at 615.

62 See Cossman, et al., *supra* note 59 at 615.

63 In the second season, viewers find out that her abusive marriage and the disturbing way in which Perry had died had deeply traumatized Celeste.

64 See Cossman, et al., *supra* note 59 at 616.

65 See Cossman, et al., *supra* note 59 at 616.

belongs at home, living under his rule.[66] Celeste and Perry do not have equal bargaining power like Halley argues. Male supremacy, domesticity, and patriarchy do not enable Celeste to have bargaining power equal to the one Perry yields in their relationship.

Importantly, Perry is a prototype of patriarchal masculinity.[67] Through its depiction of Perry and Celeste's marriage, *Big Little Lies* conveys to the viewers a message on patriarchy, patriarchal masculinity, and the violence emanating from it. Patriarchy is a political-social system that asserts that men are inherently dominating and superior to everyone considered weak, especially women.[68] Patriarchy maintains that men possess the right to dominate and rule over the weak.[69] Violence is a way to preserve this dominance.[70] Sexist violence and male dominance are necessitated, maintained, and promoted by patriarchy.[71] In all their conflicts, Celeste is badly assaulted, sometimes nearly escaping death. Viewers routinely see her and observe her bruises and wounds. To ensure that he rules the private sphere, Perry uses violence of all kinds—physical, sexual, emotional, and financial.

It is difficult for me to not see a dominance/subordination axis in their marriage. I believe she always had agency[72]-including, during violent sex, on occasions when she does not resist him and remains silently submissive to him. For example, in one of the scenes, Perry holds her from the neck and drags her from the shower across the bathroom and bedroom as if she was a suitcase. She does not fight him in this scene nor in several other scenes where he pounces on her fiercely during a fight culminating in sex because she fears more force,[73] force that could eventually kill her. Horrors and pain of a violent experience make it nearly impossible to articulate and tell the unspoken truth[74] which is why it takes her an extremely long time to interpret her sexual relationship with her husband as sexual abuse and narrate the harrowing experiences before the judge in the courtroom. By employing feminism, she produces a recorded clip of the scene discussed above as evidence for her claim of sexual abuse.

It is not a state of erotic pleasure which she enjoys with Perry but a traumatic marriage, rife with domestic violence—which she wants to leave silently. She fears that if she tells him about her desire to divorce him, he will kill her. When he finds out her plans by attending to her real estate agent's phone call in her absence, he assaults her. She is rescued by her friends. This is not the danger she is seeking in establishing and maintaining sexual intimacy. Further, in her testimony, Celeste admits that the one-night stands served as an instrument to cope with her trauma. She testifies that she is trying to cope in healthier ways to recover and fulfil her familial duties. Additionally, she narrates that there was no violence in her sexual experiences with these strange men.

Feminism neither intensifies her suffering nor is it a tool employed by her to avenge herself. Rather, feminism helps her identify the injustice and the pain of being wronged.[75] She speaks like a feminist at the point she questions Mary-Louise on her stance that Celeste and Jane were lying about Perry raping them. These

66 See Massey (1994); Kamir, *supra* note 1(in her analysis of archetypal images of female characters onscreen, Kamir notes that one such typical character is an embodiment of Eve—the wife, the mother who fully assumes her domestic duties under her husband's rule, domestic duties entail subservience to the notion that a woman belongs at home); Williams, *supra* note 36 at 20; Johnson, *supra* note 40.

67 See Hooks (2004), at 5 (the only emotion that patriarchy values and deems natural in men is that of rage, nonetheless how violent or violating it could be).

68 *Ibid* at 12–13.

69 *Ibid* at 13.

70 *Ibid.*

71 *Ibid* at 17.

72 See Ahmed (2016), at 21.

73 See MacKinnon, *supra* note 20.

74 See Bhandar (2004); Perrin and Veitch (1998); Ahmed, *supra* note 71(making sense of a wrong means reliving a wrong).

75 See Ahmed, *supra* note 72 at 22 and 27.

actions are misconstrued as using feminism to play the innocent victim and attack Perry and Mary-Louise's reputations. When a woman speaks *like a feminist*, she can very often be vilified.[76] Mary-Louise's accusations at Celeste are one such instance. To conclude, I disagree with the interpretations which can be drawn from Halley's philosophies and, relying on feminist analyses, I interpret all sex in their marriage as sexual violence.

4.4 Conclusion

Feminism needs to be everywhere because feminism is not everywhere.[77]

I began this chapter with Kamir's quote to examine how films, in this case, the television show *Big Little Lies,* construct and portray the subject and object, family, gender, sex, domestic violence in general, and sexual violence, in particular. While embarking on a philosophical analysis of the abusive marriage of Celeste and Perry Wright in *Big Little Lies*, my purpose was to assess: whether any sexual encounters between the two amounted to sexual abuse?

In fulfilling the aims of my research, I have successfully demonstrated that film, law, gender, and society are intricately related with each other. Long before *And Just Like That, Big Little Lies* made its impact in several ways. It was refreshing to watch a middle-aged female character Celeste—a mother, wife, and later a single woman following the death of her husband, being vocal about her ambitions, sexual desires, and sexual pleasure. Despite her wealth, good looks, and racial privilege, she is relatable to the average viewer in myriad ways. Despite having a successful legal career, she finds it extremely difficult to acknowledge and accept that she is trapped in an abusive marriage. The mere thought of leaving her husband scares her, because she knows that he will kill her if he discovers her plans. Many viewers can empathize with her desire to be a mother, the several miscarriages she painfully endures, and finally, her sadness at realizing the false promises of the construct of motherhood. She pines to be in the public sphere, resuming her legal career, and not "wiping her sons' noses" in the private sphere. *Big Little Lies* conveys to the viewer that motherhood should not imply being pushed into the private sphere, but unfortunately, it does—because of domesticity, traditional yet omnipresent gender roles governing childrearing and especially, in Celeste's case—a husband not participating in childrearing obligations. Besides Celeste, her best friend, Madeline, also a mother and *housewife*, is vocal about her sexual desires. While past cinema adopted the *Eve-Lilith* distinction by making mothers and housewives sexless objects,[78] *Big Little Lies* distinguishes itself from them and goes further by making Jane and Celeste allies in their shared experience of violent sex and rape.

Despite her racial and class privilege, viewers can relate to Celeste because she is not very different from other battered wives. This is so because, in conjugal relationships, consent to sex is presumed. Further, the threshold of coercion is very high. It is defined by men for women to prove that the coercion was significant enough to nullify the presumed consent. Coercion is not just limited to physical force. I believe that the male control over economic resources and the patriarchal construct of love can also be understood as coercion. The patriarchal construct of love is evident in Perry's emotional abuse of Celeste to think that he is in love with her, which is why he ardently desires her, wants to be sexually intimate with her in whatever manner he desires, wants her all to himself and his home which is why he forbids her to work or spend time with her family and friends. Perry controls and influences her thinking. This is why she perceives her sexual relationship with Perry as 'great sex' rather than sexual abuse. Perry is the subject while Celeste is the object. He dominates, she submits.

---

[76] *Ibid* at 21.

[77] *Ibid* at 4.

[78] Kamir, *supra* note 1 at 34.

The notion of domesticity as explored by Williams and Johnson adds to MacKinnon's analyses. I have argued that conformity with the discipline of domesticity produces the gendered norm of female subservience to the husband. Celeste, like other wives, cannot consent if she is subservient to Perry. She lacks autonomy. The question of consent is problematic in light of social oppression,[79] specifically, the coercive terms of Wrights' inter-personal relational arrangement.[80] The concepts of choice and consent are problematic in their relationship because Celeste never anticipated the consequences of marrying Perry, that is, non-compliance with the coercive terms of marital contract, such as not pursuing her career ultimately results in severe domestic abuse. Conformity with this discipline results in her socio-economic marginalization and dependence upon her husband, which is related to the other form of coercion used in *marital rape-economics*. Dependence and marginalization render the woman to lose her voice, if not completely, to a large extent in the private sphere. Feminism is absent in the domestic settings because Celeste is dependent upon Perry and she is unable to challenge her position as his subordinate. Domesticity creates a vicious chain of events. When she tries to deviate from the norm, he exercises his repressive power to punish her.

Halley, deciding that all feminism posits injury into subordination theories,[81] argues that we must take a break from feminism to study and analyse varied concepts. Unlike *dominance feminism* which proposes the interpretation that Wrights' marriage is sexually violent, Halley's analyses suggest a different interpretation that their sexual relationship is consensual, a state of erotic pleasure which Celeste and Perry desire and seek. Further, this interpretation suggests that feminism objectifies Celeste and treats her as injured while she is 'uninjured'.

I would like to conclude by emphatically stating that I believe Celeste is 'injured' and that she is caught in an antifeminist marriage and needs feminism to realize, identify, and narrate the wrong and injustice of sexual abuse. She finally does, by interpreting her sexual relationship with her husband as sexual abuse, unlike her past self that concealed the 'dirty secret' in her marriage by blaming some of it on herself, she is able to narrate the sexual abuse before everyone.

[79] See Fineman (2004), at 226, 219–220 (one of the essential components for a contract is autonomy of the parties to that contract). Therefore, in light of Celeste's lack of autonomy, its questionable if her marriage with Perry is a valid contract.

[80] See especially Fineman, Martha. 2004. *The Autonomy Myth: A Theory of Dependence* New York: The New Press at 226–7.

[81] Halley, *supra* note 51 at 321.

References

Ahmed S (2016) Living a Feminist Life. Duke University Press, Durham

Bernstein A (2019) War at home: how Big Little Lies deftly dissects domestic violence. The Guardian, June 17

Bhandar B (2004) Anxious reconciliation(s): unsettling foundations and spatializing history. Environ Planning D: Soc Space 22:831–845

Cossman B et al (2003) Gender, sexuality, and power: is feminist theory enough. Columbia J Gend Law 12(3):601–637

De Beauvoir S (1953) The second sex. Trans. H.M. Parshley. New York: Knopf

Fanon F (2007) The wretched of the earth. Trans. Richard Philcox. New York: Grove Press

Fineman M (2004) The autonomy Myth: a theory of dependence New York: The New Press

Foucault M (1984) Truth and power. In: Rabinow P (ed) The Foucault Reader. Pantheon, New York, pp 51–75

Foucault M (1990) The history of sexuality, an introduction: volume one. Trans. Robert Hurley. New York: Vintage Books

Fraser N (1995) From redistribution to recognition? Dilemmas of justice in a 'post-socialist' age. New Left Rev 212:68–93

Halley J (2006) Split decisions: how and why to take a break from feminism. Princeton University Press, Princeton, New Jersey

Halley J (2016) The move to affirmative consent. Signs: J Women Culture Soc 42(1):257–279

Henriques M (2020) Why Covid-19 is different for men and women. BBC Future. https://www.bbc.com/future/article/20200409-why-covid-19-is-different-for-men-and-women. Accessed 14 Aug 2023

Hooks B (2004) The will to change: men, masculinity and love. Atria Books, New York

Johnson R (2005) Law and the leaky woman: the saloon, the liquor licence, and narratives of containment. Continuum 19(2):181–199

Kamir O (2006) Framed: women in law and film: how law on screen constructs gender, dignity and honor. Duke University Press, Durham
MacKinnon C (1987) Feminism unmodified: discourses on life and law. Harvard University Press, Cambridge
MacKinnon C (1989) Toward a feminist theory of the state. Harvard University Press, Cambridge
Massey D (1994) Space, place, and gender. University of Minnesota Press, Minnesota
Munro VE (2013) Violence against women, 'Victimhood' and the (Neo)Liberal State. In: Davies M, Munro VE (eds), The Ashgate research companion to feminist legal theory, 233–248. London; New York: Routledge
Perrin C, Veitch S (1998) The promise of reconciliation. Law Text Culture 4:225–244
UN Women (2020) UN Women. COVID-19 and its economic toll on women: the story behind the numbers. https://www.unwomen.org/en/news/stories/2020/9/feature-covid-19-economic-impacts-on-women. Accessed 14 Aug 2023
Williams J (2000) Unbending gender: why family and work conflict and what to do about it. Oxford University Press, New York

An Examination of the Married Body of a Woman as Reflected Through Marital Rape in Nigeria

5

Ezinwanne Roseline Raymond

Abstract

The Nigerian Penal Code allows *'husbands to correct their wives'*. A potential inquiry over the intended role of law would question whether the law is a means of salvation or a contributor to women's objectification. The chapter asserts that the *mutual contractual consent theory* that advocates for the marital rape exemption from criminalization is a partial representation of the situation in Nigeria. Analysis of the institution of marriage within the socio-cultural context of Nigeria is crucial for gaining insights into the current manifestation of marital rape. This chapter presents a contextual framework for comprehending the non-recognition of marital rape in Nigeria by examining the objectification of women through the practice of 'bride price'. The aim is to illustrate that this practice establishes a power hierarchy within marital relationships, which, when combined with the prevalent objectification of women in Nigerian society, shapes a certain perception of a woman's body within the context of marriage, which in turn contributes to the occurrence of marital rape and violence within such unions. This chapter provides an analysis of Hale's theoretical framework and its implications for comprehending the concept of marital rape in Nigeria, focusing on consent. The influence of 'bride price' on power dynamics within marriage in Nigeria draws upon Foucault's theoretical framework of power and knowledge. This perspective offers valuable insights into the structural constraints imposed by the practice of 'bride price' and its impact on the autonomy of spouses within a marital union.

Keywords

Marital rape · Bride price · Nigeria · Power dynamics · Institution of marriage · Property theory · Unity theory · Consent theory · Sexual violence · Transaction · Bargaining · Patriarchy · Autonomy of spouses · Performative theory · Criminalization · Marital rape exception

5.1 Introduction

Marital rape has been historically recognized as legally permissible in several regions across the globe. The prevailing consensus was that a husband could not be found guilty of committing the act of rape against his wife. Most statutes qualify

E. R. Raymond (✉)
York St John University, York, UK
e-mail: raymondezinywanne@gmail.com

E. R. Raymond
Nottingham Women's Centre, Nottingham, UK

P. M. Anurag and S. Dwivedy (eds.), *Violence in Intimate Spaces*, Sustainable Development Goals Series, https://doi.org/10.1007/978-981-97-2657-8_5

rape as non-consensual sexual intercourse involving a woman who is not the perpetrator's spouse. While there are variations in the legal definition of marital rape, particularly within the United States, it can be broadly characterized as an act of non-consensual sexual intercourse perpetrated by a husband against his wife, achieved by the use of force, fear, fraud, or without consent.[1]

Rape, among other violent acts against women, is one of the most widespread, persistent, and devastating human rights violations in the world. It has been described as a shadow pandemic, with one in three women worldwide having experienced physical or sexual violence inflicted by an intimate partner or non-partner at some point in their lifetime.[2] Almost one in three (31%) women aged 15–49 have experienced physical violence in Nigeria.[3] Two out of every ten married women and girls (16%) report experiencing physical or sexual violence at the hands of their spouse or partner at some point during their lives.[4] Two in three women and girls experience violence by their husbands and boyfriends.[5] Findings from a national survey conducted in 2014 found that one in four females report experiencing sexual violence in childhood, with about 70% experiencing more than one such incident.[6] Nearly half the girls (43%) get married before the age of 18, while one in five girls is married by the age of 15 in Nigeria.[7] Child brides are 50% more likely to experience physical or sexual violence by their partner.[8]

The profound consequences of sexual assault on the physical, emotional, sexual, and reproductive well-being of women are of utmost significance. Legal systems have evolved in the recognition of marital rape as a criminal offence. As of 2019, around 150 countries, including select states within the United States, have enacted legislation to criminalize marital rape. The field of international human rights law has demonstrated consistent advancement in acknowledging intimate partner abuse as a violation of human rights and elucidating the corresponding obligations of states. However, marital rape in the context of intimate partner relationships remains controversial in many jurisdictions, including Nigeria. It is imperative to acknowledge that the occurrence of violence such as marital rape, is a multifaceted phenomenon influenced by cultural and environmental elements specific to each jurisdiction. The influence of contextual circumstances frequently shape societal perceptions of marital rape as a criminal act and determine the accountability of perpetrators as well as the response of survivors. Legal reforms, while possessing significant potential to effectuate transformation, constitute merely a component of a lasting solution. Hence, it is imperative to analyse these contextual elements and their influence on the implementation of constructive changes to legislation pertaining to marital rape. Specifically, this chapter proffers a contextual perspective to understanding the non-recognition of marital rape in Nigeria by examining the practice of bride price. The aim of this chapter is to analyse the manner in which the custom of bride price establishes a power dynamic within a marriage, which, when coupled with societal objectification of women in patriarchal Nigerian culture, presents difficulties in identifying and addressing marital rape as a criminal offence.

This chapter is divided into two distinct sections. In the first section, a concise overview is presented regarding the legal framework pertaining to rape in Nigeria, along with an examination of the theoretical underpinnings around the exemption of marital rape. This chapter provides a further examination of Hale's theory

---

[1] Bergen (1996). https://doi.org/10.4135/9781483327624.

[2] Vaeza (2020), Accessed 30 June 2023.

[3] UNICEF, Spotlight Initiative (2023), Accessed 29 June 2023.

[4] *Ibid.*

[5] *Ibid.*

[6] Women at Risk International Foundation (WARIF). Rape Stats in Nigeria. https://warifng.org/rape-stats-in-nigeria/, Accessed 20 June 2023.

[7] UNICEF, Spotlight Initiative. 2023. 16 facts about violence against women and girls in Nigeria: For the 16 days of activism https://www.unicef.org/nigeria/media/6696/file/16%20facts%20document.pdf, Accessed 29 June 2023.

[8] *Ibid.*

and explores the notion of consent within the specific setting of Nigeria. Section two delves into an analysis of the bride price system, as well as the patriarchal framework that characterizes Nigerian society. This chapter employs Foucault's theoretical framework of power and knowledge to examine the dynamics of power within the specific context of marriage in Nigeria.

5.1.1 Legal Framework on Rape in Nigeria

As early as 1993, the explicit recognition of marital rape as a form of violence against women was established by the United Nations Declaration on the Elimination of Violence Against Women (DEVAW).[9] Article 4(c) of DEVAW mandates that member states of the United Nations (UN) are obligated to demonstrate 'due diligence' in their efforts to both prevent and penalize acts of violence against women.[10] The significance of this was later underscored in the 1995 Beijing Declaration and Platform for Action, which received widespread adoption from member nations of the UN. Beyond these declarations which are non-binding on states, violence against women violates several human rights treaties which mandate nations to criminalize such acts in order to achieve their obligations of due diligence as outlined in a range of international and regional agreements. The Committee on the Elimination of All Forms of Discrimination Against Women (CEDAW) has recognized that violence against women includes marital rape[11]. These acts violate fundamental human rights, including the right to life, liberty, and security of person; the right to non-discrimination and equal protection under the law; and the right to freedom from torture. According to the Human Rights Committee's General Comment on the right to liberty and security of the person, it has been emphasized that state parties are obligated to 'respond appropriately' to instances of violence that occur in a consistent manner.[12]

Nigeria is one of the many countries that continues to uphold the marital rape exemption. Criminal offences are prosecuted based on national criminal law provisions and at the High Court at the first instance. Sexual offences, including rape, are governed by:

- the Criminal Code Act of Nigeria ('Criminal Code'), which applies in the Southern states,[13]
- the Penal Code, which applies to the Northern states,[14]
- the Violence Against Persons (Prohibition) Act 2015 (VAPP),[15]
- and other individual State laws on Domestic Violence and Sexual Related Offences, such as the Protection Against Domestic Violence Law of Lagos State, 2007, and the Ekiti State Gender Based Violence (Prohibition) Amendment Law, 2019.[16]

The Criminal Code punishes rape with life imprisonment, with or without caning. The Penal Code also punishes rape by life imprisonment; however, it includes provisions for mitigating circumstances that may result in a reduced term of imprisonment. The distinction between the Criminal Code and Penal Code, in terms of legal frameworks, is primarily rooted in geographical factors and reflects a manifestation of cultural and religious variations. According to the provisions outlined in the Violence Against Persons (Prohibition) Act of 2015(VAPP), the prescribed penalty for the offence of rape entails

[9] Randall and Venkatesh (2015)..

[10] UN Declaration on the Elimination of Violence against Women (1993), Accessed 23 August 2023.

[11] CEDAW (1992), Accessed 1 September 2023.

[12] UN Human Rights Committee (2014).

[13] *Nigerian Criminal Code* (1990).

[14] *Nigerian Penal Code* (1960).

[15] *Violence Against Persons (Prohibition) Act*, 2015.

[16] Ekiti State Gender (2019), 2019 repealed the 2011 law and incorporated the prohibition of female circumcision, genital mutilation and included provisions to uphold the rights of widows.

a minimum custodial sentence of 12 years, without a fine. The VAPP operates in the Federal Capital Territory, Abuja, and some other states in Nigeria which have either adopted it or brought similar laws, including Anambra State, Ebonyi State, and Oyo State. States which do not have the VAPP or have adopted it as a state law are still bound by the Penal Code in northern Nigeria and the Criminal Code in southern Nigeria.

While the Criminal Code and VAPP subtly make no mention of marital rape, the Penal Code clearly specifies in its provision that "*sexual intercourse by a man with his wife is not rape, if she has attained to puberty*".[17] Nigeria is party to the Convention on the Elimination of All forms of Discrimination against Women and the Maputo Protocol; however, this is yet to be incorporated within domestic laws.[18]

5.1.2 Marital Rape Exemption: Theories

English common law played a significant role historically in marital rape exemption in many countries.[19] The argument for the exemption of marital rape in English common law is grounded in three primary theories: *the property theory, the unity theory, and the consent theory.*[20] According to the tenets of property theory, women were perceived as possessions owned by males. Consequently, rape was perceived as a tortious act involving the unlawful appropriation of property that was deemed to be under the ownership of the male, either the husband in the case of a married woman or the father in the case of an unmarried woman. This perspective failed to recognize rape as a violation of the woman's fundamental human rights. Consequently, it was argued that men were deemed incapable of committing rape, as their actions were perceived as a legitimate exercise of ownership over their spouses. The concept of a woman's body as a form of property is evident in the context of adultery, which was deemed by English Lord Chief Justice John Holt as the "*the highest property invasion*".[21]

The *unity hypothesis* posits that at marriage, a couple undergoes a transformation wherein they merge into a singular entity, with the man assuming the role of this unified entity. The unity theory states that due to the conceptualization of the husband and wife as the same entity, the husband's inability to commit spousal rape stems from his inherent incapacity to perpetrate rape upon himself.[22]

The notion of *consent*, often referred to as Hale's hypothesis, has exerted significant influence in the scholarly discussion around the issue of marital rape. During the seventeenth century, Matthew Hale, a prominent British jurist, expressed in his work titled '*History of the Pleas of the Crown*'[23] "*But the husband cannot be guilty of rape committed by himself upon his lawful wife, for by their mutual matrimonial consent and contract the wife hath given herself up in this kind unto her husband which she cannot retract*". For an extended period of time, this assertion served as the rationale for the legal exemption of marital rape and the basis for the concept of spousal immunity. This line of reasoning not only deprives a married woman of her agency in relation to her spouse, but also fails to acknowledge the significant harm experienced by the woman as a survivor of sexual assault, while simultaneously denying her access to legal remedies that are otherwise afforded to unmarried women.[24] Hale posits that marriage

[17] *Penal Code Act of Nigeria*, Sect. 282.

[18] Ijeoma (2006).

[19] Fox (2013).

[20] Yllö and Torres (2016).

[21] Pillsbury (2000).

[22] Jackson (1994).

[23] Hale (1736).

[24] US Department of Justice, Office of Justice Programs. *Forcible Rape—the Crime, the Victim and the Offender*. Eds. Chappell, D., R. Geis and G. Geis. https://www.ojp.gov/ncjrs/virtual-library/abstracts/forcible-rape-crime-victim-and-offender, Accessed 9 July 2023).

is a contractual agreement wherein the exchange of wedding vows signifies the wife's implicit and irreversible permission, as well as her commitment to relinquish her right to bodily privacy. Additionally, it implies her willingness to engage in sexual intercourse with her husband at his discretion. A concise analysis of the terminology employed by Hale in his rationale is significant.

A contract represents a formal agreement, specifically in the context of a transaction involving a male and a female party. Throughout history, both in the common law tradition and in contemporary society, women have been perceived as possessions within patriarchal social structures, initially belonging to their fathers and subsequently transferring ownership to their husbands.[25] The presence of a patriarchal framework establishes an inherent imbalance in bargaining power between individuals of different genders within a marital union, hence compromising the ability to freely negotiate conditions within the confines of the marriage contract.

The *concept of consent* holds significant importance within *social contract theories* of political legitimacy, as evidenced in the works of renowned thinkers, including Plato, Thomas Hobbes, and John Locke.[26] The concept of consent is invoked in a variety of contexts in morality and law and its legal definition often varies by location and context. The significance of consent as a moral imperative in determining the validity or permissibility of various behaviours and activities, particularly in the context of sexual encounters, is widely recognized. Arguably, consent plays along two dimensions of our moral thought: first concerning our interpersonal moral relationships, and, on the other hand, the justifiability of our actions.[27]

Against this background, it is important to examine the role of acceptable definitions of consent in normative behaviour. The # *MeToo Movement* has played a significant role in shaping the legal and cultural frameworks surrounding consent in the context of sexual relationships.[28] The philosophical discourse frequently grapples with the ambiguity surrounding the correlation between consent and permissible action. Public education on rape focuses mainly on '*universal*' understandings of rape without looking at broader sexual cultures or taking the local context into account. This often creates a disjuncture between the definitions and meanings held in social groups, raising a question of what kinds of actions are perceived and classified as rape, coercion, or violence by those who experience them. Although it is widely understood that many women across cultures choose not to call non-consensual sex with their boyfriends and partners 'rape', the meanings and the extent to which a woman feels violated are under-researched in African settings.[29]

Specifically, the traditional models of consent fail to adequately account for the role of context in the dynamics of a marital relationship. Current literature on marital rape often overlooks the unique cultural circumstances surrounding this issue, as well as the specific nuances associated with the concept of consent within these contexts. In a patriarchal society such as Nigeria, consent undermines sexual autonomy and reduces sexual relations to a matter of 'giving' and 'taking'. According to Jennifer Nedelsky, as opposed to consent, frameworks of sexual practice based on autonomy fundamentally promote equal participation, co-determination, and erotic flourishing and agency. Practices of eliciting and giving consent are often regarded as superficial, having less to do with respecting the autonomy of the other person, and might even be oppressive, leaving very little room for the pursuit of acceptable

[25] Scott et al. (2016).

[26] Zaitchik (1982).

[27] Healey (2018).

[28] Sadler-Venis, J. Sexual offence laws: #MeToo movement drives new consent-based definitions. https://www.ibanet.org/article/386A45E6-0A58-4A7F-8741-3CE58A50F8C4, Accessed 30 June 2023.

[29] Wood et al. (2007).

alternatives.[30] Awareness of the cultural context of marital rape, a crime in which consent is significant, should be indispensable in an argument for the ethical significance of marital rape, both in theory and practice. This chapter aims to fill this gap in the existing literature. The next section examines the context of Nigerian society, with a particular focus on the bride price system prevalent in Nigeria. It explores the implications of this system on the dynamics of power within marital relationships.

5.1.3 Bride Price System in Nigeria[31]

Bride price, generally known as the exchange of materials or money from the groom to the bride's family, constitutes a crucial part of marriage in African cultures.[32] A woman is often regarded as unmarried, even if she has children, until the man pays her bride price.[33] Historically, bride price took the form of labour provided by the groom to the bride's family.[34] In the modern cash economy, it has principally taken the form of cash payment to the bride's family.

Advocates of the bride price contend that this custom transcends mere tradition and functions as an instrument of ratification of the marriage.[35] It is argued that payment of bride price serves multiple purposes, including the affirmation of a woman's worth and femininity, acting as recompense for the bride's family for the loss of labour, fostering a harmonious connection between the two families, and serving as a commitment from the groom to ensure the bride's well-being. It is regarded as an honour, a symbol of good faith, and a demonstration of commitment, respect, and appreciation by the groom to the bride and her family. Customarily, payment of bride price is proof of recognition of marriage and grants the man the entitlement to consider the woman as his 'wife'. Additionally, it affords his family a valid basis for asserting their rights over the offspring resulting from the marriage.

The practice of bride price is criticized by feminist scholars for its commodification of women. Ancient bride price was often considered a direct payment for the bride's virginity.[36] To understand the dynamics of the bride price, the chapter will examine two major features of its practice that potentially impact the autonomy of the woman and establish a foundation for an unequal power relationship in a marriage—*firstly,* the negotiation of bride price and *secondly,* the return of bride price.

Negotiation of bride price is typically a bargaining exercise where parties to the marriage have the final say on the bride price. The parties mutually determine the venue for the negotiation, which is typically the bride's residence but may be altered for the sake of convenience. The 'spokesperson' for each party, who is predominantly a male, is tasked with mediating between the parties' differing interests concerning the precise bride price and the payment method (lump sum or instalments). Factors that impact the decision of the bride price during negotiation are the bride's education and sometimes the characteristics of other members of her family. Education of the girl child is regarded as an advantage and is emphasized to improve the bargaining power of the girl's family while negotiating the bride price. In most cultures, participants in the negotiation space are typically restricted to males and consist of the groom, the senior men in the clan, parents, and relatives of both parties. Women, on the other hand, can express their opinions only in private,

[30] Nedelsky (1996); *See also* Lillehammer (2020).

[31] There is a lack of consistency in literature with respect to the use of terms for marriage payments. Terms such as dowry, bride wealth, and bride price are often used interchangeably to mean payments between bride and groom's family. For this chapter, bride price shall mean marriage payment from the groom's family to the bride's family.

[32] Papps et al. (1983).

[33] Ruth (2015), Accessed 3 July 2023.

[34] Nwoke (2009).

[35] Goldschmidt (1973).

[36] Anderson (2007).

and though their opinions may be adopted, they cannot express the same in the negotiating space. According to a participant in a study on bride price by Chen et al. (2023),[37] "*My father, not me, determined the amount of bride price without discussing it with me. A total of 300,000 gifts still cost very high. I'm the only daughter and spoiled at home, but that did not give me the liberty to participate in the final negotiation*".

The significance of the links between space and power dynamics between men and women has been recognized in several academic literature.[38] This gendering of *space* and *location* for the bride price negotiation reflects and influences the way in which societies construe and comprehend gender. It reduces women to commodities whose worth is not only quantified in monetary or material terms but is also subject to negotiation by the 'owners'. The spatial hierarchy in question gives rise to the gendered power dynamics that exist between men and women; these dynamics concurrently form the foundation of the patriarchal system.[39]

Return of bride price is prevalent in some parts of Nigeria. In the event of divorce or a woman's intention to separate from her spouse, customary practice dictates that she and her family are obligated to restore the bride price and any accompanying material possessions that were bestowed upon her family. This serves as evidence of the termination of the union. The act of returning the bride price carries a social shame for both the woman and her family since it symbolizes a perceived inadequacy or shortcoming on the part of the woman's parents. This phenomenon might be attributed to the patriarchal nature of Nigerian society, particularly within the Igbo tribe, where women are commonly held responsible for marital failures and frequently lack familial support.[40] The prevailing patriarchal ideology often stigmatizes women who have experienced marital dissolution as negative influences on other women, resulting in their social isolation and rejection by both familial and social networks.

The act of refunding the bride price in the event of a marriage dissolution has been consistently supported by Nigerian courts in a substantial number of instances. In the case of *Bawa v Bawa*,[41] the Customary Court rendered a decision mandating the return of the bride price. The court justified its ruling by emphasizing the sanctity of marriage as an institution that warrants universal reverence. It further asserted that the exploitation of marriage for personal gain or the pursuit of specific benefits should not be condoned or promoted. In the case of *Eze v Omeke*,[42] the Customary Court rendered a decision stating that the dissolution of a customary law marriage is rendered ineffective if there is no subsequent order for the return or acceptance of the bride price or dowry. Nevertheless, the court has unequivocally denounced the reinstatement of bride price, deeming this custom as morally objectionable and in violation of principles of inherent fairness. The significance of the practice of bride price return cannot be overstated. Scholars have discerned that the restitution of bride price subsequent to a dissolution of marriage might impose restrictions and curtail a woman's agency within an abusive relationship, particularly when considering the exorbitant expenses associated with bride price.[43] When determining the amount to be repaid, various variables are taken into account, such as the length of the marriage, the existence of children, and the essential, inherent, and altruistic services provided by the woman during the subsistence of the marriage.

[37] Chen (2023).

[38] Flather (2013).

[39] Massey (2013).

[40] Elochukwu (2021), Accessed 11th September 2023.

[41] *Tabitha Bawa v. Bawa Waziri* (unreported) delivered on 24 June 2011. CCKJ/CV/14/2011 (HW Emmanuel J. Samaila—Judge and Mr. Luka Magaji & Mr. Inda Tache—Members).

[42] Eze v Omeke (1977).

[43] Eves (2019).

5.1.4 Patriarchy and Marriage in Nigerian Society

The notion of patriarchy is not a novel concept and was described by Engels as "*the world historical defeat of the female sex*".[44] In the late twentieth century, feminist theories began to expand the understanding of patriarchy beyond an ancient civilization. According to Alda (2013),[45]

> Patriarchy is a form of mental, social, spiritual, economic and political organization/structuring of society produced by the gradual institutionalization of sex-based political relations created, maintained and reinforced by different institutions linked closely together to achieve consensus on the lesser value of women and their roles. These institutions interconnect not only with each other to strengthen the structures of domination of men over women but also with other systems of exclusion, oppression, and/or domination based on real or perceived differences between humans, creating States that respond only to the needs and interests of a few powerful men.

The terms '*gradual institutionalization and consensus on the lesser value of women*' in the above definition are key to understanding how patriarchy is reproduced. Gradual institutionalization suggests that patriarchy, as observed within the family unit, is not an inherent or innate characteristic. Rather, it is acquired through socialization and perpetuated deliberately over time, becoming deeply ingrained within behaviours, practices, and societal structures. The concept of '*consensus regarding the diminished worth of women*' encompasses not only the unequal power dynamics between men and women, but also the shared intellectual agreement within a given culture that women possess a lesser value than men. This agreement is manifested through many practices, beliefs, customs, and interpersonal connections.

Patriarchy manifests in diverse forms within the Nigerian context, encompassing sociocultural practices. Marriage holds prominent cultural significance in certain regions of the nation, extending beyond a mere social convention, as it symbolizes the passage into a culturally prescribed state of masculinity.Marriage is often regarded as a representation of accountability and personal growth and is held in high esteem within society for individuals of both genders; a sense of accomplishment for males, but for women, it is commonly perceived as a form of privilege. In Nigeria, there exists a prevalent socialization process wherein young girls are encouraged from an early age to aim towards marriage, with the belief that it should be their foremost concern. The prevailing cultural traditions in certain regions of Nigeria regarding the naming of children impose restrictions on women's sexual expression and reinforce and perpetuate traditional notions of femininity. Females are bestowed with names that embody gender dynamics, encompassing notions of spousal significance, prospective marital roles, the significance of matrimony, procreation, and motherhood.[46]

In research conducted by Eyo (2023),[47] a 52-year female participant stated that:

> Marriage is an essential obligation in the life of everybody in our society. Every girl-child is a future wife, and her name is a constant reminder of her role as a dutiful wife that represents traditional values and customs. She grows up with this knowledge that enables her to fit into the principle of ideal womanhood. It is the name that guides the bearer into this orthodox wifely devotion. She starts early in life to imbibe strong feminine qualities such as obedience, loyalty, and faithfulness, which are taught by the example of her mother.

Butler's conceptual framework, known as the '*performative model*', offers valuable insights into the practice of assigning gendered names to women. In their seminal publication on gender[48], Butler argues that gender is performative rather than inherent. They further emphasize that gender is not simply a set of actions, but rather a series of repeated stylizations of the

[44] Engels (1972). *See also* Lerner (1988).

[45] Facio (2013), Accessed 20 August 2023.

[46] Mensah (2023).

[47] *Ibid.*

[48] Butler (2006).

body that occur within a strict regulatory framework. These stylizations gradually solidify over time, creating the illusion of a natural and essential form of existence. Over time, the woman gradually internalizes her longing for fulfilment within the institution of marriage. The individual in question derives her sense of worth and personal identity from her marital partnership, with this awareness being deeply ingrained as a significant element of her social development. Consequently, a woman is thus emotionally equipped for a prospective life with her spouse, whom she has been socialized to value in order to attain social recognition within the community. Additionally, after a marriage, a woman is considered a member of her husband's household (which explains why the majority of women change their names), as her marital home is considered her sanctuary—a location where she can find solace, protection, and companionship. Being married signifies a woman's completion; therefore, her matrimonial union is considered to be the cessation of her '*incompleteness*'.

On the other hand, stereotypes surrounding singlehood among women in Nigeria pose challenges for unmarried women in terms of emotional and practical autonomy. Women who achieve financial independence often face social stigma, as they are frequently associated with having older men as their financial sponsors or are unjustly labelled as '*ill-behaved*'. Single women face challenges while attempting to secure rental housing, as landlords often exhibit hesitancy in offering their properties due to the prevailing cultural norm that regards marriage as a need for upholding societal standards of decency. Unmarried women are sometimes subject to suspicion of engaging in prostitution and being irresponsible. Consequently, several landlords require communication with a woman's spouse or father, who is perceived as being responsible for her, prior to letting out their properties.[49] This presents a complex situation when an adult woman encounters difficulties in locating a suitable romantic companion. In certain instances, unmarried women may experience vulnerability and become subject to violent relationships as a result of their earnest pursuit of social approval. Women may experience a sense of compulsion to engage in desperate behaviours, such as entering into unhealthy relationships, in order to attain social status or validation from others.

Several reports of harrowing cases of violence against women and girls continue to emphasize sexual and gender-based violence as the most prevalent human rights violation in Nigeria. During the lockdown in 2020, it was reported that the National Human Rights Commission received about 11,000 reported cases of rape.[50] There exists a widely held perception that women frequently experience instances of sexual harassment in public spaces due to their choice of attire, which is deemed by societal norms as excessively revealing for women. This phenomenon is more prevalent among unmarried women, as there is a societal expectation for married women to attire themselves in a manner that caters to the preferences of their spouses. Due to this rationale, certain employers and organizations enforce dress codes specifically targeting women.

The marginalization of women and the tendency to assign blame to victims in cases of sexual and violent crimes exemplify the challenges faced by women. The system and law enforcement consistently fall short in their support of women and girls, resulting in significant barriers for survivors seeking access to justice. In the context of prosecuting rape cases, it is frequently observed that the accused party may propose marriage to the victim by way of redress and retribution for the offence committed. This statement is grounded in the prevailing social stigma experienced by rape survivors in Nigeria, which is further exacerbated by the widely held assumption that a man would be unwilling to pay the customary bride price for a woman who

[49] BBC (2018), Accessed 3 July 2023.

[50] Amnesty International (2021), Accessed 15 August 2023.

has been subjected to sexual violation. In order to mitigate instances of sexual assault and harassment, women often seek protection from their male relatives, fathers, or husbands. Child marriages, a pervasive regressive socio-cultural practice in Nigeria, are influenced by both push and pull factors. Nigeria currently has an estimated 22 million child brides.[51] In the northern western and eastern regions of the nation, around 68% and 57% of women between the ages of 20 and 49 were wedded before reaching the age of 18, respectively.[52] Research has indicated that child marriage constitutes a significant determinant of intimate partner violence, given that individuals who enter into marriage at a young age are more prone to limited educational opportunities, impoverished living conditions, and adherence to conventional gender roles[53] These matrimonial unions are frequently distinguished by substantial disparities in the ages of the spouses, unequal distribution of power, limited social integration, and lack of autonomy.

Conversely, in the case of men, marriage frequently entails a costly financial transaction involving the payment of a bride price and a comprehensive set of requirements imposed by the bride's family. The magnitude of bride prices can exert an influence on saving behaviours and yield substantial consequences for households. The financial obligations associated with the payment of the bride price, adherence to traditions, and hosting a wedding ceremony, when applicable, may impose constraints on the marriage prospects of men, particularly in a nation such as Nigeria, characterized by elevated inflation rates and widespread poverty. The escalating bride prices in the marriage market may give rise to distortions that have the potential to impede the marriage prospects of young men, particularly those who belong to marginalized communities, experience financial hardship, and have challenges sustaining themselves within an economically unstable environment. This phenomenon places excessive societal expectations on males, leading to the emergence of social hierarchies based on marital status inside their respective social networks. Certain individuals employ different methods in order to fulfil these requirements, as their failure to provide the bride price may result in a loss of social standing and esteem. In the context of a patriarchal society such as Nigeria, there exists a prevailing perception that a successful marriage is characterized by the husband assuming the major role of providing full financial support for his wife and children. Given the considerable challenge of meeting this elevated societal expectation, married men who are unable to do so experience significant psychological distress due to the associated shame. These challenges are further exacerbated by the societal stigma associated with deviating from established norms, which in turn leads to apprehension regarding potential ostracism from social circles. There is a significant gap in academic study about the comprehensive understanding of the deleterious effects of patriarchal institutions on individuals of both genders, which can be attributed to the prevailing socio-cultural expectations.

5.1.5 Existence of Entrenched Power Relations

If rape is understood primarily as an expression of power rather than a sexual act, it becomes imperative to analyse the phenomenon of marital rape by considering the power dynamics that exist within the institution of marriage and the family unit. Foucault[54] posited that power is constructed through the legitimization of specific forms of knowledge and notions of 'truth'. He contended that cultural power structures are justified and maintained through a complex interplay of beliefs that are widely accepted as truth by individuals across different social hierarchies.

[51] UNICEF (2018), Accessed 15 August 2023.

[52] Girls not Brides. Child Marriage Atlas: Nigeria https://www.girlsnotbrides.org/learning-resources/child-marriage-atlas/atlas/nigeria/, Accessed 15 August 2023.

[53] UNICEF. (2005), Accessed 15 August 2023.

[54] Foucault (2008).

Consequently, disentangling the interconnectedness of these belief systems and power dynamics becomes exceedingly challenging, as they mutually reinforce and rely upon one another in a profound manner. In order to comprehend this concept, it is crucial to emphasize that Foucault portrays power dynamics as not solely hierarchical, but also as multidirectional, intersecting, lateral, or reciprocal.

The phenomenon of bride practice encompasses a complex system of beliefs that is universally accepted by both genders as an inescapable reality in Nigeria. The concept of bride price gives rise to a power dynamic inside the familial sphere, indicating the emergence of a '*new moral economy*'. In this context, the male perceives his payment of bride price as a fulfilment of his responsibilities, while the woman, viewed as a commodity that has been exchanged, assumes her own set of obligations.[55] In light of this context, a man (who has fulfilled the customary practice of paying the bride price) enters into a marital union with a cognitive perception of possessing ownership, authority, and entitlement to the utilization and gratification of his spouse, whom he has financially compensated for. Certain men experience distress due to the exploitation perpetrated by the bride's family, subsequently directing their frustration towards their spouses through various means, such as neglect and acts of violence, following the wedding ceremony. It has been observed that men often express sentiments such as "*I paid bride price to reassert my ownership rights*"'or "*to validate their confidence and social standing within their peer group*".

In contrast, the woman whose bride price is paid possesses a cognitive awareness of fulfilment and occasionally privilege when entering the marital union. Despite being subjected to the authority of her husband, she has a sense of fulfilment in terms of her purpose and worth, ultimately achieving a prominent position as a married lady within her social milieu. From a societal perspective, the act of marriage bestows upon her a sense of respectability and affords her an alleged safeguard provided by her spouse. This phenomenon is not solely a product of societal norms, but also a result of the socialization process that shapes women's behaviour. The tacit comprehension between male and female individuals has a substantial role in shaping the gender-based power dynamics that underlie the institution of marriage.

The family, set up through marriage, is the smallest social unit and the origin of most power interactions from a bottom-top perspective. This phenomenon is demonstrated through the nuanced and tacit mechanisms by which power dynamics and influence manifest within the context of marriage and family. As an illustration, women who serve as primary earners transfer their financial resources to their spouses in public settings, enabling their husbands to uphold their societal standing or perceived role as the primary provider. This phenomenon is also evident in the manner in which a married woman feels her own self-worth and superiority over single women, even in instances where she finds herself in an abusive marital relationship. This phenomenon bears resemblance to the manner in which mothers of brides employ various strategies to ensure their daughters acquiesce to the customary tradition of bride price or to persuade them to marry their perpetrators in order to evade social ostracization. Similarly, it mirrors the manner in which mothers exert influence upon their daughters to enter into child marriages as a form of recompense for the family or as a means to circumvent the ignominious circumstance of being unable to marry. The phenomenon of women's invisibility within the institution of marriage is evident in Nigerian wedding ceremonies, when the role of the father, or in his absence, an older male figure, involves escorting the daughter down the aisle and formally presenting her to the groom. This ritual symbolizes the transfer of ownership from the father to the husband.[56]

[55] Chen, J. and W. Pan. 2023, Bride Price and Gender Role in Rural China. Heliyon. 9 (1) e12789: 1–9. https://doi.org/10.1016/j.heliyon.2022.e12789.

[56] Barnes (2014).

Women in Nigeria face a scarcity of resources as a result of the adverse effects of discriminatory legislation and practices that hinder their access to educational, employment, and marital possibilities. Women face various socio-economic disadvantages, encompassing limited access to production resources, unequal rewards for their work, inequitable distribution of consumption, income, and goods, restricted authority and power, and limited participation in cultural, political, and religious activities. Gender plays a significant role in shaping individuals' behaviour and influencing the outcomes of social interactions. Frequently, women, including those in abusive households, tend to rely on their spouses as a result of apprehension over their ability to sustain themselves independently. This is exemplified in a narrative that recounts the traumatic experience of Ndidi, who endured sexual assault perpetrated by her biological father at the age of eight. Ndidi apprised her mother of the incident of sexual assault; however, her mother refrained from taking any measures due to apprehension and reliance on the father. Following a period of four years characterized by severe abuse, Ndidi managed to escape from her situation and subsequently obtained assistance. In the Nigerian context, women face limited alternatives outside the institution of marriage due to societal norms that discourage the recognition and celebration of single women's accomplishments. In order to mitigate their marginalization within the social framework, women actively participate in the perpetuation of the prevailing patriarchal ideology.

5.2 Marital Rape: A Form of Unequal Power Relation

The practice of bride price engenders an asymmetrical power dynamic inside the institution of marriage, fostering a perception of entitlement, dominance, and possession in male conduct, hence heightening women's susceptibility to mistreatment within the marital union. This disposition and inherent feeling of possession is frequently manifested in acts of physical, sexual, and mental violence, as well as instances of spousal rape. Ambekar (2009) posits that marital rape fulfils various purposes, such as functioning as a socially accepted means to penalize women, a strategy to assert masculinity and uphold a patriarchal societal structure, a mechanism to 'resolve' domestic disputes, and a manifestation of male sexual gratification (Sexual Violence Research Initiative, 2007). A research investigation conducted in Oyo state, Nigeria, during the year 2018 revealed that approximately 14% of female participants in the study reported instances of marital rape. Additionally, the study revealed that married women who autonomously made decisions on their sexual interactions with their spouses faced greater susceptibility to marital rape compared to those who engaged in sexual activity based on their husbands' requests. This link underscores the prevalence of male dominance in marital dynamics, particularly with respect to sexual concerns. It reveals a tangible depiction of how the agency of married women is suppressed and invalidated.

Marital rape constitutes a violation of women's fundamental rights, including the right to life, dignity, freedom from torture and discrimination, and the right to health. Marital rape poses a significant health burden among married women in Nigeria.

Survivors of marital rape are less likely to get support from crisis centres, family, friends, and the police as this is often counter-productive for women; revictimized by the patriarchal Nigerian criminal justice system shaped by the existing notion that marital rape does not constitute an offence in Nigeria. Also, the desire to maintain their '*honour*' within their community and social circle adversely impacts women's ability and will to seek help and escape abusive relationships.[57]

[57] Femi-Ajao (2018).

5.3 Proposed Reforms

The struggle to criminalize marital rape is intricately linked to the wider fight for human rights for women within intimate relationships and society at large. Marital rape is a prevalent form of gender-based violence that is rarely the subject of scholarly investigation, as it is both legally and culturally sanctioned in the majority of sub-Saharan African nations, particularly Nigeria. It is recommended that a multidimensional strategy incorporating both top-down and bottom-top approaches is adopted to efficiently fight this growing menace. A top–bottom approach would involve lobbying and campaigning for legal reform on marital rape in Nigeria, specifically articulating and evidencing issues such as burden of proof, definitions, corroboration, and other relevant procedural issues that might be challenging in the unique context of a marriage. The development of reporting mechanisms that incorporate a trauma-informed approach, acknowledging the unique obstacles and difficulties faced by women who have experienced marital rape, is of utmost importance.

These mechanisms should also be inclusive, ensuring that all individuals have equal access to reporting avenues, and are culturally acceptable, taking into account diverse cultural norms and values. By implementing such mechanisms, the risk of re-traumatization for women survivors can be minimized, thereby promoting their well-being and ensuring their rights are upheld. Furthermore, it is crucial to establish a comprehensive body of information and evidence in order to effectively guide campaigns, legal advocacy, and research efforts focused on understanding trends, prevalence rates, and the various elements that contribute to the issue at hand. Additionally, it is important to examine the responsibilities played by different sectors in addressing this issue in a coordinated manner.

When confronted with difficulties that are firmly rooted in cultural practices, it is advised to employ a grassroots approach. This approach plays a crucial role in the reformation of potentially problematic practices, such as the bride price system, by fostering a participatory environment that empowers individuals to become active agents in driving their own transformative processes. The proposed strategy is a grassroots movement aimed at fostering behavioural change, re-education, and the integration of human rights principles into cultural practices.

Active participation and engagement with local associations, peer groups, religious groups, school leaders, and village heads/chiefs plays a crucial role in educating various influential groups of individuals. Foucault's examination of power and knowledge holds significant importance in the transformation of the narrative within Nigeria.[58] According to Foucault, the concept of power cannot be discussed in isolation from knowledge. The individuals responsible for the creation of knowledge, such as village elders, market associations, peer groups, religious groups, and school leaders, possess intersecting manifestations of power within the societal framework. Enabling individuals from the local community, particularly women who have personally experienced violence and marital rape, to assume positions of authority and influence, will establish a secure environment that deeply connects with and motivates community members, thereby enhancing the accessibility of services. The establishment of support facilities within communities to facilitate the expression, socialization, and acquisition or reacquisition of values that promote behavioural transformation among males is very crucial. It is imperative to emphasize that the criminalization of marital rape necessitates complementary endeavours at the community level to modify individuals' attitudes and behaviours through processes of learning, unlearning, and incorporating positive practices into existing cultural frameworks, rather than attempting to completely overhaul the culture. The integration of both approaches will progressively cultivate a robust collective determination, culminating in

[58] Foucault, M. 2008. Power/knowledge. In The New Social Theory Reader, eds. Seidman, S. and J.C. Alexander, 73–79. London: Routledge.

a readily attainable legislative transformation that garners widespread public endorsement, thus fostering heightened adherence to legal principles.

Moreover, the notable legal precedent set by Denise Clair's landmark case, wherein she effectively pursued a civil action for compensation against the defendant after a failed criminal trial, provides an avenue to examine civil action as a viable alternative for survivors of rape seeking justice.[59] The rigorous standard of proof beyond a reasonable doubt, the use of evidential procedures, and the insistence on corroboration frequently result in limited access to justice for survivors within the criminal court system. Hence, it is advisable to examine the feasibility of pursuing civil litigation as a potential recourse for those who have experienced rape and other forms of sexual offences.

5.4 Conclusion

Current discourse surrounding marital rape in Nigeria offers valuable perspectives on the frequency of marital rape and the necessity for legal reforms to criminalize this abhorrent behaviour. Despite the extensive and ongoing advocacy for legislative reform, there exists a significant scarcity of scholarly studies about cultural practices within Nigeria. This lack of empirical investigation contributes to the reinforcement of perpetrators of marital rape, as it allows for their continued impunity and lack of accountability. This chapter focused on the bride price system, specifically exploring its distinctive characteristics, such as the bargaining process and the return of the bride price upon the dissolution of a marriage. This chapter provided a comprehensive analysis of marital rape within the specific cultural context of Nigeria, with the intention of contributing to the ongoing scholarly discussion. It explored the psychological attitudes of both men and women within a marriage, the imbalanced power dynamics that arise from the bride price system, and how these dynamics manifest in interpersonal relationships within the marital union. The anticipation is that the insights gained from this chapter will serve as valuable guidance for activists, policymakers, and scholars in recognizing areas where evidence is lacking in the pursuit of sustainable legislative reform and the mitigation of marital rape and its consequences.

[59] DC (2017). *See also* Adams (2018), Accessed 16 November 2023.

References

Adams L (2018) Woman brings civil case against man cleared of raping her https://www.bbc.co.uk/news/uk-scotland-43044323

Amnesty International (2021) Nigeria: a harrowing journey: access to justice for women and girls survivors of Rape in Nigeria https://www.amnesty.org/en/documents/afr44/4959/2021/en/

Anderson S (2007) The economics of dowry and brideprice. J Econ Perspect 21:151–174. https://doi.org/10.1257/jep.21.4.151

Barnes MW (2014) Our family functions: functions of traditional weddings for modern brides and postmodern families. Qual Sociol Rev 10(2):60–78

BBC, Lagos (2018) Why single Nigerian women battle to rent homes. https://www.bbc.co.uk/news/world-africa-45169688

Bergen RK (1996) Wife Rape: Understanding the response of survivors and service providers. Sage Publications, USA

Butler J (2006) Gender trouble: Feminism and the subversion of identity. Routledge, New York and London

CEDAW (1992) General Recommendation No. 19: Violence against Women. Adopted at the Eleventh Session of the Committee on the Elimination of Discrimination against Women. UN Doc. A/47/38 https://tbinternet.ohchr.org/_layouts/15/treatybodyexternal/Download.aspx?symbolno=INT%2FCEDAW%2FGEC%2F3731&Lang=en

Chen J, Pan W (2023) Bride price and gender role in rural China. Heliyon 9(1):e12789: 1–9. https://doi.org/10.1016/j.heliyon.2022.e12789

DC v (First) DG & (Second) DR [2017] CSOH 5

Eds. Scott BK, Cayleff SE, Donadey A, Lara I (2016) Women in culture: an intersectional anthology for gender and women's studies. 2nd edn. Wiley Blackwell

Ekiti State Gender Based Violence (Prohibition) Amendment Law (2019)

Elochukwu A (2021) Stigma and mental health impact of divorce on women: a Nigerian perspective. https://www.rightsofequality.com/stigma-and-mental-health-impact-of-divorce-on-women-in-nigeria/

Engels F (1972) The origin of the family, private property and the state. International Publishers, New York
Eves R (2019) 'Full price, full body': norms, brideprice and intimate partner violence in highlands Papua New Guinea. Cult Health Sex 21(4):1–14
Eze v Omeke (1977) 1 ANSLR 136 cited in Nwogugu, E.I. 2014. Family Law in Nigeria. 3rd edition. Hebn Publishers
Facio A (2013) What is patriarchy? https://www.learnwhr.org/wp-content/uploads/D-Facio-What-is-Patriarchy.pdf
Femi-Ajao O (2018) Intimate partner violence and abuse against Nigerian women resident in England, UK: a cross-sectional qualitative study. BMC Womens Health 18:1–13
Flather AJ (2013) Space, place, and gender: the sexual and spatial division of labor in the early modern household. History Theory. 52(3):344–360. https://doi.org/10.1111/hith.10673
Foucault M (2008) Power/knowledge. In: Seidman S, Alexander JC (eds) The new social theory reader. Routledge, London, pp 73–79
Fox V (2013) Historical perspectives on violence against women. J Int Women's Studies 4:15–34
Girls not Brides. Child Marriage Atlas: Nigeria https://www.girlsnotbrides.org/learning-resources/child-marriage-atlas/atlas/nigeria/
Goldschmidt W (1973) The Brideprice of the Sebei. Sci Am 229(1):74–85
Hale Sir. M (1736) History of the pleas of the crown. 1 Hale PC (1736) 629
Healey R (2018) Consent, rights, and reasons for action. Crim Law Philos 13:499–513. https://doi.org/10.1007/s11572-018-9484-7
Hudson VM, Matfess H (2017) In plain sight: the neglected linkage between brideprice and violent conflict. Int Secur 42(1):7–40. https://doi.org/10.1162/isec_a_00289
Ijeoma AN (2006) The convention on the elimination of all forms of discrimination against women and the status of implementation on the right to health care in Nigeria. Human Rights Brief 13(3):34–39
Jackson L (1994) Marital rape: a higher standard is in order. William Mary J Women Law 1(1):183–216
Lerner G (1988) The creation of patriarchy. OUP, USA
Lillehammer H (2020) Autonomy, consent, and the "Nonideal" case. J Med Philos 45(3):297–311. https://doi.org/10.1093/jmp/jhaa006
Massey D (2013) Space, place, and gender. Wiley
Mensah EO (2023) Husband is a priority: gender roles, patriarchy and the naming of female children in Nigeria. Gender Issues 40:44-64.https://doi.org/10.1007/s12147-022-09303-z
Nedelsky J (1996) Violence against Women: challenges to the liberal state and relational feminism. Political Order. 38:454–497
Nigerian Criminal Code (1990)
Nigerian Penal Code (1960)
Nwoke MB (2009) Bride price and implications for Women's Rights in Nigeria: psychological perspective. Gender Behav 7(1):2078–2087. https://doi.org/10.4314/gab.v7i1.45030
Papps I, Davis J, Grossbard-Shechtman A, Mair L, Pryor FL, Reyna SP, Gratton NE, Schneider HK, Tapper N, Wilder WD (1983) The role and determinants of bride-price: the case of a Palestinian village [and Comments and Reply]. Curr Anthropol 24(2):203–215. https://doi.org/10.1086/202966
Penal Code Act of Nigeria, Section 282
Pillsbury SH (2000) Judging Evil: Rethinking the law of murder and manslaughter. NYU Press, New York
Randall M, Venkatesh V (2015) Criminalizing sexual violence against women in intimate relationships: state obligations under human rights law. Amer J Int Law 109:189–196
Ruth O (2015) Without bride price, there is no marriage https://nigerianobservernews.com/2015/08/without-bride-price-there-is-no-marriage/
Sadler-Venis J, Sexual offence laws: #MeToo movement drives new consent-based definitions. https://www.ibanet.org/article/386A45E6-0A58-4A7F-8741-3CE58A50F8C4
Tabitha Bawa v. Bawa Waziri (unreported) delivered on 24 June 2011. CCKJ/CV/14/2011 (HW Emmanuel J. Samaila—Judge and Mr. Luka Magaji & Mr. Inda Tache—Members)
UN Declaration on the Elimination of Violence against Women (DEVAW). December 1993. Article 4(c). UN Doc. 48/104 20. https://www.ohchr.org/en/instruments-mechanisms/instruments/declaration-elimination-violenceagainstwomen#:~:text=For%20the%20purposes%20of%20this,of%20liberty%2C%20whether%20occurring%20in
UN Human Rights Committee (2014) General Comment 35: Article 9—Liberty and Security of Person, para. 9, UN Doc. CCPR/C/GC/35
UNICEF, Spotlight Initiative (2023). 16 facts about violence against women and girls in Nigeria: For the 16 days of activism https://www.unicef.org/nigeria/media/6696/file/16%20facts%20document.pdf
UNICEF (2005) Early marriage: a harmful traditional practice- a statistical exploration https://data.unicef.org/resources/early-marriage-a-traditional-harmful-practice-a-statistical-exploration/
UNICEF (2018) Child marriage in west and central Africa at a glance. https://www.unicef.org/chad/media/246/file/Child-Marriage-in-WCA-At-a-Glance.pdf
US Department of Justice, Office of Justice Programs. Forcible Rape—the Crime, the Victim and the Offender. Eds. Chappell, D., R. Geis and G. Geis https://www.ojp.gov/ncjrs/virtual-library/abstracts/forcible-rape-crime-victim-and-offender
Vaeza M-N (2020) Addressing the impact of the COVID-19 pandemic on violence against women and girls. UN Chronicle. United Nations. https://www.un.org/en/addressing-impact-covid-19-pandemic-violence-against-women-and-girls

Violence Against Persons (Prohibition) Act (2015)
Women at Risk International Foundation (WARIF). Rape Stats in Nigeria. https://warifng.org/rape-stats-in-nigeria/
Wood K, Lambert H, Jewkes R (2007) "Showing roughness in a beautiful way": talk about love, coercion, and rape in south african youth sexual culture. Med Anthropol Q 21(3):277–300. https://doi.org/10.1525/maq.2007.21.3.277
Yllö KE, Torres MG (2016) Marital rape: consent, marriage, and social change in global context. OUP, USA
Zaitchik A (1982) Hobbes's reply to the fool: the problem of consent and obligation. Political Theory 10(2):245–266

The 'Joy' of Motherhood, the Violence in Motherhood: A Decolonial Feminist Analysis of Sexual and Reproductive Rights

6

Brototi Dutta

Abstract

Drawing strands from feminist theoretical contestations around 'motherhood' and located within the context of intersectional queer decolonial third world experiences and identities, this chapter will examine 'motherhood' as an institution and its intersections with law and its instrumentalities. Beginning with a feminist critical exploration of the terms 'joy' and 'violence' as used in the context of motherhood and by 'motherhood' as an institution, the chapter attempts to bring to the fore, and therefore, asks the question: what does it obfuscate and what is its corollary? The chapter then goes into an exploration of what 'violence' means in the context of 'motherhood' as an institution. It probes the layers of discrimination and violence embedded in 'motherhood' as an institution, using reproductive rights as the broad framework for analysis. Specifically, the way this is brought into sharp focus in cases involving marginalized 'bodies' of women and others, capable of becoming pregnant and 'mothering'. This is explored through discussion on obstetric violence, coercive sterilization practices, rights of queer persons to marry and form families, and denial of one's reproductive autonomy. The chapter looks into these issues within the overarching role of law as an instrument of social change, but also as an instrumentality of the State that it employs in specific and intentional ways.

Keywords

Motherhood · Popular culture · Reproductive rights · Feminist analysis · Pregnancy · Coercive sterilization · Reproductive autonomy · Mothering · Obstetric violence · Safe motherhood

In popular culture, 'motherhood' has been a recurring theme to denote, variously, the joys, the sacrifices, and the unique contribution of women as mothers; often, to communicate images of empowered women who deftly balance competing commitments. One recalls the television advertisements of the 1990s with the ever smiling "mother" expertly navigating between health drinks and detergents to make decisions for her family. As the world moved from television to living in the online space, these images of middle-class mothers have given way to mom influencers who invite

B. Dutta (✉)
Advocacy Adviser for India-Asia Program, Centre for Reproductive Rights, New Delhi, India
e-mail: brototi@gmail.com

P. M. Anurag and S. Dwivedy (eds.), *Violence in Intimate Spaces*, Sustainable Development Goals Series, https://doi.org/10.1007/978-981-97-2657-8_6

us into their homes and let us experience their everyday lives. Underlying these diverse set of images, however, is an understanding of 'motherhood' that continues to be located within a set of heteronormative patriarchal codes that promote the perceived 'joys' of motherhood and in the process, push to the margins, any experience that is not aligned to this idea of the 'normal'. Adrienne Rich (1986) drew attention to the two distinct worlds that motherhood dwelt in—one which defined '*the potential relationship of any woman to her powers of reproduction and to children; and the institution, which aims at ensuring that that potential – and all women – shall remain under male control*'.[1] Andrea O' Reilly's work over the years has built on this to advance what is now a distinct field of scholarship—'*motherhood studies*',[2] with three overlapping domains; motherhood as an *institution* (that is maintained by patriarchy), motherhood/*mothering* signifying women's lived experiences (and now, expanded by narratives of queer and postcolonial lived experiences, amongst others) and their journey of conforming to or resisting the patriarchal ideology, and lastly, motherhood as *identity* or the ways in which the experience of motherhood affects women's sense of self and identity and '*how her sense of self is shaped by the institution of motherhood and the experience of mothering, respectively*'.[3]

Feminist theory has however, had a complex and uneasy relationship with motherhood studies, beginning with radical feminism's rejection of motherhood as inherently oppressive and akin to '*selling oneself to slavery*' (Simone de Beauvoir 1949, 1964; Shulamith Firestone) and has taken more moderate forms in recent feminist scholarship with romanticized ideas that often draw upon patriarchal tropes (Bell Hooks, 135).[4] Matricentric feminists (such as Rich, Ruddick, Collins) have pointed out that the absence of motherhood narratives in mainstream feminist academic scholarship leads one to conclude that '*feminist theory is still to a large extent determined by universalist and essentialist histories of motherhood that are the basis of*

[1]Adrienne Rich went on to demonstrate that the construction of motherhood (in its sense as an institution) was neither natural or inevitable. Rather it was deeply ideological – shaped and domesticated by patriarchy. In the book, Of Woman Born, Rich notes, "The patriarchal institution of motherhood is 'not the human condition' any more than rape, prostitution, and slavery are." Rich, 1986 (33). In her 2021 introduction to *Of Woman Born*, Eula Biss notes the significance of Rich's analysis of a systematic devaluation of care work. Rich points out that the institution of motherhood affects everyone in different ways, and those who care for children – whether others or their own – does work that is devalued by the institution. Her statement that "The labour of childbirth.

[2]According to the description of an institute focusing on motherhood studies within the Boston University, "motherhood studies" is based on understandings that recognize that mothers' lives are shaped differently based on intersecting factors of race, class, gender, and sexuality. This in turn, is recognizing that institutionalized "good mothering" assumes and promotes privileged motherhood, primarily by reinforcing White, at-least middle class, cisgender, heterosexual privilege and an even-more intensive ideology of good mothering, and any mother who "fails" to meet the standards of intensive mothering is policed and labeled a "bad mother." (The Institute for the Study of Motherhood Scholarship).

[3]Andrea O' Reilly (ed.), Twenty-first Century Motherhood: Experience, Identity, Policy, Agency (2010), 3.

[4]In the introduction to a special issue on Feminism and Motherhood in the "fourth wave" feminism context, Charlotte Beyer traces feminist theory's engagement with analysis of motherhood, including matrophobia or the "fear of becoming one's mother" that Amber Kinsley has referred to in her work, to argue the need for proactive attention and reframing of narratives. She also refers to Amy Westervelt's 2018 article, "Is Motherhood the Unfinished Work of Feminism?", in *The Guardian* where Westervelt argues that motherhood is seen as such a problematic issue that it is often glossed over or completely avoided in fourth wave feminist scholarship and then makes the crucial point that "What some theorists forget [...] is that ideas and expectations around mothering impact all women, whether they have children or not". Beyer, Charlotte ORCID: 0000-0002-2701-5443 (2019) Motherhood and 21st Century Feminism: Reaching out across the Divide. Feminist Encounters: A Journal of Critical Studies in Culture and Politics (Double Issue: Feminism and Motherhood in the 21st Century), 3 (1–2). p. 2. An analysis of motherhood is therefore, imperative to the intersectional feminist analysis of the ways in which constructions of expectations around "motherhood" impacts beyond biological motherhood and cis-gender identities.

much feminist theorising of gender, femininity, and motherhood' (Takseva, 179). As Braithwaite has raised the problematic in the broader context of critiques of western white feminism, '*whose feminism and whose women's studies is being called upon, or passed on, and where and by whom*?' (Braithwaite et al., 31).

Drawing strands from these contestations and located within the context of intersectional queer decolonial third world experiences and identities, this chapter will examine '*motherhood*'. It will focus on '*motherhood*' as an institution and delve into what seems to be considered in popular imagination, its key constituent and one that lends motherhood its moral credence: the 'joy' of motherhood. The chapter brings to the fore the feminist(s) critiques of what joy means, not as an experience or identity, but from the perspective of motherhood as an institution and therefore, asks the question: what does it obfuscate and what is its corollary? The chapter then goes into an exploration of what 'violence' means in the context of 'motherhood' as an institution. It probes the layers of discrimination and violence embedded in 'motherhood' as an institution with its socio-cultural connotations, using reproductive rights as the broad framework for analysis. Specifically, the way this is brought into sharp focus in cases of obstetric violence, coercive sterilization practices, and denial of one's reproductive autonomy, and their intersections with one's social location and identities is an area that this paper seeks to explore within the overarching role that the law plays as an instrument of social change but also as an instrumentality of the State that it employs in specific and intentional ways.

For the purposes of this chapter, law therefore refers to its normative avatar i.e., the constitutional guarantees and international human rights and public health standards, and also to its institutional avatar i.e. the force of its institutions such as the police, prosecution, and courts that may be brought to bear on an individual. This is because more often than not, the State seeks to enforce discriminatory norms against persons at the margins and ensure compliance through the institutions of law. This has been referred to as the violence of law (Cover, 30; '*Violence and the Word*').[5] Legal scholars have powerfully explored the violence of the law in the context of carceral and punitive bias of our laws, including for marginalized groups such as women, prisoners, juveniles,[6] same-sex relationships, and in cases of mass violence.[7]

6.1 Exploring 'Joy' and 'Violence'

Much is said about the 'joy' of motherhood, such that motherhood is ubiquitous as a morally superior being with their happiness and self-worth linked to their role as a mother. This supposedly benign construction of motherhood and the preoccupation with the joy that every mother within this institution was supposed to feel as if by nature preordained, has been the subject of careful scrutiny by early feminists and the very foundation on which is laid the ongoing feminist intersectional critiques of anti-abortionist policies and other forms of regression in recent time in advancing reproductive justice. These feminist critiques drew attention to the false idealization of women as mothers within patriarchy which is then used to exploit and victimize

---

[5] In his seminal work, Justice Accused, Robert Cover examined the then US Supreme Court's treatment of anti-slavery regulations on universities and in the process, concluded that the state's norms are not necessarily (morally) superior. The backing of force and the power to suppress that the State simply mean that the government's norms are capable of killing off norms of other communities (Cover, Minow and Ryan 1993).

[6] Martha Minow's work on child soldiers.

[7] Martha Minow's work (Minow, 1998) analyzing criminal trials such as Nuremburg, Tokyo, and the International Criminal Tribunals for Yugoslavia and Rwanda as well as Truth and Reconciliation Commission models such as South Africa TRC as modes of transitional justice explores ideas of "vengeance" as limiting and the need to move towards a framework of "forgiveness" and "are thus, more suited to achieving social reconciliation than trials". See Laurel Fletcher, Between Vengeance and Forgiveness: Facing History After Genocide and Mass Violence, Berkeley Journal of International Law (Vol. 19:428).

them. This discomfort is expressed in Adrienne Rich's words when she notes,

> *I do not see the mother with her child as either more morally credible or more morally capable than any other woman. A child can be used as a symbolic credential, a sentimental object, a badge of self-righteousness. I question the implicit belief that only "mothers" with "children of their own" have a real stake in the future of humanity.* (Rich 1986, xxiv)

Writings from intersectional, decolonial, queer, and transnational feminist perspectives have since then, added a rich complexity to this analysis—leading one to ask questions about a linear understanding of motherhood as an institution constructed by patriarchy without taking into account its interactions with race, class, religion, indigeneity, disability, age or relationship status. These critiques also then open the space for us to interrogate how this construction of the *institution* of motherhood affects the *experience* of motherhood—that which I refer to in this chapter as the journey from the 'joy' of motherhood to the 'violence' in motherhood, often depending on the specific intersectional location or identity that one inhabits in.

When asked about their one priority ask for quality Sexual and Reproductive Health and Rights (SRHR) services as part of White Ribbon Alliance's What Women Want campaign, the language we encounter from a randomized sample of 1000 responses from India by women aged 15–55 plus is telling. '*Respectful behaviour of medical staff*', '*No caste discrimination and no Verbal Abuse*', '*timely treatment*' or less waiting time, '*No denial of services by providers*' were some key demands of the women. Motherhood is a special and joyous experience for most persons who are capable of becoming pregnant (pregnant persons). For some though, it is an uncertain, undignified, and often violent experience, especially if the person belongs to the margins of the society. Overmedicalization and lack of a rights perspective within the health system, particularly the public health system, often means that pregnancy and childbirth is treated as a purely medical issue within which narratives of dignity and bodily autonomy rarely exist. Juxtaposed against this is socio-cultural construct of motherhood in South Asian contexts that is primarily geared towards ensuring safe childbirth and neonatal health rather than the mother's overall well-being. Right to available, accessible, affordable, and quality maternal health including to '*safe motherhood*' must be seen in the continuum of women and girls' lives, which are often marked by deprivation, violence, and discrimination. This discrimination plays out at individual, familial, institutional, and systemic levels and intersects with their social location and identity (Yamin 2010).

In India too, the last decade or so has been marked by a gradual shift from a population-control driven reproductive rights agenda to recognition of maternal health concerns as fundamental women's rights, largely aided by higher judiciary's rulings. But the significantly high reported cases of maternal deaths tell us that a new approach to understanding 'motherhood' and the institutional approach to maternal health, especially obstetric violence, is needed. This chapter will examine these questions through desk review and reading of judgments to make sense of the violence embedded in the institution of 'motherhood'. An analysis of the linkages between 'motherhood' and violence within the framework of the law will be undertaken through a combination of primary and secondary sources: official data available in the public domain and reading of key judgments of the higher judiciary (including the Supreme Court of India and various High Courts), as well as a reading of media reportage, research and academic reports/articles, reports/publicly available documentation of civil society organizations working on this and related issues.

6.2 International Human Rights Norms

Every person has the right to highest attainable standard of health, which includes the right to dignified and respectful healthcare during pregnancy and childbirth and the right to be free from violence and discrimination (Center for

Reproductive Rights 2014).[8] These rights are inextricably and inalienably linked to a pregnant person's autonomy over their bodies as also their mental and physical well-being and choices. It includes when, where, and how to conceive, carry a pregnancy to term, give birth and during the post-partum stage. The standards around the right to dignified and respectful care during pregnancy and childbirth have evolved incrementally with the monitoring of the health-related indicators of the *Millennium Development Goals* and in the recent jurisprudence of key United Nations Treaty Monitoring Bodies (UNTMBs) such as the Committee on the *Elimination of Discrimination Against Women* (CEDAW Committee),[9] the *Human Rights Committee* (HRC), and the *Committee Against Torture* (CAT) as well as regional human rights instruments. Tracing its history, however, reinforces that this was never the core concern of States or the global public health community. Earliest global human rights instruments such as the *Universal Declaration of Human Rights* or even the *UN Declaration on Elimination of Violence Against Women* (DEVAW) did not articulate and name the violence associated with childbearing and childbirth. It was in fact, the childbirth activism movement in Latin America in the 1990s that brought to focus pervasive and systematic incidents of 'obstetric violence'[10] and called for dignified and respectful care. In Brazil, human rights and public health advocates initiated what came to be known as the humanized childbirth movement which translated into official Government policies, while Argentina defined 'obstetric violence' '*as the appropriation of women's body and reproductive processes by health personnel, which is expressed by a dehumanizing treatment, an abuse of medicalization and pathologization of natural processes, resulting in a loss of autonomy and ability to decide freely about their bodies and sexuality, negatively impacting their quality of life'*.[11]

This definition of '*obstetric violence*' while used in the context of women's bodies is equally symptomatic of the '*dehumanization*' and '*medicalization*' of other marginalized bodies that are capable of getting pregnant or experience

[8]Over the years, these overarching standards have been applied in specific contexts to seek State accountability for cases of maternal mortality, lack of access to quality maternal healthcare, and instances of violence and discrimination. The underlying and interlinked social determinants that exacerbate discrimination against specific groups and marginalized persons has been highlighted by scholars, advocates, and international human rights and public health mechanisms. In the context of maternal mortality for instance, research and practice documents the ways in which patterns of maternal mortality reflect disparities in resources, access to health services and discrimination. Even within countries that have relatively moderate or low maternal mortality rates, wide disparities in maternal mortality rates persist among populations, as groups of women who have historically been marginalized commonly experience a substantially higher likelihood of dying during pregnancy and childbirth. Young women and adolescents also represent a particularly vulnerable subpopulation throughout the world. Complications in pregnancy and childbirth are the leading cause of death among adolescent girls in most low-income countries. (Center for Reproductive Rights 2014).

[9]The CEDAW Committee in its General Recommendation 24 has highlighted State's obligations that "require all health services to be consistent with the human rights of women, including the rights to autonomy, privacy, confidentiality, informed consent and choice." CEDAW Committee, General Recommendation 24 (1999), available at: http://tbinternet.ohchr.org/_layouts/treatybodyexternal/Download.aspx?symbolno=INT/CEDAW/GEC/4738&Lang=en (last accessed 25th August 2023).

In a first of its kind decision by a treaty monitoring body on maternal mortality, the CEDAW Committee in *Alyne da Silva Pimentel v. Brazil (2014)*, found that Brazil had discriminated against Alyne on the basisof her gender, race, and socioeconomic status. Alyne was an Afro-Brazilian woman who died following pregnancy and post-natal complications due to denial of emergency obstetric care. Most importantly, the Committee recognized that these violations reached system-level factors of neglect. CENTER FOR REPRODUCTIVE RIGHTS, Breaking Ground: Treaty Monitoring Bodies on Reproductive Rights 2020 (2020), p.11.

[10]Incidents of.

[11]Maternal Health Task Force, Harvard Chan School Center of Excellence in Maternal and Child Health, https://www.mhtf.org/2017/04/11/respectful-maternity-care-a-basic-human-right/ (last accessed 25th August 2023).

motherhood, including trans persons, bisexuals and lesbians, women with disabilities, sex workers, and others. While examining this issue from the perspective of pregnant women (primarily since much of the existing literature and norm-setting has taken place in this context), this chapter will continue drawing linkages in relation to other marginalized bodies that may not conform to cis-het framework of family formation.

Going back to international human rights and the evolution of respectful and dignified maternal healthcare, experts have noted that despite recent efforts including a joint statement in 2015 by UN and regional human rights mechanisms explicitly calling on states to address '*acts of obstetric and institutional violence*', many forms of mistreatment remain unaddressed or inadequately analyzed under international human rights law (Khosla et al. 2016).[12] Before this, the *World Health Organisation* (WHO) in a 2014 statement on mistreatment during childbirth and its associated human rights violations that was endorsed by several organizations globally, called for greater action, dialogue, research, and advocacy (WHO 2014). Human rights bodies have specifically recognized the intersections of discrimination and violations based, for instance, on one's ethnicity (Roma women), economic status (inability to pay hospital fees), age (stigma and verbal abuse faced by adolescent girls), or HIV status (involuntary sterilization) (African Commission on Human and People's Rights 2013).

[12] Amongst others, the UN and regional human rights experts highlighted acts of obstetric and institutional violence faced by women in healthcare facilities including forced or coerced sterilization procedures, refusal to administer pain relief, disrespect and abuse of women seeking healthcare and reported cases of women being hit whilst giving birth. Available at https://www.ohchr.org/en/statements/2015/09/joint-statement-un-human-rights-experts-rapporteur-rights-women-inter-american?LangID=E&NewsID=16490 (last accessed 25th August 2023).

6.3 (Un)wanted Bodies and Motherhood

The axes along which this violence often manifests is rooted in hetero-normative paternalistic frameworks. As in the case of laws and policies relating to gender and sexuality, the rights and entitlements are then framed around narratives of 'deserving' and 'undeserving' women.

Women in prisons bear the full force of the carceral legal system's violence at all times but particularly if they are pregnant and lactating. Manisha's case in 2010 is well documented and triggered immediate response from the prison authorities but also from the judiciary. In 2012, Manisha delivered her baby on her own in the prison toilet using razors she had bought. By the time the prison authorities had broken the doors open, she had allegedly taken steps to end the new born baby's life. While the authorities claimed she had not informed them or anyone else about her pregnancy status, the incident led to widespread indignation including from medical practitioners that it was unlikely that the prison authorities were unaware of her status and that she was denied the much needed prenatal care. In the immediate aftermath, a committee was set up to look into the lapses and put in place accountability mechanisms. This led to a '*buddy system*' being established in many prisons but the enquiry also identified overcrowding of prisons as a key reason for lack of documentation and support systems for vulnerable prisoners (Shantha, The Wire, August 2020). In Manisha's case, the State's violence (through the prison system as its instrumentality) was likely not intentional; instead, it was located within an overall apathy that nonetheless stems from an understanding that a prisoner is a deviant and therefore, not deserving of the State's care. A female prisoner's experience of pregnancy and motherhood is therefore, mediated by stigma, discrimination, apathy and abuse based on the overall carceral framework within which the prisons system functions and which is not conceptually geared towards rights-based care. Conversations around bodily autonomy and dignity hold very little meaning within this framework.

It may have been that Manisha did not disclose her pregnancy status to fellow prisoners and the authorities because she did not want to carry on with it after her family abandoned her and hoped that it will lead to a spontaneous abortion. Maybe she anticipated being granted pre-trial bail and continued till her bail application was rejected when she had already reached her third trimester. On the whole though, it was an intersectionality of systemic, institutional, and societal factors that converged to deny her the ability and choice to seek safe abortion care and then, much needed prenatal and obstetric care.

A corollary of the intentional violence of carceral frameworks on pregnant women in prisons can be found in instances of incarcerating women in prohibitive abortion regimes and denial of emergency obstetric care—a practice common in several Latin American countries. In 2008, a woman named Manuela was convicted of aggravated homicide after an obstetric emergency and later died while incarcerated in El Salvador. Her case was one of the first that was brought before the *Inter-American Court of Human Rights* (IACHR) and in a landmark decision, the IACHR found El Salvador responsible for her death and of violating her rights to life, personal liberty, fair trial, privacy, equal protection, judicial protection, and health under the Inter-American Convention and the Convention of *Belem Do Para*.[13] It was recognized that by creating a legal framework that criminalized abortion under all circumstances, the State unjustly persecutes women seeking healthcare during obstetric emergencies. The decision sheds light on the way in which the power of the law and its attendant institutions is brought down to create an atmosphere of fear and leads to denial of essential services much beyond what might have a limited scope on paper—emergency healthcare for obstetric emergency in this instance. As many such penal laws across country contexts, including India's, demonstrate non-state (peaceful) actors including doctors, counsellors, first responders etc. are often drafted into this *criminalising* project of the State.

Since then, a robust jurisprudence on obstetric violence and other forms of discriminatory treatment during pregnancy and motherhood as a form of gender-based violence within repressive regimes has been developed in Latin America. Recently, the IACHR explicitly named "obstetric violence" as a form of gender-based violence under applicable international law in the case of *Britez Arce* et al. *v. Argentina*.[14]

In India too, the Supreme Court of India and various High Courts have developed some progressive jurisprudence on access to maternal health including providing timely, affordable, and high quality maternal health care, access to the full range of contraceptive methods in a non-coercive and target-free manner, and preventing child marriage amongst others. The higher judiciary has also held the State accountable for denial of decisional and bodily autonomy of women with disabilities, including their decision to abort or to carry with a pregnancy as well as coercive sterilization practices. The next section will examine the narratives that the courts have developed and

[13] IACHR, Report No. 153/18, Case 13.069. Merits. Manuela and family. El Salvador. December 7, 2018, available at http://www.oas.org/en/iachr/decisions/court/2019/13069FondoEn.pdf (last accessed 25th August 2023).

[14] The IACHR went on to define "obstetric violence" as "...a form of gender-based violence (...), exercised by health care providers against pregnant women, during access to health services that take place during pregnancy, childbirth and postpartum, which is expressed mostly, but not exclusively, in a dehumanizing, disrespectful, abusive or negligent treatment of pregnant women; in the denial of treatment and full information on the state of health and applicable treatments; in forced or coerced medical interventions; and in the tendency to pathologize natural reproductive processes, among other threatening manifestations in the context of health care during pregnancy, childbirth and postpartum." https://reproductiverights.org/inter-american-court-human-rights-protections-pregnant-women-latin-america/#:~:text=In%20its%20ruling%2C%20the%20Court,children's%20rights%20and%20judicial%20protection. (last accessed 25th August 2023).

to what extent this enables us to argue for recognition of diverse claims of marginalized bodies to dignity and autonomy in motherhood.

Before looking at the judicial narratives, let us examine a few instances where the State and its institutions have put in place repressive policies and actively coerced to prevent what it perceives as '*undesirable*' bodies from motherhood.

6.3.1 Population Policies, Sterilization, and the Privilege of Motherhood

Population policies the world over are inherently grounded within a Malthusian-inspired[15] negative narrative of the inverse relationships of population growth with agricultural and industrial production, the state of the environment, and State welfare entitlements, to name a few. A logical corollary of this negative framing therefore, is the justification of coercive tools such as involuntary/coercive sterilization as well as more benign but effective forms of disincentives such as disqualification from higher education, state entitlements, or Government jobs.

In July of 2021, the Government of Uttar Pradesh published a draft UP Population (Control, Stabilisation and Welfare) Bill, 2021 for public consultation and feedback (Livelaw 2022). The draft Bill exemplifies the *carrot and stick* approach that has historically been the feature of many population control policies. On the one hand, it proposes a set of incentives for those who adhere to the two-child norm and opt for 'voluntary sterilization' to higher education and Government jobs, loans, health insurance, and reduced fees for public utilities. On the other, it bars those who contravene the two-child norm from State welfare schemes, elected bodies, government employment, receiving any kind of Government subsidy including limits on free ration. Uttar Pradesh is of course not the first state to advance a population control law or policy; states like Andhra Pradesh, Madhya Pradesh, Haryana, Odisha, Rajasthan, and recently, Assam have enforced the two-child norm for elected panchayats, urban local bodies, and also for entry and promotions of employees in public services and to decide the eligibility for government's welfare programs and services (Dash, September 2021). The UP Bill however, went a step beyond the realm of elected bodies and Government employment to key welfare programs and access to higher education, loans, and fees for public utilities. The Bill also distinguished itself from other such policies by laying down a detailed set of criteria supported by illustrative scenarios for how the disincentives would operate in cases of polygamous marriages. It has been critiqued for reinforcing a fertility-driven approach that violates women's reproductive autonomy (Centre for Public Policy Research 2021). In a country where sterilization is gender-based and there are cultural/patriarchal stereotypes around childbearing and masculinity, the provisions of the Bill is likely to force

[15] Thomas Robert Mathus, an English Economist, is now considered with notoriety for his essentialist ideas on population growth. His propositions predicated on the idea that populations continue to increase till there's availability of food, and after that, population growth can be checked by what he referred to as 'positive' checks in the form of natural disasters/disease and by a preventive check which he described as a "foresight of the difficulties attending the rearing of a family" (Rao, 1995). Poverty according to Malthus, therefore, was a natural and desired state and had nothing to do with structural, institutional forces. Since the early nineteenth century, Malthusian ideas of population growth were used by the British to explain poverty in India and therefore, to justify and gloss over the systematic destruction of its indigenous weaving industry and trade. Globally, these ideas lent well to the growing concerns around racial purity that became the basis of the eugenics movement that later, metamorphosed into a population control movement. The birth control narratives were also complicated by a coming together of various influences and critiques, including as one knows, socialist and radical feminist engagements with women's work (Rao and Sexton, 2010). Elsewhere, Mohan Rao analyses the continuing influence of Malthusian thinking in narratives about immigration and what he refers to as a "sub-discipline of 'strategic demography'" that connects growth of Islamic fundamentalism in the "youth bulge" theory. Rao points out that the search for biological metaphors to what are political and social problems fails to explain the rise of "Protestant fundamentalism" in the United States which has neither a youth bulge nor significant population growth (Rao, 2008).

the woman to disproportionately bear the brunt of sterilization procedures (The Wire 2021). The religion-based population control approach that is at the centre of the proposed Bill has also been the subject of criticism from a cross-section of experts (Dash 2021).

As many experts have pointed out, available official data relating to fertility and other health related indicators debunk the supposed population growth in states such as Uttar Pradesh and the need to control it to *"stabilize the population of the State for promotion of sustainable development with more equitable distribution"* [Livelaw, The Uttar Pradesh Population (Stabilization, Control, and Welfare) Bill 2022]. For instance, the total fertility rate (TFR) for India has in fact, declined from 2.2 in 2016 to 2.0 as per National Family Health Survey-5 (NFHS-5) and is therefore, currently below the replacement rate. Most importantly, the TFR data analysis from NFHS-5 highlight that population growth is more proximately linked to factors such as women's level of schooling and economic status. While states such as Uttar Pradesh and Bihar continue to have relatively higher TFR than states in the south and west of India, it is significant that overall, the NFHS-5 data shows that fertility has declined amongst all age cohorts of women in the reproductive age-group. This then clearly reinforces the need to address the underlying determinants of health within an enabling framework of reproductive and decisional autonomy based on availability and accessibility to the full range of sexual and reproductive information and services, rather than a coercive anti-natalist approach that seeks to define who is deserving of procreating and to what extent.

It also attests to what has been identified as the resurgence of an anti-natalist/pro-natalist narrative in many countries across the world. Because most low and middle income countries have been historically driven by the goals of lowering fertility rates, population policies have become synonymous with achieving the desired fertility rate, which then translates exclusively to control of women (and pregnant persons) bodies and their reproductive autonomy. For high income countries, increasing pronatalist sentiments are not only driving progressive parental leave, maternity care, and child care services but also coercive policies aimed at migrant communities or so-called non-indigenous population. The systematic human rights abuse and State violence against Roma women in Europe in the form of coercive sterilization practices combined with substantial financial incentives has been well documented since the 1980s when it first came to mainstream attention.[16] In November 2021, the Government of Slovakia adopted a resolution with an unconditional apology to women of Roma origin '*who were illegally subjected to sterilisation from 1966 to 2004, and they were provided with compensation*'.[17] Despite the international scrutiny and recommendations from European regional and national human rights bodies such as the *European Court of Human Rights* (ECtHR),[18]

---

[16] It was this research which was published as a factsheet that first documented and highlighted the systematic reproductive rights violations against the Roma women. The research found "clear and consistent patterns of health-care providers who disregarded the need for obtaining informed consent to sterilization and who failed to provide accurate and comprehensive reproductive health information to Romani patients, resulting in the violation of their human rights." (p. 14); United Nations Development Programme (UNDP), Nowhere to Turn: Gender-based Violence Against Roma Women (2018), available at: https://www.undp.org/sites/g/files/zskgke326/files/migration/eurasia/NowhereToTurn_Roma_UNDP_RBEC.pdf.

[17] https://www.ohchr.org/en/news/2023/05/experts-committee-elimination-discrimination-against-women-commend-slovakia-adoption. The text of the resolution specified that "The government condemns sterilisation as a means of regulating the birth rate of the socially disadvantaged, which took place mainly among Roma women," See: Čítajte viac: https://spectator.sme.sk/c/22789783/government-apologises-for-sterilisation-of-women.html.

[18] In 2011 and 2012, the European Court for Human Rights (ECtHR) in a series of rulings confirmed that several hospitals around Slovakia violated Roma women's right to freedom from inhuman and degrading treatment and their right to a private and family life. Decisions in *V.C. v. Slovakia* (November, 2011), *N.B v. Slovakia* (June, 2012), and *I.G., M.K. and R.H. v. Slovakia* (November 2012). See European Court of Human Rights, Factsheet: Roma and Travellers, December 2022, available at: https://www.echr.coe.int/documents/d/echr/fs_roma_eng#:~:text=In%20this%20case%20the%20applicant,degrading%20treatment)%20of%20the%20Convention.

Roma women and girls continue to bear the brunt of historical and continuing discrimination targeting their reproductive rights, including their right to pregnancy and motherhood. This ensures State accountability for this systematic violence has been a long journey for reproductive rights and women's rights advocates. In the 2011–2012 series of cases, the ECtHR found involuntary sterilization during a caesarean birth to be of the level of severity to qualify as 'degrading' treatment under Article 3 and the absence of safeguards for a Roma woman's reproductive health to be Slovakia's failure to fulfil its obligation to protect the right to respect for private and family life under Article 8 of the *European Convention*. However, the EtCHR limited itself to looking at individual violations and found that there was no evidence of the systematicity of the practice in question, which would constitute a violation of the guarantee of prohibition of discrimination under Article 14 of the Convention. It thus, refused to examine whether the health care professionals had acted in the manner they did because of structurally discriminatory policies influenced by racial or ethnic prejudices. In contrast, in an earlier decision relating to a prejudicial law that affected Roma children in schools, the EtCHR not only found a violation of Article 14 but did not go into the individual facts of the cases on the basis that as the legislation had been established to have a disproportionately prejudicial effect on the Roma community, it was sufficient for the applicants to only establish that they were in fact, part of that community (Goldston 2010: 325).[19]

In India too, State-sanctioned coercive sterilization practices have been well documented, especially against tribal minority groups and which led the Supreme Court of India in 2009 to issue guidelines directing the State to prohibit what euphemistically came to be referred to as 'camps'.[20] Rather than limiting its directions to specific instances of violations however, the court went beyond to hold the Indian State accountable and require the development of a uniform set of guidelines for both male and female sterilization, including requirement of informed consent, punitive action for violations, and compensation for victims.[21] The issue of unsafe and coercive sterilization procedures came up again before the Supreme Court in a public interest litigation filed in 2009. With its decision, the court went on to recognize reproductive rights both as part of the right to health as well as an aspect of personal liberty under Article 21 of the Indian Constitution, which includes the right to "access a range of reproductive health information, goods, facilities and services to enable individuals to make informed, free, and responsible decisions about their reproductive behaviour."[22] The court specifically recognized the disproportionate impact that target-driven and incentive-based policies have on women from marginalized and vulnerable communities given the lack of real choices and alternatives that they may have because of their socio-economic conditions. It went on to direct the State to eliminate sterilization camps within a fixed time frame but also undertake reforms of the primary health care system and formulate a gender-responsive National Health Policy.[23]

The decisions relating to coercive sterilization were part of a progressive jurisprudence that emerged from the courts in India since the 2000s with the courts framing the right to reproductive autonomy of women, including the right to decide whether to procreate or not, to refuse to participate in sexual activity, and concomitantly, to use appropriate birth-control methods including access to the full range of contraception as an inherent part of the right to life and

[19] D.H. and others v. Czech Republic (Application No. 57325/00) (European Court of Human Rights, 2006).

[20] *Ramakant Rai v. Union of India*, (2009) SCC 16 565.

[21] Ramakant Rai (2009).

[22] Devika Biswas v. Union of India (2016) 10 SCC 726/733, in A Casebook, (2019:17).

[23] Devika Biswas in Casebook (18).

liberty under Article 21 of the Constitution.[24] Over the years, several sub-national (state level) policies creating disqualifications for those with more than two children from serving in local governance institutions, from public employment, or in educational institutions were challenged before the courts on the grounds that these violated Article 21 of the Indian Constitution. These challenges brought to the fore the tension between the fundamental right to privacy as a constituent of the right to life under Article 21 and the argument that population control measures were essential to achieve the goals enshrined in the Directive Principles of State Policy.[25] In contrast to the approach in cases relating to sterilization practices, courts in India, including the Supreme Court of India, have consistently upheld family planning and the two-child norm as a legitimate State goal, and found that disqualification based on number of children satisfied the test of reasonable classification and had a rational nexus with the objectives of promoting public health, family welfare, and population control.[26] Is it then that the judiciary (as an institution of the State) operating as it does within the patriarchal value system, remains completely invested in the dominant State ideology? In the cases where it does seem to take positions in opposition to advance the development of a competing norm or value, especially in relation to marginalized persons or groups, what considerations shape the court's decision and specific to our enquiry here, how does it use the force of its legitimacy to accomplish this endeavour?

Generally though, rulings of the higher judiciary have built upon and expanded the scope of specific fundamental rights with the effect that we have today, a vibrant articulation of sexual and reproductive rights within the constitutional framework. The courts drew upon international human rights standards relating to bodily autonomy, right to privacy and family formation, right to equality and non-discrimination, and the right to sexual and reproductive information and services to shape the contours of these rights within the domestic sphere. A nine judge bench of the Supreme Court of India in *K.S. Puttaswamy* (also referred to as the 'privacy' judgment) held the right to privacy as a fundamental right. Speaking through a plurality opinion (with five other judges delivering separate but concurring opinions), the court located privacy within the constitutional guarantees of dignity, personal liberty, and non-discrimination. It went on to carve out the right to reproductive choice from an intersection of the rights to privacy, dignity, and bodily integrity under Article 21 relying on its earlier decision in *Suchita Srivastava.* The decision acknowledged that privacy, at its core, includes the preservation of personal intimacies including sexual orientation, thus paving the way for the *Navtej Singh Johar* decision as some scholars note (Jain and Shah 2020). The separate opinions specifically recognized the choice to procreate or to abort as well as making an informed choice regarding sterilization as an aspect of a woman's right to privacy. In *Navtej Singh Johar*, a five-judge bench of the Supreme Court unanimously read down Sect. 377 of the Indian Penal Code that penalised sexual activity '*against the order of nature'*, excluding consensual sexual relationships between adults, whether same-sex or not.[27] As has been argued elsewhere, by decriminalising the stigma attached to the practice of homosexuality through this judgment, the court enabled transgender and same sex persons to be able to report non-consensual acts and violence

[24] See Suchita Srivastava v. Chandigarh Administration, (2009) 9 SCC 1.

[25] For instance, in Mukesh Kumar Ajmera v. State of Rajasthan (1997); Smt. Renuka Sahal v. State of Rajasthan (2015); B.K. Parthasarathi v. State of Andhra Pradesh (2000).

[26] Javed v. State of Haryana (2003) 8 SCC 369, in Casebook (18).

[27] Navtej Singh Johar v. Union of India, (2018) 10 SCC 1, see https://main.sci.gov.in/supremecourt/2016/14961/14961_2016_Judgement_06-Sep-2018.pdf.

perpetrated against them, including of rape.[28] The decision is also significant for the concurring opinion of Chandrachud, J. (as he was then) in which he critiqued the court's decision in *Air India v. Nergesh Meerza* (1981) as stereotyping and essentializing gender roles related to pregnancy and motherhood, which lead to discrimination against women. The opinion notes,

> *It holds that the burdens of health and family planning rest solely on women. This perpetuates the notion that the obligations of raising family are those solely of the woman....A discriminatory act will be tested against constitutional values. A discrimination will not survive constitutional scrutiny when it is grounded in and perpetuates stereotypes about a class constituted by the grounds prohibited in Article 15(1).*
>
> (Navtej Singh Johar, concurring opinion, Chandrachud, J. 438)

Taken together, these landmark judgments have evolved an impressive jurisprudence, breathing fresh air into a '*transformative constitution*'[29] and advancing an intersectional queer feminist approach to sexual and reproductive rights. While celebrating these gains from a marginalized community perspective, one tends to exercise adequate caution especially in the context of the recent dissonance seen in relation to the right to safe abortion in India. These will be discussed briefly later in this chapter.

6.4 Queer Bodies and Motherhood

On 17th October 2023, the Supreme Court of India through a five-judge bench issued its ruling in what has become well known as the 'marriage equality case'.[30] Seeking recognition of the right to marriage of members of the LGBTQI+community, the petitions challenged the constitutionality of the *Special Marriage Act*, 1954 on the ground that exclusion of the LGBTQI+community from the ambit of this secular law violates their rights to equality, freedom of expression, and dignity. The petitions relied on *Navtej Johar* and the earlier *NALSA* decisions of the court which had recognized non-binary gender identities and consensual sexual and reproductive choices of same-sex persons. While the court's decision affirming that there is no fundamental right to marry and thus, rejecting the challenge to constitutionality of the *Special Marriage Act* and marriage equality for queer persons disappointed (Narrain 2023), the petition and the judgment were significant for many reasons.

Drawing upon a decision of the court in *Deepika Singh*[31] in the context of denial of maternity leave where she had in earlier instances availed childcare leave for her nonbiological children, some of the petitions articulated the argument for recognition of "chosen families"—understood as nonbiological kinship bonds, whether legally recognized or not, and deliberately chosen for the purpose of mutual support and love. Chosen families have often been embraced within lesbian, gay, bisexual, and transgender (LGBT) communities (Gates 2016). Citing with approval, the framing of 'atypical families' in Deepika Singh, the court noted,

> *Queer relationships may constitute one's family. Persons in such relationships are fulfilling their innate and human need to be a part of a family and to create their family. This conception of a family may be atypical but its atypical nature does not detract from the fact that it is a family.... These atypical manifestations of the family unit equally constitute the fundamental groups of society. The Constitution accounts for plural identities and values. It protects the right of every person to be different. Atypical families, by their very nature, assert the right to be different. Difference cannot be discriminated against simply because it exists. Articles 19 and 21 protect the rights of every citizen and not some citizens.*
>
> (*Supriyo*, para 229)

[28] Shraddha Chaudhary, Navtej Singh Johar v. Union of India, Love in Legal Reasoning (2019), http://nujslawreview.org/wp-content/uploads/2020/01/12-3-4-Chaudhary.pdf.

[29] See Navtej Singh Johar (2018), 95.

[30] Supriyo @ Supriya Chakraborty and Anr. v. Union of India 2023 INSC 920 https://main.sci.gov.in/supremecourt/2022/36593/36593_2022_1_1501_47792_Judgement_17-Oct-2023.pdf.

[31] *Deepika Singh v. Central Administrative Tribunal*, Civil Appeal No 5308 of 2022 (2022).

Although the court (through its separate opinions that constituted a majority) in *Supriyo* went on to refuse to read down the *Central Adoption Resource Authority* (CARA) guidelines to allow unmarried couples to adopt,[32] the somewhat solidification of the idea of 'atypical' families or 'chosen' families and the entitlements that flow from that is a powerful advancement towards recognition of 'atypical' bodies and possibly, 'atypical' motherhood and parenting. Another recent area of contestation (and convergence) relates to access to assisted reproduction, including surrogacy. While this merits a separate discussion which is outside the remit of this chapter, it is important to note here that despite some fissures within the feminist(s) analysis of surrogacy, especially in the context of decolonial discourses around bodily autonomy and exploitation, its implications "*reach far beyond its effects on individual childbearing behavior and population development*" to that alter understandings of social representation of motherhood, parenthood and reproduction, as well as for '*gender relationships on the private, societal, and global level*'. (Neyer and Bernardi 2011: 163) It adds important nuances to the discussion on motherhood both as an institution and as an experience—and how the State and its instrumentalities construct desirability within the larger narratives of State interest.

6.5 Abortion Rights and Some Recent Anxieties

While much has been said about the global regression on abortion rights, especially in the United States of America with the US Supreme Court decision in *Dobbs v. Jackson Women's Health Organisation* (2022) that reversed half a century old protection afforded by the court's landmark decision in *Roe v. Wade*, this chapter will neither delve into this issue in detail nor address the global nature of its scope. However, one would be greatly amiss in not referring to two recent decisions of the Supreme Court of India that follow two contrasting trajectories in its understanding of reproductive autonomy and most importantly, in its treatment of what the law considers as a desirable pregnancy and motherhood and the potential violence that it may consequently subject a pregnant person to.

In *X v. Principal Secretary, Health & Family Welfare Department*[33] (henceforth, X v. Principal Secretary), the Supreme Court of India purposively interpreted the *Medical Termination of Pregnancy Act*, 1971 (as amended in 2021) to extend the right to safe abortion until 24 weeks of gestation to unmarried women on the ground of "material change in circumstances". The provision under the Act had limited this ground to divorced women and widows. Explaining its rationale, the court noted,

> *The law should not decide the beneficiaries of a statute based on narrow patriarchal principles about what constitutes "permissible sex", which create invidious classifications and excludes groups based on their personal circumstances. The rights of reproductive autonomy, dignity, and privacy under Article 21 give an unmarried woman the right of choice on whether or not to bear a child, on a similar footing of a married woman.* (para 121)

Applying an intersectional analysis to the issue, the court emphasized that *'(T)rue realization of reproductive autonomy is possible only by addressing problems in the societal contexts within which individuals, particularly women, are situated. It is not only social stigma which prevents women from realizing the right to health but also caste and economic location.'* (*X v. Principal Secretary*, para 129). Referring to the scope of reproductive autonomy and health, the decision affirmed that *'(R)eproductive health implies that women should have access to safe, effective, and affordable methods of family planning and enabling them to undergo safe pregnancy, if they so choose.'* (para 130) The court

[32] The current position of the law therefore, is the same as before - that a person in a same-sex relationship can adopt in their individual capacity but not as a couple.

[33] Civil Appeal No 5802 of 2022, decided by the Supreme Court on 29.09.22.

also expanded the understanding of 'woman' to include trans and non-binary persons under the ambit of the law, thus, moving a step closer to the realization of an overarching recognition of pregnant persons' right to reproductive autonomy, including access to safe abortion. A part of the constellation of recent constitutional jurisprudence advancing the rights to equality and dignity, *X v. Principal Secretary* has been lauded for its progressive vision and articulation of reproductive rights, especially in the context of regression in countries such as the United States of America following the reversal of *Roe v. Wade* in the *Dobbs* decision.

While there was much to congratulate ourselves for in *X v. Principal Secretary* ruling, the Supreme Court's recent ruling in *X v. Union of India and Anr.*[34] has taken us back a few steps, if not brought us closer to a complete U-turn. Most importantly, the court by providing a space for arguments around foetal viability (which is not at all considered in the Act itself), has given rise to newer anxieties within an otherwise progressive legal framework. In this case, the Supreme Court was dealing with a petition by a married mother of two, who sought medical termination of pregnancy after 24 weeks of gestation, which is permitted only to save the woman's live or in case of '*substantial foetal abnormalities*'. The court rejected the pregnant woman's plea on the ground that the medical examination found the foetus to be viable and not suffering from any abnormality, and that there was no threat to the woman's life. In framing the proceedings in the court (the proceedings before the three-judge bench led by Chandrachud, CJI, was livestreamed) solely in terms of viability of the foetus and whether the foetus was likely to be harmed because of the life-sustaining medication the pregnant woman was on, the judgment laid bare a key anxiety of the patriarchal state with the right to abortion.

That despite having a relatively liberal legal framework and progressive constitutional jurisprudence on reproductive autonomy, an 'ideal' woman (understood to be cis-gendered and in a heteronormative socially sanctioned marriage with pre-existing children) could not refuse (or reject) 'motherhood' solely on the basis of her mental health or that she feels herself 'incapable' of child rearing. In this case, the petitioning pregnant woman had sought abortion on the ground that she was suffering from post-partum psychosis for which she was under medication. 'Motherhood' it seems, once taken on cannot be rejected, unless the State and its instrumentalities consider her undesirable, because she is a minor, unmarried, has a disability, or has had a "change in circumstances", amongst others. The violence of 'motherhood', therefore, extends much beyond those that are labelled 'undesirable'; given the circumstances, the institution of 'motherhood' coerces 'desirable' bodies and 'fit' mothers—and in a sense, demarcates the limits of reproductive autonomy and justice. The decolonial intersectional queer feminist project therefore, must engage with this inherent problematic as it engages with law and constructions of 'motherhood'.

6.6 Conclusion

In 1986, Adrienne Rich wrote that '*The labor of childbirth has been a form of forced labor…*' Since then, feminist scholars, practitioners, and women and persons capable of being pregnant, especially from black, indigenous and postcolonial perspectives, have reimagined the ability and experience of childbirth and mothering in different ways. In the Indian context, feminist scholars and thinkers such as Mary John, Uma Chakravarti, Jasodhara Bagchi, Tanika Sarkar and others have developed a rich analysis of the "*social and ideological construction of a woman as a mother in the iconography of India as a nation in the making*" (Agnihotri 2020) and interacted closely [and sometimes, in complex ways as Jasodhara Bagchi notes in her book

[34] X v. Union of India and Anr., 2023 INSC 919, https://main.sci.gov.in/supremecourt/2023/42181/42181_2023_1_24_47700_Judgement_16-Oct-2023.pdf.

'*Interrogating Motherhood*' (2017)[35]] with the activism that the women's movements undertook on issues such as unpaid care work, sexual violence, intimate partner violence, surrogacy, and assisted reproduction amongst others.

India also has a history of progressive jurisprudence such as rulings in *Suchita Srivastava* that recognized bodily and decisional autonomy of women in making choices about their own reproduction and motherhood while seeking to address State's coercion that manifested in sterilization policies. However, as I discuss in the foregoing analysis, the institution of motherhood finds newer and more sophisticated ways of bearing down on and prescribing who, when, where, and how one gets to become a mother and undertake 'mothering'.

The COVID-19 pandemic further exacerbated pre-existing inequalities with women, girls, and persons marginalized because of their ethnicity, religion, socio-economic status, disability status, and sexual orientation having been disproportionately impacted. According to the United Nations, as a result of the pandemic, health of women generally was adversely impacted through the reallocation of resources and priorities, including sexual and reproductive health services. (United Nations 2020) It also found that globally, women make up 70 percent of the health workforce and are more likely to be front-line health workers as also the majority of health facility service-staff—and as such are more likely to be exposed to the virus (United Nations 2020). Data from the pandemic years and its aftermath has also demonstrated the impact on unpaid care economy and informal/low-paid sectors that is where women, girls and other marginalized persons are disproportionately located. These inequities are mirrored in the Indian context too.[36]

The increasing shift towards anti-rights rhetoric in mainstream media and policies, globally and in India, is likely to have severe repercussions first and foremost on marginalized 'bodies', including of women and girls. Globally, we are witnessing an emboldening and increasing sophistication of anti-rights narratives (which are increasingly co-opting much of the rights language that feminist and intersectional movements have fought to create), as seen in the aftermath of the United States Supreme Court decision in *Dobbs v. Jackson Women's Health Clinic* (2022) that overturned half a century-old constitutional right to abortion as guaranteed by earlier decisions of the court in *Roe v. Wade* (1973) and *Planned Parenthood of Southeastern Pennsylvania v. Casey* (1992). At the same time, several jurisdictions such as Nepal, South Korea, Argentina, and Mexico have witnessed landmark progress towards liberalization of abortion access. There have been significant norm-setting towards seeking State accountability for maternal deaths and discriminatory access to maternal healthcare as also obstetric violence in several countries in South America and Africa. The "right to reproductive health and other reproductive matters" is enshrined in the Interim Constitution of Nepal (2007) and is further strengthened in the Safe Motherhood and Reproductive Health Rights Act, 2018,[37]

[35] Jasodhara Bagchi in Interrogating Motherhood (2017) notes, for instance, "Feminist understanding of motherhood has been central to the unfolding of Indian society from the moment of insertion into the global capitalist system through the colonizing process to the present day, when it is directly under the thumb of a market-driven neo-liberal regime of globalization." (p.xxvi referred in Agnihotri, 2020).

[36] UN Women's data shows that during the pandemic, women's share of unpaid care work in India grew by nearly 30 per cent and more girls than boys were left out of school during the pandemic and 65 per cent of parents surveyed were reluctant to continue the education of girls and resorting to child marriages to save costs. Reports of domestic violence, child marriage, cyber violence and trafficking of women and girls increased within the first few months of the pandemic. (UN Women, 2021).

[37] The Safe Motherhood and Reproductive Health Rights Act, 2018 was enacted to "respect, protect and fulfill woman's safe motherhood and reproductive health rights as guaranteed in the Constitution" and to provide "safe, quality, affordable and accessible maternal and reproductive health services". The Act amongst others, prohibits forced use of contraceptives and family planning measures, guarantees safe abortion, and stipulates that services under the law must be disabled and adolescent friendly.

which provides the foundation for advocating for a justice-centric vision of reproduction and motherhood.

There is thus, much to be cautiously optimistic about, while remaining vigilant about oppositional narratives in an increasingly polarized world, in terms of the ways in which some attempts (mostly in courtrooms) are being made to re-imagine the engagements of law and its institutions with 'motherhood', specifically when looked at using sexual and reproductive health and rights as the frame.

References

Abrams P (2015) The bad mother: stigma, abortion and surrogacy. J Law Med Ethics. https://doi.org/10.1111/jlme.12231

African Commission on Human and Peoples' Rights (2013) Resolution on involuntary sterilisation and the protection of human rights in access to HIV services. ACHPR/Res.260(LIV)2013. https://achpr.au.int/index.php/en/adopted-resolutions/260-resolution-involuntary-sterilisation-and-protection-human-rights-ac

Agnihotri I (2020) Book review: Jasodhara Bagchi, interrogating motherhood. Indian J Gend Stud 27(1):167–172. https://doi.org/10.1177/0971521519891476

Albertson Fineman M, Karpin I, Lhamon CE (1996) Mother as trope in feminist legal theory. In: Source: The Yale Law J (Vol 105, Issue 5). The Yale Law Journal Company, Inc. (X v. Union of India and Anr., 2023)

Bohren MA, Vogel JP, Hunter EC, Lutsiv O, Makh SK, Souza JP, Aguiar C, Saraiva Coneglian F, Diniz ALA, Tunçalp Ö, Javadi D, Oladapo OT, Khosla R, Hindin MJ, Gülmezoglu AM (2015) The mistreatment of women during childbirth in health facilities globally: a mixed-methods systematic review. PLoS Med 12(6). https://doi.org/10.1371/JOURNAL.PMED.1001847

Center for Reproductive Rights (2014) Realizing states' obligations to prevent and address maternal mortality from risk to rights. www.reproductiverights.org

Center for Reproductive Rights (2023) Legal analysis: what dobbs got wrong. https://reproductiverights.org/what-dobbs-got-wrong/

Center for Reproductive Rights, & Poradna pre obcianske a l'udské práva, in consultation with I. Z. (2003) BODY AND SOUL forced sterilization and other assaults on Roma reproductive freedom in Slovakia

Centre for Public Policy Research (n.d.) UP Population (Control, Stabilization, and Welfare) Bill, 2021- a better or a bitter pill to swallow! Retrieved December 11, 2023, from https://www.cppr.in/articles/up-control-stabilization-and-welfare-bill-2021-a-better-or-a-bitter-pill-to-swallow#_ftn1

Chandra A, Satish M (2019) Reproductive justice in India. Center for Reproductive Rights

Cho S, Crenshaw W, Mccall L (2013) toward a field of intersectionality studies: theory, applications, and Praxis. Source: Signs 38(4):785–810. https://doi.org/10.1086/669608

Cover RM, Minow M, Ryan M, Sarat A (1993) Narrative violence and the law: the essays of robert cover. University of Michigan Press

Crenshaw K (1996) Mapping the margins: intersectionality, identity politics, and violence against women of color. In: Kelly Weisberg D et al. (Ed), Applications of feminist legal theory (pp 363–377). Temple University Press. http://www.jstor.com/stable/j.ctt14bs8md.30

Diamond-Smith N, Treleaven E, Murthy N, Sudhinaraset M (2017) Women's empowerment and experiences of mistreatment during childbirth in facilities in Lucknow, India: results from a cross-sectional study. BMC Pregnancy and Childbirth, 17.https://doi.org/10.1186/S12884-017-1501-7

Faheem A (2022) The nature of obstetric violence and the organisational context of its manifestation in India: a systematic review. Sexual Reproductive Health Matters 29(2). https://doi.org/10.1080/26410397.2021.2004634

Ferree MM (2010) Filling the glass: gender perspectives on families. J Marriage Fam 72(3):420–439. https://doi.org/10.1111/j.1741-3737.2010.00711.x

Few-Demo AL (2014) Intersectionality as the "new" critical approach in feminist family studies: evolving racial/ethnic feminisms and critical race theories. J Fam Theory Rev 6(2):169–183. https://doi.org/10.1111/jftr.12039

Few-Demo AL, Allen KR (2020) Gender, feminist, and intersectional perspectives on families: a decade in review. J Marriage Fam 82(1):326–345. https://doi.org/10.1111/jomf.12638

Gates TG (2016) Chosen families. In: Carlson J, Dermer SB (Eds), The SAGE Encyclopedia of marriage, family, and couples counseling. SAGE Publications, Inc. https://doi.org/10.4135/9781483369532.N74

Jain D, Shah PK (2020) reimagining reproductive rights jurisprudence in India: reflections on the recent decisions on privacy and gender equality from the supreme court of India. Colum J Gender & L 39(2):1. https://doi.org/10.7916/cjgl.v39i2.5673

Kannabiran K (2006) Three-dimensional family: remapping a multidisciplinary approach to family studies. Econ Pol Wkly 41(42):4427–4433

Kapur R, CB (2019) Subversive sites 20 years later: rethinking feminist engagements with the law. Unpublished

Khosla R, Zampas C, Vogel JP, Bohren MA, Roseman M, Erdman JN (2016) International human rights and the mistreatment of women during childbirth. Reproduct Health Res. https://www.hsph.harvard.edu/hhrjournal/wp-content/uploads/sites/2469/2016/12/Kholsa-final-1.pdf

Khullar M (ed) (2005) Writing the Women's movement: a reader - google books (M. Khullar, Ed.; reprint). Zubaan

Law and Pluralism - Bicocca. (n.d.). Retrieved December 10, 2023, from https://www.lawpluralism.unimib.it/en/focus/forced-sterilisation-of-roma-women-echr-violations-and-criminal-implications

Mackinnon CA (2013) Intersectionality as method: a note. Source: Signs 38(4):1019–1030. https://doi.org/10.1086/669570

Ministry of Health and Family Welfare (2016) National family health survey - 4: India fact sheet. 1–8. http://rchiips.org/nfhs/pdf/NFHS4/India.pdf

Mohanty CT, Russo A, Torres L (1991) Third World women and the politics of feminism. Third World Women Politics Feminism. https://doi.org/10.2307/40149059

Narrain A (2023) Marriage equality judgement: overlooking fundamental rights. Supreme Court Observer. https://www.scobserver.in/journal/marriage-equality-judgement-overlooking-fundamental-rights-justice-bhat-on-marriage-equality/

Narrain A, Bhan G (2005) Because I have a voice: queer politics in India (Narrain A, Bhan G, Eds.; 1st ed.). Yoda Press

Neyer G, Bernardi L (2011) Feminist perspectives on motherhood and reproduction. Historical Soc Res 36(2):162–176. https://doi.org/10.12759/hsr.36.2011.2.162-176

Rao M (1994) An imagined reality: Malthusianism, Neo-Malthusianism and Population Myth. Econ Political Weekly 29(5):PE40–PE52. http://www.jstor.org/stable/4400725

Rao M (2008) Review: playing god: the global population control movement. Econ Political Weekly, 28–30. https://www.jstor.org/stable/40278023

Rao M, Sexton S (2010) Markets and Malthus. Population, Gender and Health in Neo-Liberal Times, 368

Rich A (2021) Of woman born: motherhood as experience and institution (3rd ed.). Virago Press. (Original work published 1986)

Sadler M, Santos MJ, Ruiz-Berdún D, Rojas GL, Skoko E, Gillen P, Clausen JA (2016) Moving beyond disrespect and abuse: addressing the structural dimensions of obstetric violence. Reprod Health Matters 24(47):47–55. https://doi.org/10.1016/J.RHM.2016.04.002

Sarat, Austin., & Kearns TR (1992) Law's violence. 261

Sen G, Reddy B, Iyer A, Heidari S (2018) Addressing disrespect and abuse during childbirth in facilities. Reprod Health Matters 26(53):1–5. https://doi.org/10.1080/09688080.2018.1509970

Shrivastava S, Sivakami M (2020) Evidence of "obstetric violence" in India: an integrative review. J Biosoc Sci 52(4):610–628. https://doi.org/10.1017/S0021932019000695

Takševa T (2018) Motherhood studies and feminist theory: elisions and intersections. J Motherhood Initiative Res Commun Involvement 9(1). https://jarm.journals.yorku.ca/index.php/jarm/article/view/40489

The Indian Ban on Commercial Surrogacy - Women's Policy Journal (n.d.) Retrieved October 2, 2020, from https://wpj.hkspublications.org/2020/06/19/the-indian-ban-on-commercial-surrogacy/#_ednref16

Two-child Norm: Curtailing Welfare, Weaponising Demography I Economic and Political Weekly (n.d.) Retrieved December 10, 2023, from https://www.epw.in/journal/2021/35/commentary/two-child-norm.html

UNDP Europe and Central Asia (2018) Nowhere to turn gender-based violence against Roma women report of a field study of Roma communities in Albania, Montenegro and the former Yugoslav Republic of Macedonia Roma. https://www.undp.org/eurasia/publications/nowhere-turn-gender-based-violence-against-roma-women

UN Women (2021) Your questions answered: women and COVID-19 in India. UN Women. https://www.unwomen.org/en/news/stories/2021/7/faq-women-and-covid-19-in-india

Vacaflor CH (2016) Obstetric violence: a new framework for identifying challenges to maternal healthcare in Argentina. Reprod Health Matters 24(47):65–73. https://doi.org/10.1016/J.RHM.2016.05.001

Verloo M (2013) Intersectional and cross-movement politics and policies: reflections on current practices and debates. Source: Signs 38(4):893–915. https://doi.org/10.1086/669572

Why experts say India does not need a population policy I Research News - The Indian Express (n.d.) Retrieved December 10, 2023, from https://indianexpress.com/article/research/from-before-independence-indias-many-experiments-with-population-control-7976458/

World Health Organization (2014) The prevention and elimination of disrespect and abuse during facility-based childbirth. https://apps.who.int/iris/bitstream/handle/10665/134588/WHO_RHR_14.23_eng.pdf

X v. Union of India and Anr. (2023). https://main.sci.gov.in/supremecourt/2023/42181/42181_2023_1_24_47700_Judgement_16-Oct-2023.pdf

Yamin AE (2010) Toward transformative accountability: applying a rights-based approach to Fulfill maternal health obligations. Sur Int J Human Rights. https://sur.conectas.org/en/toward-transformative-accountability/

Natal Family Violence: Crisis Interventions and Paths to Survival with LBT Persons

7

Niharika Banerjea, Kolika Mitra, and Poushali Basak

Abstract

This chapter engages with those queer and trans persons who are at the forefront of facilitating survivors of natal family violence out of their familial homes. Lesbian, bisexual, and transmasculine (LBT) identifying persons survive unique forms of natal family violence related to their gender-sexual intersectional locations. The chapter collaboratively engages in experiential-analytical documentation of crisis intervention in natal family violence. Eight of the authors named in this chapter from the COVID-19-induced lockdown have been directly involved with organizing 'paths to survival' along with LBT persons who have migrated from various districts in West Bengal to safer spaces. How do we deploy 'crisis intervention'? What does it mean to organize 'paths to survival'? What effects do these have on the mental health of the organizers? We conducted a reflexive focus group discussion amongst ourselves to understand the meaning of intervention, the process, and what it means to navigate families and police along the way. We do not seek to break the silence by publicizing the particular instances of natal family violence, but by engaging with the expectations of the organizers as they seek to create liveable lives with/for their peers who are looking for a way out of natal family violence. This chapter discusses the affective and methodological dimensions of intervening in instances of natal family violence, and what it may mean for survival and liveability. We expect to join critical voices who are working to break the heteropatriarchal status quo surrounding natal family homes in the absence of anti-discrimination laws.

Keywords

Crisis intervention · Natal family violence · Queer and trans persons in Kolkata and West Bengal · Liveability · Scholar activism · Collaborative methodology · Aggression · House-arrest · Forced marriage · COVID-19 · Path to survival · LBT persons · Caste · Class · Livelihood · Strategy · Health · Mental health · Safe space · Co-survivor · Social reproduction · Heteronormative · Identification documents · Liveable life · Chosen family

N. Banerjea (✉)
Jindal Global Law School, O.P. Jindal Global University, Sonipat, India
e-mail: niharika.banerjea@jgu.edu.in

K. Mitra
Rabindra Bharati University, Kolkata, India

P. Basak
Advanced Centre for Women's Students, Tata Institute of Social Sciences, Mumbai, India

P. M. Anurag and S. Dwivedy (eds.), *Violence in Intimate Spaces*, Sustainable Development Goals Series, https://doi.org/10.1007/978-981-97-2657-8_7

7.1 Introduction

Lesbian and transmasculine identifying persons encounter and survive unique forms of natal family violence related to their gender-sexual, caste, and class locations. This chapter is an experiential-analytical piece on intervening in natal family violence in West Bengal, India, from the standpoint of persons identifying as queer, non-binary, and lesbian.[1] Academic discourses typically focus on marital violence within domestic spaces and activists and scholar activists have recently begun to document the particular forms of violence LBT[2] persons face in their natal homes.[3] Our chapter takes a specific angle and narrates the processes of intervention to survive natal family violence. How do we deploy 'crisis intervention'? What does it mean to organize 'paths to survival'? What effects do these have on the mental health of the organizers? By reflecting on 'crisis intervention', we try to bring forth the complexities and challenges in methodologies, activist work and co-creating liveable spaces. Crisis intervention in queer and trans persons' lives deeply entangles not only those who are facing natal family, the police, and different vectors of institutional violence but also those who commit to supporting and accompanying queer and trans individuals out of crisis situations. The named members of the activist forum and organization, Sappho for Equality,[4] here, who occupy the position of some socio-political and economic capital, go through significant emotional and physical obstacles when engaging in such work. This chapter discusses the affective and methodological dimensions of intervening in instances of natal family violence and what it may mean for survival and liveability.

Eight of the named authors of this chapter, since the COVID-19-induced lockdown, have been directly involved with organizing 'paths to survival' along with LBT persons who have migrated from various districts in West Bengal to safe spaces. What does it mean to organize 'paths to survival'? What kind of absences and structural apathy exist when discussing natal family violence? What effects do these have on the mental health of the organizers? We came together in the summer of 2023 and conducted a *reflexive focus group discussion* to narrate and share the intervention process. We aimed to discuss and document the processes of intervention when families in collusion with state apparatuses and local neighbourhood groups seek to close themselves off from any form of arbitration or interference from those seeking 'paths to survival'. We do not seek to break the silence by publicizing the particular instances of natal family violence, as our intention is not to create portraits of suffering. Looking at 'paths to survival' as a core way to create and imagine liveable spaces, we expect to join critical voices who are working to break the heteropatriarchal status quo surrounding natal family homes in the absence of anti-discrimination laws.

7.1.1 Methodological Sensibilities

Our chapter is co-created from a patchwork of voices; all those named have consented. The first three authors took the lead in transcribing, writing, and close reading. Those acknowledged in this chapter, are our co-thinkers and co-discussants. All named voices in this chapter are related to each other, not by blood or marriage but through ties of *queer kinship*. We are a motley group of people across class, caste and place. Our stories of intervention and survival are also

[1] This chapter does not engage with the history or global circulation of these identity terms, and all those named know their complex existences either through their lived experiences, their academic training or a mixture of both. We deploy the identity terms here to be strategically legible.

[2] Lesbian, bisexual and transmasculine.

[3] For a recent report, see Apnon Ka Bahut Lagta Hai (Our Own Hurt Us the Most): Centering Familial Violence in the Lives of Queer and Trans Persons in the Marriage Equality Debates 2023.

[4] Sappho for Equality is an activist forum and organization for the rights of lesbian, bisexual and transmasculine identifying persons. It is common for queer and trans collectives and organisations in the Indian context to work with specific groups of people, even when their membership is broad, due to different histories of oppression. For more see https://www.sapphokolkata.in. All authors in this chapter are members of the activist forum.

acts of listening and sharing and a form of 'collaborative witnessing' (Ellis and Rawicki, 2013) of natal family violence on their queer and trans members. The witnessing happens at a meeting point of trans and queer folks who are at the forefront of natal family violence and those who are not at present.

We understand the focus group discussion as একসাথে কথা বলা (eksathe kotha bola/talking together) to underscore a research practice that thrives on compassionate listening and collective meaning-making. Minai and Shroff (2019), in the tradition of Linda Tuhiwai Smith and Eve Tuck's work, make a call to "ethical responsibilities and intimate relationalities that this contemporary moment requires of us" (2019, pp. 32). In doing so, they deploy *yaariyan* (friendship), *gupshup* (a mode of speaking), and *baithak* (a mode of space) to theorize their "queer feminist care as research practices" (2019, pp. 32). To this, we add our mode of একসাথে কথা বলা (eksathe kotha bola/talking together) to theorize crisis intervention in the face of natal family violence in ways that are legible to those who are at the forefront of the intervention. In this way, *yarariyan*, *gupshup*, and একসাথে কথা বলা (eksathe kotha bola/talking together) are not modalities (although they are also that) of conversation but spaces of theorization that include street corners, benches, tables, balconies, rooms, etc. Navin Minai and Sara Shroff underscore that these spaces need not be read as margins; they may also be constituted through contextually dominant power relations. And so, we do not claim our methodological practice as an authentic, non-hierarchical, academic work mode. Instead, we situate ourselves in the genre of writing that centres co-authorship as a collaborative sensibility that is explicit about the many voices that inform our writing, thereby also forging and renewing relations of solidarity (Banerjea, Browne et al. 2016; El Kotni, Dixon and Miranda 2020; Koni and Nagar 2006). So, our focus group discussion is perhaps a more academic way of putting our একসাথে কথা বলা (eksathe kotha bola/talking together); at the same time, the practice of একসাথে কথা বলা (eksathe kotha bola/talking together) exceeds the academic formalization. A most banal and common communication modality, talking,[5] in its formalized understanding as a focus group discussion functioned to generate knowledge to be shared publicly for an edited volume. This chapter is thus a public sharing of a collective discussion in the intimate space of a room in Chetana, a gender-sexuality resource centre of Sappho for Equality, in a modest middle-class neighbourhood in Kolkata. When our sharing of crisis intervention narratives becomes available for academic consumption, we hope it will connect with those who are attentive to the role of the natal family in maintaining violent and historically oppressive structures. What is left unsaid in this public sharing are informal relational intimacies that emerge and dissipate as they appear in a safe room in Chetana, over a cup of tea and samosas. Not all bits of knowledge are transcribed and available for academic consumption. Navin Minai and Sara Shroff indicate this as the "trust and safety" that underpins works suffused with "intimate informalities" (2019, pp 37). The trust and safety that are our concern include both the survivors of natal family violence and the intervention team.

Through their absent presence, the survivors alluded to in this chapter are all 18–25 years of age, from both subordinate and dominant caste[6] backgrounds, once living in various districts of West Bengal, but now in anonymous locations in Kolkata. We start by discussing what crisis intervention means and introduce the team and their thoughts and experiences. Following that, we discuss paths to survival, including its strategies and what liveable spaces may mean to the intervention process. The chapter does not conclude with any grand claims, instead, requests the reader to reflect on how natal families are

[5] Talking can be read as an ableist term; we use this to indicate not just words uttered but also non-verbal gestures that bind us through the collective sharing through guiding questions.

[6] We use the terms subordinate and dominant caste in line with Sumit Baudh's (2017) call to state upfront the systemic domination and subordination within caste and caste-ist structures.

predicated on violent heteronormative projects and intervention as an emotional and physically laborious collective process, at the request of those who are at the forefront of this violence. We argue that crisis intervention is not a problem-solving exercise but a meeting point for different queer and trans people trying to create a survival network and a liveable life.

7.2 Crisis and Its Intervention

What does a crisis look like? Conceptual historians suggest that there may not be an inherent meaning to the term; the academic needs to focus on what is "conjured up when different discursive communities speak or write the word 'crisis'?" (Freeden, 2017, pp 17), including sociologists, political economists, and psychiatrists. A conceptual and theoretical history of the English term is outside the scope of this chapter. That said, we are more interested in the term's enabling potential to intervene in instances of natal family violence. While situated within western analytical thought,[7] NGOs often use this term to intervene through circuits of capital and funding, and Sappho for Equality is no exception. Yet, when we brought forth this term in our discussion this summer, we found ourselves thinking about the need to broaden its understanding to speak specifically to instances of natal family violence. House arrest, confinement, inability to access the phone, inability to access food and health care, verbal and physical abuse, forced marriages, sexual violence, and inability to access one's official documents are all instances of everyday forms of violence meted out by many natal families, sometimes for years, on their children who express different desires. When we attempt to interrupt this flow of violence at the request of a person who is confronting such violence, we are intervening. This section details thoughts and recitals concerning intervention with persons identifying as lesbian, queer, and non-binary. Built into these words are critiques that contextualize already existing interrogations of the natal family in queer and trans praxis. We ask the readers to engage with care with the narratives as collective responses to institutional behaviour—*the natal family's propensity for violence*.

7.2.1 Meaning

> It is the need of the individual person that defines what a crisis is. Is the person [who is reaching out to us] feeling a crisis, and how? We have to understand what the person is asking for, against all the mistrust they face [from their natal family]... When we receive that phone call, the person trusts the one who picks up the phone, and we have to understand what the person needs... It is not only a crisis but the development of a trust, with the collective.
>
> Ree

Our entry point into the meaning of crisis is when we come to know specific instances of various forms of violence meted out by natal families on their children. The need to intervene only arises when a person reaches out to us. Natal families, when responding to their children via violence, perceive a crisis in the heteronormative order. That which has disrupted the family order has to be restored, and violence is a response to the disruption. The natal family order stretches beyond the immediate family members, to include the police and legal personnel, all of whom favour the parents' demands over their children, whether they are legally adults or not. There is, thus, no exact moment when a crisis can be marked as such. It is a series of moments, layered upon each other, wrapped in perceptions of threats to the natal family, unworkable realities for queer and trans persons, and the slow loss of life energies.

While a crisis may not have a clearly marked moment, intervention does. An intervention involves responding to a call for facilitation and/or support from persons struggling to move toward a liveable life. There is never one kind of response. As Shreosi elaborates:

> Crisis intervention also happens through phone calls [when a call is received from a person], as we may not be able to reach the person concerned

[7] See Tangjia, 2014; Koselleck and Richter 2006 for elaborations.

> as the person is confined [in the house]. This involves sustained and continual peer emotional support, through phone calls. We watch to see if the person has lost access to the phone, or if they have access to food, medical help, etc. During phone calls, we often keep hearing voices in the background, and the person whispers, indicating they are in a vulnerable position…During phone calls, listening carefully is a practice. To listen and to be able to identify what is going on [as the person is not in a position to clearly state what is going on due to the possibility of being overheard and resultant violence]; is there a restricted movement, is the person not allowed to continue their studies and so on.

Crisis intervention is a response to suffering or a condition of precarity induced and instituted through the natal family order. When a person communicates that precarity, we have a crisis needing intervention. As Koyel elaborates:

> A crisis is that which the person perceives as a crisis. When someone connects with us and says 'I need help' then we try to see how we can mitigate the situation, not always trying to fix it, because most things are not fixable, but to see what kind of emotional support we can provide or at a later date reaching out with more concrete solutions. We also evaluate how much we can promise with the volunteer support that we have.

The extent of the intervention, while dependent on the person who has reached out from the confines of the natal family, is influenced and informed by the emotional and strategic resources and labour of the persons who have volunteered to be part of this process. These are not written down anywhere but accumulated and embodied through one's own and other's experiential knowledge, shared in collective spaces and recalled and activated during a situation. The intention is to facilitate support and not to seize the situation. In Ankana's words:

> So I really feel that not interfering in the individual agency, how we can help that person who does not have those resources [that we have], and how we can brainstorm to create more resources.

Trust helps stick the connection between us and the person on the other side of the phone. It may be built over several phone calls, as familiarity is generated, or often, it is unfamiliarity that aids in connecting. Soham explains:

> There can be a person who calls because they do not know me. 'I stay in Bangalore, I am sharing with you, because you will not judge me, you do not know me, and there is no space for me to know you. But trust has to be created. We have to explain that we can be trusted. A person who wants to leave their home and barely knows about us, fears may exist in that person that they may be trafficked they may be harmed. If the person cannot trust their family members, how can they be expected to trust us, whom they do not know? So, we have to work to generate that trust constantly.

7.2.2 The Team

> [During the lockdown] the number of phone calls in the helpline increased, so much so that it became unmanageable. It was impossible for one person to run the helpline. We would often bring another volunteer member into the call [with the consent of the person on the line] to have a conference call if we felt that having another person [who can address a specific issue] would be helpful. So, there weren't any specific directions we had set down for ourselves; it was haphazard. We quickly realised that we had to figure out some practical, logistical issues to reach the person who had contacted us…Much of this involved how to talk to police personnel and anticipate legal issues.
>
> Shreosi

A dedicated crisis intervention team was never on the agenda. During the pre-COVID-19 induced lockdown days, a response would occur as and when a person reached out. The lockdown intensified instances of natal family violence against queer and trans persons.[8] We would hear from persons who were told they would be forcibly married off the next day, and therefore needed to leave the natal family home immediately and several other instances of violent threats. We soon realized that just mental health support over the phone would not

[8] As is well documented now, the lockdown also intensified and burst open violence on economically marginalised Dalit persons of all genders, caste Hindu cis women, and Muslim persons. For elaborations, see Patil 2021; Sen 2020; EPW Engage 2020; Tieri and Ranjan 2023.

be enough; we needed to take concrete steps toward physical support. A crisis intervention team organically emerged out of the volunteers available at the moment to address immediate mental health concerns, house arrests, and homelessness of persons who had managed to leave their houses. Gradually, we started setting in place more formal procedures to safeguard our volunteers as well as the persons with whom we were in contact. It was similar to 'capacity building' but on the go, as we learnt that crisis intervention has nuanced angles that we could not anticipate. There was no formal induction of volunteers either; those who came together to help each other during the COVID-19 induced lockdown to address the moments of crisis formed a team as the logistics were formalized. Later on, our organization set up a temporary residence, where persons assigned gender female at birth who reached out to us and were becoming homeless could opt to stay for 3 months or more if needed.[9]

Upon talking to each other and looking back, we realize that a sensibility of collective care and empathy solidified the team formation process. Ree elaborates:

> I can link myself with every crisis. I may not have encountered intense violence, but I have been present [in Sappho for Equality's efforts] since the start, and crisis existed then. A crisis exists now with similar scenarios [of house arrests, forced marriage, food and money deprivation, corrective rape, etc.]. In those days, people would die, and they would come to us as news of death. We would only get to know that someone was in crisis when the news of their death reached us. And we would feel despondent that we could not do anything. What are we doing if, as a collective, we cannot prevent one's death? So, we have to stand beside whatever the intensity of the crisis. The pandemic threw us into disarray with constant phone calls for help.

But there were times when we doubted ourselves. Can we actually do anything in the face of such intense violence? Exhaustion and doubts about whether we could reach any resolution haunted us. In such times, coming together as a volunteer team helped. We shared our doubts and exhaustion as much as we figured out and planned the logistics within the strict lockdown measures, trusting each other to keep the minutiae of those logistics within the team and not reveal them in anticipation of any counter-violence as we set in action the particularities of the intervention. Collective care does not mean a problem will be solved, but it does mean that the personal is refracted through the collective while attempting to respond to and address someone else's call. The response and address, as Koyel said, is 'according to one's ability'. When deliberations occur, the team is well aware that the end point of the crisis is not a successful intervention,[10] as the elements and perceptions of a crisis exceed the moments of actual intervention. As Reshmi says:

> A crisis does not present itself as something we intervene in, then disappears. A crisis is ongoing; even after we intervene, it can continue. What we do is reach out to an immediate call. If I am marginalised in some sense, so is that person, and we intervene when there is a call for help.

Anyone is prone to injury; thus, a crisis can occur at any time. But situations that emerge from a person's intersecting marginalizations determine if one will be injured. While Ankana states that the person in crisis could have been her, she also says, "Because we have some privileges, perhaps we are not facing what others are facing now". Thus, the team neither claims to feel proud of what they do nor despondent when they cannot find a suitable solution. The sharing of the crisis at hand, providing space for each other to share one's feelings, comprehending distress, figuring out modalities of support, and strategizing about when and how to intervene—this is what drives the volunteer team of seven to eight active persons. A shared politics of understanding and commitment drives doing 'crisis intervention' and nurturing the support system.

[9] The 3-month time is given to facilitate the person's finding suitable employment and residence of one's own.

[10] In the short term, the success or failure of an intervention is measured by whether the team can do what the person asking for intervention wants.

The current team's composition includes both paid employees[11] and volunteer members. The entire team is referred to as a volunteer team because no formal procedure requires that paid employees be part of the team. All members identify as queer, non-binary, trans, and lesbian persons; they are from oppressed as well as dominant caste and class backgrounds. Some are part of the team because they happened to be involved in addressing a crisis during the lockdown and went on to continue. Others may feel a sense of solidarity toward peers who are in crisis. Soham elaborates with their words:

> I call myself queer. If I observe from my specific location, I see that the shift from gay to queer is a journey that I have undertaken. From that vantage, when I look around, I see the conditions of people; I see what situations they are in. From here, I feel a sense of solidarity. There is also a sense of happiness when I imagine I can be of use to someone in a position more vulnerable than me. Maybe for someone like me, even though I have had a complex journey, I have not had to be 'rescued', and herein lies my privilege. I feel a sense of solidarity when I see a crisis through its caste, class and geographical location. I then feel that I must be there for the crisis intervention.

The sense of 'have to be there' for an intervention must be emphasized. It is a personal-political connection and commitment. The volunteer identifies with the survivor to an extent where it necessitates that they involve themselves in the crisis work. While emotionally one is perturbed, which is one primary reason to do such voluntary work, it is not only that emotion drives action. Rather, it is an ethical commitment, a politics of life, from where such voluntary actions are seen as responsibilities. But in that ethical, political commitment, we also go through many moral dilemmas and emotional ups and downs.

7.2.3 Vulnerabilities

> I do not let myself be bothered too much [by the crisis at hand]. I have explained to myself very strategically that I cannot be bothered by every crisis because then I will not be able to live. I like to intervene in my capacity as a human being, and not necessarily always as a queer trans person. I know that I will go [for an intervention] and reach out to someone similar.
>
> Soham

The persons in the crisis intervention team act within the context of their vulnerabilities. One's mental and physical health informs intervention and attempts to create a liveable life. Also, the forces that impede a liveable life spill over to the team; their bodies and memories are challenged, triggered, and pushed to perform in the present to create a safe path out of the natal family violence of the person who has asked for support. Ankana, Koyel, Ree, Reshmi, Soham, and Shreosi shared their affective narratives.

Ankana talked about her self-doubt and anxieties in the face of intervention, saying, "I ask myself if I am prepared to do this"? However, since time is a big factor in the intervention process, there isn't any scope to search for the answers to the questions that come up in one's mind. The sedimented narratives to legitimize violence forcefully challenge the team, so much so that Ankana personally often "feels lost; lost in front of the language of the institution, its overpowering nature". How does one answer to the police in a non-confrontational but assertive way when they dominate the conversation, say that there is no crisis and that parents know best what is good for their children? How does one communicate to a parent, a sibling, or a neighbour—who are often violent with the team members, and sometimes in collusion with the police—that they cannot put a person under house arrest, deny them food, sedate them, forcibly marry them off? Such concerns, as Shreosi indicated, were never part of one's privileged middle-class upbringing; cis women are taught in caste Hindu and middle-class families to stay away from trouble. Therefore, sometimes, she rehearses how she will speak to the police and the kinds of words she will use because, during a conversation, the police will say several things before she can think of a fitting reply. Ankana often wonders if they have any power to answer a call for help. With each intervention, they

[11] Some of the paid employees are queer, trans and non-binary identifying.

are (un)learning how to communicate, and it is always a dilemma as to how much they can or are prepared to intervene and help. After each crisis, the team has a small feedback meeting to see who could have done what, with a view to the next intervention. Even that fails sometimes, as crisis often unfolds in multiple layers. In one recent instance, the team had to save themselves from a violent mob when they visited someone who had called them for help. In another instance, they were locked up in a room in a person's house who had called for help. Reshmi shared her fear of claustrophobia in this situation, saying such situations are additional crises.

Navigating an intervention is, therefore, never a personal matter; as Ankana says, "Not being able to understand which exact path to follow, we only try to navigate those crises as a team…coming back from a shaken disintegrated position". Despite communication challenges with the police, the team attempts to work with the law in general and the police in particular. Ree says, "We prefer to walk the path of the available law, and during every step of the process, we keep the person informed about what is available". This is necessary as the police are not always conversant with the legal frames of reference and resort to normativities that push the person violated by the natal family deep into the familial home, giving false assurances to the team that they will look into the matter. So, different kinds of strategies on the spot have to be devised. Sometimes, the team braces itself to be beaten up; simultaneously, they are in a telephonic network with peers, friends, and other members of Sappho for Equality during the intervention to keep a circle of protection, information, and advice active. Ree explains, "This is also part of our team intervention".

7.3 Paths to Survival and Liveability

Organizing paths to survival out of natal family violence is a necessity for those who reach out and for us who are involved in the work. We have a political commitment to connect with queer and trans people who do not have access to formal education, knowledge systems, and socio-political and economic resources. Not all forms of connection work are legible. It has taken considerable effort to coherently organize our speech and actions in the known format of crisis intervention. Instead of defining what is a pathway to survival, we ask how such pathways are perceived and ethically organized. Our tales of crisis intervention can add to queer theorizations of vitalities and care, but in a format that is not about rescue, rehabilitation, and protection. While the team has to interact regularly with state agencies in the language that they understand, at the same time, there is an insistence that support is what we are trying to build, while taking responsibility for building solidarities with queer and trans persons from oppressed class-caste-religious-ethnic backgrounds.

Is crisis intervention an act toward a liveable life? What relationalities are possible after an intervention is formally over? Can liveable spaces be created from such intervention? Liveability, deployed here as জীবনের মতো জীবন (Jeebonder mato jeebon/A life that is like a life), relates to desires, actions, and speech that can reside in spaces between life and death, in normative conditions of the everyday, and political becomings (Banerjea and Browne, 2023; Butler 2004a, b). When it is difficult even to hold a dream, imagining a life that is like a life beyond one's safety may not always be possible. In crisis intervention, survival is key; but liveability does not linearly follow survival and is deeply constitutive of the desire to reduce trauma and enable access to economic and social resources.

7.3.1 Leaving the Natal Family

> [Leaving the natal family] is a survival strategy. If I do not leave now, I will never be able to leave; this feeling works in the decision to leave. Not that the person can always imagine a clear future or expects it. The redressal from violence is an immediate means to survive; when one's back is against the wall over a period of time, there comes a time when I will think, either I die, or I am out of this

> place. After that, I will figure out what to do, but only after I am out. Because sometimes the situation is such that there is no time. Of course, some people also plan it out, the need to find a job in Kolkata, rent a place, and so on. Whatever it is, that the person will not take the violence is a firm decision; leaving is a better option than forced marriage.
>
> Koyel

A *jansunwai*, closed-door public hearing organized by People's Union for Civil Liberties (PUCL) and National Network of LBT women and Transpersons was held on April 1, 2023, following which a report titled, *APNON KA BAHUT LAGTA HAI (Our Own Hurt Us the Most): Centering Familial Violence in the Lives of Queer and Trans Persons in the Marriage Equality Debates* was publicly released. This report details the various forms of natal family violence that LBT persons undergo at the hands of their families of birth, and most often in collusion with neighbours and law enforcement agencies. The lockdown heightened these realities. In Shreosi's words:

> [The family members] kept a tab on who their child/sibling was talking to. They could hear everything when the person would try to speak in the bathroom in the small confines of one's house, as going out briefly to talk was impossible. They are constantly asked by their family members why they are 'like that'; because of them, 'the family cannot show their faces to other people…cannot get their elder sister married. So, the option is to keep on trying to live in that place of domestic violence or leave.

Forced marriages, too, did not stop during the lockdown. As Ree stated:

> In the pandemic, everything stopped. The train wheels stopped, cars stopped, but marriages did not stop. This is one of the most intense sides of violence. The family understood their 'daughter' is different, so the immediate solution was to marry them off forcibly. And since it is the pandemic, the 'daughter' can be married off with very little money as the government had said that families can conduct marriage with about 50 people. So, this is a big reason [as to why more persons wanted to leave during the lockdown]…If the person has been married off and is a transmasculine person, he has to leave after lots of emotional and physical violence…In the lockdown some families have also thought that if the person can be married off, then at least it will also be one less mouth to feed.

When the natal family stops access to resources that are sometimes limited,[12] initiates house arrest, monitors their child or sibling's clothes, restricts mobility, and forces them to marry, restricts food, and hides their official documents, such as educational certificates and government ID cards, it securitizes itself against breaches in communities organized on caste and religion. Endogamy, the essence of the caste system,[13] and a key function of the natal family, is breached when the family's young member is seen as moving outside the functional folds of procreation, intergenerational transference of property, and the continuation of the lineage. The person assigned gender female at birth, who is out of place, thus becomes a non-functioning member, who then needs to be restored in place through enactments of violence.

The decision to leave can thus be read as part of an intense social struggle in which movement toward an unfamiliar but hopeful space is the desired goal. This hopeful space, at times, is filled with an imagination of love/ing another. Those with access to the news media sometimes take note of the possibility of same-gender persons living together. Persons often ask us the legal implications of wanting to stay together, or if there is any provision in law to get married. Soham said,

> Love is an important point. Why will it not be? The person may think that if I stay on in my family, then either I will be pushed into marriage or even if I am not, my entire life I will have to live by compromising myself; will I not want to fulfil my expectations, will I not want to hope, not want to romance, love and be romanced and loved?

7.3.2 Strategies for Survival

> The steps [in intervention] are not chronological or planned linearly. Most of the time, things happen simultaneously. One member of our

[12] Many of the persons who seek intervention are from low-income households.

[13] See Ambedkar (1916) for an analysis of caste endogamy as the essential function and feature of the Hindu caste system.

> team may be speaking to the person [who has sought assistance], the other may be talking to the police, and another person may be trying to locate a supportive peer of the person in the area. Still, another may look after the logistics, such as which route to take to reach the person. Whatever we do, we try to document the process as well, either in a written or audio-visual form, as best as we can.[14]
>
> Ankana

The strategies for intervention are also strategies for survival. Logistics, in their banality, are steeped in power. We carry out our intervention anticipating micro and macro aggressions from the family, neighbours, and police. Talking to the police is one of the initial steps, which, despite being difficult, is essential to push law enforcement to seek protection from violence rightfully and thus make them accountable. Sometimes other state agencies such as the Women's Commission or West Bengal Transgender Persons Development Board have had to be approached to ease the situation with the police. Since the likelihood of house arrest and holding of official documents by the natal family is very high, we try to find out if the person has access to his/their/her documents, and if not, how that can be retrieved. Without documents, the chances of finding livelihood options after the person has left the natal family become slim. Survival and ethics demand that we keep the person in the planning process and that he/she/they are comfortable with any strategies that we are proposing. There is no way of knowing if a strategy will succeed or fail. Even after planning everything smoothly, the person may be unable to leave the natal family home. Spontaneous planning, including asking for help from familiar persons in the trans and queer networks, is a common move and source of support. Often, taking help from a loose network of people helps, especially when the geographical distances are large.

A strategy is not static, but changes according to the situation with people available to support and help. Sometimes, a strategy is developed in the moment of its action. To cut a path through a violent familial order, a strategy presents itself as an essential intervention element rather than a cautious material step, not fully determined in advance. Sometimes Kolika's Transgender Development Welfare Board membership card helps to push the police to take notice. Whatever the strategy, the goal is to create a safe space out of the natal family and a path to access to emotional and economic security. But the first order of care revolves around the person's mental and physical health. Soham elaborated:

> At the start, roti, kapra, makan [bread, clothes, shelter] and mental health support. Mental health support is crucial as the person who has left their home, with little or no chance of returning, maybe traumatised. Physical health is a simultaneous cause of concern, and support related to doctor's visits is extended. The person usually then thinks about how they want to live, and what kind of livelihood options may be available given their formal educational qualifications, if any, and other skills, or no market skills, etc.—we have such discussions with them. From there, we think about what kind of livelihood opportunities may be or can be created, like a small tea shop, depending entirely on what they imagine for themselves or gradually figuring out. If together we see that some 'skill development' is required, like knowing how to utilise a computer, we try to assist accordingly. Amid this, acquiring identification documents that are missing is necessary.

The effort is thus to take small but significant steps towards a liveable life, but with the person's consent and desires. We support but are cautious not to take the lead when the person is figuring out what they want to do with their life after they have left their natal family homes. At this stage, connecting with others who have left their natal family homes may create networks, some developing into kinship later. Simultaneously, assistance is provided in acquiring skills for livelihood options.

Survival and liveability are a collective affair, through moments of co-creating strategical paths that exceed beyond moments of leaving the natal family home to entering Sappho for Equality's temporary residence. Survival cannot work unless safety is assured. Reshmi

[14] Documentation is often needed in anticipation of any harm to the person or crisis intervention team members.

emphasized that the natal family often does not rest until they can connect with their young adult. So they take the help of the police or political party members to 'catch them', take them back to the family or even send them to rehabilitation centres under the pretext of mental unwellness. The person, thus, has to be kept safe at all times. Shreosi, in marking the rage of the natal family, said:

> If they manage to contact us, the family shows their rage, indicating that the person is their property. If we have 'touched their property' we will face their rage. Rage includes telling us, and sometimes with the help of the police, that the parents are crying, they care and are concerned, and this is considered a big thing. The nation is grieving as the parents are grieving! The natal family is in a race with us on the pretext of concern and care!

Safety is a collective concern for the crisis intervention team as well, as they, too, are at risk. We, therefore, are careful to only share Chetana's address and phone number with those who come in contact with us during the course of the intervention. So, while we are engaged in the person's survival, we are also ensuring our own survival.

7.3.3 Liveable Spaces

> Once the survivor comes here [temporary residence], it's a new place. On top of that, they have to find a livelihood while simultaneously building friendships; all of this is very difficult. An entirely new space, where they were and where they are now. All [survivors and us] are fighting for something.
>
> Reshmi

Survivors of natal family violence who come in contact with the crisis intervention team are searching for liveable spaces, to renew their living. However, this is not linear. Even when trying to make a new family, survivors are woven into emotional entanglements that are sometimes hard to maintain, reconfigure or break with their natal family. It is not easy to develop and sustain new friendships when people arrive with trauma, vulnerabilities, and insecurities. Thus, sharing and caring for each other, with anyone, in addition to a partner (with whom many times people escape violent homes) becomes an uphill task. Building newer relationships and friendships often takes a lot of time and space. Team members put in sustained effort to maintain physically safe spaces when people come with diverse emotional and physical hurt and injuries. Through their own histories, the crisis intervention team have arrived at a space where they lean more toward the idea of a 'chosen family'[15]. As Koyel explained:

> My personal imagination is to nurture a space of friendship, of a chosen family. The survivors have more complex emotions. Many are desperate to return to their natal family, expecting more understanding and acceptance… Sometimes they shed tears while looking at a photograph of an aunt, or a sister… There is sometimes an expectation that acceptance will follow if a livelihood is acquired. It is difficult for a survivor to forge new relationships with others. So we cannot expect they will be able to create [liveable spaces] quickly. A sense of trauma, loneliness, and helplessness works with a sense of relief.

On the one hand, there is a sense of distress in being violated, and on the other, the cutting of natal family ties brings in the sense of intense severance. Many survivors wish to return to their natal families if they could. Mourning the disconnection with the mother is common; even if some do not want to return, they may still want to know how their mother is doing. The natal family thus haunts, neither to fulfil nor disappear. A liveable space is never outside but constitutive of the natal family, perhaps until the person is engaged in surviving and finding one's own.

The temporary residence is a transitional space and a spatial entry point toward a life out

[15] The term 'families we choose' was first introduced in academia by Kath Weston in the early 1990s to talk about enduring relationalities that exist outside of blood and marriage ties. While 'chosen family' is used by many Sappho for Equality members, especially when desiring to indicate queer kinship, not all are comfortable with the term 'family' as it is built upon existing or new hierarchies.

of natal family violence. At a time, the residence has space for eight persons. Our organization assists with household infrastructure and groceries, but the everyday running of the temporary household is the responsibility of the residents. It is an emotionally intense space; the residents witness desperation, joy, mistrust and care, among its residents and about the team members and other volunteers of Sappho for Equality. It is too early to say if solid caregiving structures can emerge beyond this. It is a seed that holds potential and provides an anchor for survivors in the present. To expect survivors to visualize something larger when taking immediate care of their material and affective realities, such as means of regular caregiving, alternative living arrangements, and communal living structures, is to hoist our imaginations onto an already precarious condition. The way that heteronormative families, in their varying capacities of privilege, intend to or can acquire material resources, for survivors is an uphill task. As Shreosi explained:

> For queer trans persons, especially if they are from subordinate caste, class and religious backgrounds, it is anyhow difficult to get livelihood options, so building alternative spaces immediately after they are out of their natal family homes, especially one that is sustainable, is a huge challenge.

After a few months, some who have come to know each other in that residence have, after arranging for a livelihood, got together to rent a place. This is a nascent step towards another home, fraught with disharmonies and material interdependencies. Koyel explains that it is difficult to rebuild trust with a stranger, even when being a co-survivor, when the natal family, which is supposed to embody trust, is the primary cause of violation and trauma.

The team, while witnessing the intense effects of the survivors, holds open their own patches of liveable spaces, with their vulnerabilities and resources, through the various moments of intervention. They are often asked by survivors what they are to each other, and terms like *bandhu* (friend), *bhai* (sibling) are used to explain, with details of how that provides comfort and safety. The team shares aspects of their stories, their lives, and the minutiae of building relationalities, including friendships, romantic relationships, and relationships with no name. Sometimes, the existing class-caste differences with a few team members are stark; at other times, the differences form moments for alliances, with, as Soham says, 'humility'. These are small ways of enabling a world space without legal guarantees. Still, they carry a certain intentionality and imagination of contributing to a future that has destroyed caste-class normativity concerning social reproduction.

7.4 Conclusion

This chapter engaged with those queer and trans persons who are at the forefront of facilitating survivors of natal family violence out of their familial homes. The tales of crisis intervention shared in this essay are not to be read as rescue narratives; rather, we implore the readers to think about how natal families are predicated on contextualized heteronormative projects. Families do not work alone, but as scholars of postcolonial sexualities have demonstrated, they are imbricated with projects of community and nation-building.[16] While we have not presented a detail of this imbrication, we have alluded to the micro effects of this in queer and trans lives. Making an explicit connection is the occasion for another chapter; for now, let our act of co-sharing enable raising questions about the tendencies of natal families to preserve heterosexist and casteist practices, which have often been disregarded in the Indian context. Not every survivor can be expected to become an activist, says Ree, but there is a hope that gradually, some of them would, through their struggle to survive and live, be able to offer space to others. This is not an individual transactional process but is deeply embedded in the dynamics of power and resources. Crisis intervention is not a problem-solving exercise but a meeting point for different people trying to create a support

[16] For elaborations see Abbas and Ekine 2013; Puri 2022.

network and a liveable life. Hence, it is a modality of reciprocal solidarity in the face of violence. There will always be an excess to what we presented here; what is turned into an academic product for publication will not show the deep affects, including those around emotional labour and conflictual shared understanding, that are not amenable to conceptualization.

Acknowledgements The authors would like to acknowledge the assistance received from Ankana, Koyel Ghosh, Ranjita Biswas, Ree, Reshmi, Soham, and Sreyoshi in preparing this chapter.

References

Abbas H, Ekine S (eds) (2013) Queer African Reader. Pambazuka Press, Nairobi

Ambedkar BR (1916) Castes in India: their mechanism, genesis and development. Lecture presented at An Anthropology Seminar taught by Dr. A. A. Goldenweizer in Columbia University. http://www.columbia.edu/itc/mealac/pritchett/00ambedkar/txt_ambedkar_castes.html. Accessed 22nd Sept 2023

Apnon Ka Bahut Lagta Hai (Our Own Hurt Us the Most): Centering Familial Violence in the Lives of Queer and Trans Persons in the Marriage Equality Debates. A Report on the findings from a closed-door public hearing on April 1, 2023, Organised by PUCL and National Network of LBI women and Transpersons. http://orinam.net/content/wp-content/uploads/2023/04/JS_Report_23_04_23.pdf. Accessed 21st Sept 2023

Banerjea N, Browne K (2023) Liveable lives: living and surviving LGBTQ equalities in India and the UK. Bloomsbury Academic, UK

Banerjea N, Browne K, Bakshi L, Ghosh S (2016) Writing through activisms and academia: challenges and possibilities. In: The Routledge research companion to geographies of sex and sexualities, pp 175–184

Baudh S (2017) Invisibility of "other" Dalits and silence in the law. Biography 40(1):222–243

Benson K, Nagar R (2006) Collaboration as resistance? Reconsidering the processes, products, and possibilities of feminist oral history and ethnography. Gend Place Cult 13(5):581–592

Butler J (2004a) Undoing gender. Psychology Press

Butler J (2004b) Precarious life: the powers of mourning and violence. Verso, NY

Ellis C, Rawicki J (2013) Collaborative witnessing of durvival during the Holocaust: an exemplar of relational autoethnography. Qual Inq 19(5):366–380. https://doi.org/10.1177/1077800413479562

El Kotni M, Dixon LZ, Veronica M (2020) Introduction: Co-authorship as feminist writing and practice. Member Voices, Fieldsights, February 6. https://culanth.org/fieldsights/introduction-co-authorship-as-feminist-writing-and-practice

Engage EPW (2020) COVID-19, domestic abuse and violence: where do Indian women stand. EPW Engage

Freeden M (2017) Crisis? How is that a Crisis!?: Reflections on an overburdened word. Contrib Hist Concepts 12(2):12–28

Koselleck R, Richter MW (2006) Crisis. J Hist Ideas 67(2):357–400

Minai N, Shroff S (2019) Yaariyan, baithak, gupshup: queer feminist formations and the Global South. Kohl: J Body Gend Res 5(1):31–44

Patil SM (2021) Gender equity and COVID-19: Dalit standpoints. Econ Pol Wkly 56(11):1–10

Puri J (2022) Sexuality, state, and nation. In: Introducing the new sexuality studies. Routledge, pp 685–692

Sen R (2020) Stay home, stay safe: interrogating violence in the domestic sphere. Econ Polit Wkly 55

Tangjia WANG (2014) A philosophical analysis of the concept of crisis. Front Philos China 9(2):254–267

Tieri S, Ranjan A (2023) Covid-19, communalism, and Islamophobia: India facing the disease. Soc Identities, 1–17

Weston K (1997) Families we choose: lesbians, gays, kinship. Columbia University Press

8 Navigating Intimate Spaces of Violence: Global Legal Responses on Female Genital Mutilation/Cutting

Varsha Mohan

Abstract

International human rights law recognizes Female Genital Mutilation/Cutting (FGM/C) as a form of violence against women and girls and focuses on the urgency to eradicate this harmful cultural and religious practice through enactment of laws, supplemented by psychological and health support services. FGM/C operates within private-intimate spaces in the family and community. It is committed to control female sexuality and suppress female sexual desire. The violence of FGM/C is examined in this chapter as emanating and operating within patriarchal social structures and not simply as violence practiced and confined within the narrow walls of a specific culture or religion. The chapter presents an overview of the current global legal responses to address and eradicate FGM/C. In doing so, the chapter explores intimate spaces occupied by minor girls and their families, the tussle between individual, family, community, religion, culture and law and the challenges faced by States in navigating the complexity of rights regimes and criminal regimes to determine legal interventions that are likely to be effective, with the objective of assessing best practices emerging from several jurisdictions that have legislated on the subject.

Keywords

Cut · Female genitalia · Non-medical procedures · Control female sexuality · Criminalization · Child abuse · Private intimate spaces · International human rights law · Violence against women and girls · Family · Community · Religion · Culture · Tradition · Khatna · Khafd · Trauma

8.1 Introduction

I feel that God made my body perfect the way I was born. Then man robbed me, took away my power, and left me a cripple. My womanhood was stolen. If God had wanted those body parts missing, why did he create them?

I just pray that one day no woman will have to experience this pain. It will become a thing of the past. People will say "Did you hear, female genital mutilation has been outlawed in Somalia?" Then the next country, and the next, and so on, until the world is safe for all women. What a happy day that will be, and that's what

This chapter has benefited immensely from discussions with Prof Shama Banoo Hussain Abbasi, Assistant Professor, Jindal Global Law School, O.P. Jindal Global University, Sonipat, India.

V. Mohan (✉)
Jindal Global Law School, O.P. Jindal Global University, Sonipat, India
e-mail: Vmohan@jgu.edu.in

P. M. Anurag and S. Dwivedy (eds.), *Violence in Intimate Spaces*, Sustainable Development Goals Series, https://doi.org/10.1007/978-981-97-2657-8_8

I'm working toward. In'shallah, if God is willing, it will happen.—Waris Dirie, Desert Flower[1]

Though it is impossible to predict if the focus accorded to Female Genital Mutilation/Cutting (FGM/C) and its elimination as a goal under Sustainable Development Goals (SDG)[2] by the United Nations (UN) will provide an impetus towards its end in the world, it has, however, elevated the conversation on FGM/C to an area of critical concern, as the world moves forward with its articulation of FGM/C as a serious form of violence against women and children. The practice is an affront to the norm of equality and non-discrimination under international human rights law.[3] The World Health Organization (WHO) uses the umbrella term *Female Genital Mutilation* (FGM) to encompass *procedures that involve total or partial removal of female genitalia or other injuries to the female genital organs for non-medical reasons.*[4] Further, WHO has unambiguously stated that *female genital mutilation is universally unacceptable because it is an infringement on the physical and psychosexual integrity of women and girls and is a form of violence against them.*[5] The Office of the High Commissioner for Human Rights (OHCHR) estimates the number of girls and women that face FGM/C each year at three million, while one hundred and forty million have already been subjected to the practice,[6] calling it *one of the most widespread and systematic violations of the universal human right to personal integrity, abusing their physical and psychological integrity and damaging their lives irreversibly*. FGM/C has now been acknowledged and placed fairly and squarely as *a harmful traditional practice not based on any religion, medical or social promise*, but a practice that is a *reproductive health concern and a human rights violation that is an affront to human dignity.... The geographic reach of which extends well beyond those countries that have been historically considered to be its bastions.*[7] These harmful practices are based in unequal gender structures, while unequal access to education, wealth, health and employment are seen as critical factors that perpetrate the practice of FGM and deter efforts at eradication.[8] The UN Commission on the Status of Women during its 54th Session passed a resolution focusing on the urgency for member States to end FGM/C through enactment of legislation and to develop psychological, health support services to end this form of violence against women and girls.[9]

---

[1] Dirie and Miller (1998).

[2] Transforming Our World: The 2030 Agenda for Sustainable Development, A/RES/70/1 UN, sustainabledevelopment.un.org, SDG Goal 5 to '*achieve gender equality and empower all women and girls*' under 5.3 aims at eliminating '*all harmful practices, such as child, early and forced marriage and female genital mutilation*'. https://sustainabledevelopment.un.org/content/documents/21252030%20Agenda%20for%20Sustainable%20Development%20web.pdf.

[3] Under the Convention on Elimination of All Forms of Discrimination Against Women, 1979 (CEDAW), Part One Article 1–6; General Recommendation No 14 on Female Circumcision,1990; General Recommendation No19 of the CEDAW Committee Declaration on Elimination of Violence against Women, 1992, Article 2; and United National Convention of the Rights of the Child, 1989 (CRC), Articles 6 and 24(3).

[4] WHO, https://www.who.int/news-room/fact-sheets/detail/female-genital-mutilation. Accessed 28 September 2023.

[5] *Ibid. at 129.*

[6] https://www.ohchr.org/en/stories/2012/09/female-genital-mutilation-over-3-million-women-and-girls-are-risk.

[7] Ibid.

[8] Isha Dyfan, Chief of the Women and Gender Section, UN Human Rights Office. As a speaker on a panel discussion during the session of the Human Rights Council titled, '*Harmful Traditional Practices, Rhetoric or Reality*'.

[9] *Ending female genital mutilation*, The Commission on Status of Women, E/CN.6/2008/L.2/Rev. 1. *Recalling also general recommendation 14, concerning female circumcision, adopted by the Committee on the Elimination of Discrimination against Women at its ninth session; paragraphs 11, 20 and 24(l) of general recommendation 19, concerning violence against women, adopted by the Committee at its eleventh session; paragraphs 15(d) and 18 of general recommendation 24, concerning Article 12 of the Convention on the Elimination of All Forms of Discrimination against Women on women and health, adopted by the Committee at its twentieth session, and taking note of paragraphs 21, 35, and 51 of general recommendation 14 concerning Article*

WHO classifies FGM into four types—type 1 involves the removal of the prepuce and visible/sensitive part of the clitoral hood; type 2 is the total or partial removal of labia majora and minora; type 3 is infibulation by covering of the vaginal opening, removal and repositioning of the labia minora and majora and narrowing of the vaginal opening by creating of a covering seal; type 4 includes all other harmful procedures to the female genitalia for *non-medical purposes,* for example, pricking, incising, piercing, scraping and cauterization. Certain communities have indicated that they practice 'only' type 1 which they 'claim' as being the least invasive, and thus, undeserving of the negative focus drawn to it. The chapter is firmly grounded in the understanding and construction of all forms of FGM/C as an 'act' intended to control female sexuality and curb female sexual desire. FGM/C operates within patriarchal notions of male dominance and female subordination and strict rules of paternity. The principal reason is the suppression of sexual desire to ensure that the girl child remains chaste during the passage between adolescence and marriage and then to ensure chastity after marriage. This is the only way to keep her an 'honorable woman.' FGM/C of every type is a form of 'child abuse' as it is performed on the body of minor girls and women and there can be no justification of this harmful practice.

Societies that practice FGM/C are ever evolving, they are not homogenous or uniform. These debates take place at the community, local, national, and international levels and are mostly spearheaded by non-government organizations or community-based efforts. Governments of States have responded to these voices by initiating action using different approaches, the outcome of State response is therefore variable. Diverse perspectives on FGM/C and its cultural origins have strengthened responses by way of special enactments on FGM/C, or by incorporating measures within existing legal frameworks. The States that have legal provisions addressing FGM/C have done so by categorizing the practice as a crime against bodily integrity and violence on woman and children. Laws in most States approach FGM/C as a serious crime, thereby negating the impact of culture, tradition or religion as possible justifications. However, keeping in mind that the practice operates within cultural, geographical or religious sensibilities, criminalization through laws, while an essential first step, may not be an adequate measure in itself to eradicate the practice.

The very nature of FGM/C ensures that this form of violence operates strictly within the confines of the family and community. The principal 'actors' are therefore drawn from these private-intimate spaces. *Who are these actors that ensure the perpetration and execution of FGM/C?* Most commonly they are the immediate and extended family, a professional cutter, the clergy/imam and sometimes medical professionals. The victims/survivors of FGM/C are principally minor girls. The practice is shrouded

12 of the International Covenant on Economic, Social and Cultural Rights11 adopted by the Committee on Economic, Social and Cultural Rights at its twenty second session, Recognizing that female genital mutilation violates, and impairs or nullifies the enjoyment of the human rights of women and girls, Recognizing also that female genital mutilation is an irreparable, irreversible abuse that affects one hundred to one hundred and forty million women and girls alive today, and that each year a further three million girls are at risk of undergoing the procedure. Reaffirming that harmful traditional or customary practices, including female genital mutilation, constitute a serious threat to the health of women and girls, including their psychological, sexual and reproductive health, which can increase their vulnerability to HIV and may have adverse obstetric and prenatal outcomes as well as fatal consequences, and that the abandonment of this harmful practice can be achieved only as a result of a comprehensive movement that involves all public and private stakeholders in society, Recognizing that negative discriminatory stereotypical attitudes and behaviours have direct implications for the status and treatment of girls and that such negative stereotypes impede the implementation of legislative and normative frameworks that guarantee gender equality and prohibit discrimination on the basis of sex; https://www.un.org/womenwatch/daw/beijing15/outcomes/crp/crp10e.pdf.

in secrecy, there is little or no penetrability into the community and family spaces. It is critical to note that in all cases the voices against FGM/C are survivor-led movements.[10] What are the voices of these *reformists*[11] saying? *How can the actors be stopped?*

The challenge in legislating on religious, cultural and traditional practice juxtaposed with parental rights to ensure protection of minor girls is that the law must enter private spaces; the home and the community. This poses challenges as criminal law has strict evidentiary rules, the task of holding private actors responsible is daunting since it involves not just entering intimate spaces but also poses the dilemma in prosecuting parents and close family and community for inflicting harm on children who they have the responsibility of protecting and nurturing. While law may take its course and prosecution can bring the actors to the doorstep of justice, what happens next? The State at this point must assume the role of *parens patriae*[12] to ensure that the child at risk or a child who has been subjected to FGM/C must be removed from the violent space and provide child protection and bring them under the social welfare process. The criticality and sensitivity required in empathizing with the position of parents[13] and family within the context of fear of stigma and ostracization exerted by their community and religion, cannot be overemphasized. The violence of FGM/C is examined in this chapter as emanating and operating within patriarchal social structures and not simply as violence practiced and confined within the narrow walls of a specific culture or religion.

With this understanding, the chapter will engage and focus on addressing the following: the 'spaces' and 'relationships' within which the violence takes place and the *legal responses* from several jurisdictions across the world. In doing so the chapter explores the violence tied to the act of FGM/C in intimate spaces occupied by minor girls and their families within the limited context of the Indian experience of FGM/C and its practice among Bohra Muslims in India. This intimate space is a religious-cultural landscape, complicated by family ties between the people who practice FGM/C and the young girls who are *cut*.[14] As law navigates this intimate space, tussle between individual, family, community, religion and culture can be anticipated. The chapter then delves into the critical challenges that States' face in navigating both, the intricacies of rights regimes and criminal regimes to ascertain what form of legal intervention is likely to be effective in eradicating the practice. The objective is to indicate best practice emerging from these jurisdictions that can provide direction for States that are yet to legislate on the subject.

8.2 Navigating Spaces of Violence: Family, Community, Relationships and Trauma

In 2017, a show titled *Spotlight: Horror of Female Genital Cutting*,[15](*Spotlight*) curated by Indian journalist and media personality Barkha Dutt brought to the fore the practice of FGM/C

[10] Blank (2021).

[11] Ibid.

[12] The doctrine of *parens patriae* states that a state or court has a paternal and protective role over its citizens or others subject to its jurisdiction. This doctrine is also one in which all orphans, dependent children and persons deemed incompetent are within the special protection and under the control of the state. This doctrine narrowly is also used in juvenile justice cases where the state is given the power to intervene and act for the welfare of the child thus replacing the negligent parent or guardian.

[13] The fear of community/religious leaders and the practice of excommunication in some cases.

[14] '*the cut*' has been used interchangeably with FGM/C in this chapter.

[15] *We the Women, Horror of Female Genital Cutting*.2017. https://youtu.be/WKS_R-9th-10th2017,zBLE?si=praHDPwK09fGd8JD. Accessed 27 Nov 2023. The interview referenced was conducted for *We the Women*, in collaboration with UN Women.

and its prevalence in India, specifically among the Bohra Muslim community. The show 'spotlighted' individual campaigners against FMG/C from this community.[16] At the start of the show it was clarified that "*religious orthodoxy of all faiths militates against women*," and that the show does not intend to ostracize a specific religion, but is an effort to project the courage of women who have raised their voice against the practice. The voices on the show belonged to individual survivors and those who are spearheading survivor-led movements against FGM/C in India. This section of the chapter is based on the understanding of spaces of violence, complex relationships and trauma of FGM/C shared through the rich narratives of young girls and women on this show '*Spotlight*'. While this show was about the specific regressive practice of FGM/C against women from one community in India, it must be acknowledged that *Bohra community is one of the most cultured and educated* and that women from this community have achieved much in their professional lives.[17]

The women on the show report that the 'cutting' is almost always conducted in unhygienic conditions by midwives and not doctors. The process and its execution are shrouded in secrecy and deception. One of the survivors starts her story by explaining that her grandmother tricked her into the *khatna*[18] procedure under the pretense that they were going to buy chocolates.[19] The survivor then describes with disbelief, how her grandmother led her into a dark and dingy room where a lady was waiting, and this lady asked her to spread her legs. She says, "*My grandmother was there, and she was watching…*," clearly pointing to how the person she trusted until then, was complicit in the pain and trauma caused to her. The stories of all survivors indicate that the practice is conducted surreptitiously by a woman, clearly not trained in medical procedures, in unhygienic, harmful conditions. Girls are 'cut' around 7 years of age, but the real impact of FGM/C is felt by them later, as young women. The women who facilitate this practice believe it to be a necessary *rite of passage for young girls.* While the experience of *khatna* relates to a single traumatic incident in their childhood, all survivors agreed that its impact lasts a lifetime.

A woman shares that she and her cousin were taken by her mother to a neighbours' house for the 'cut' and she was *told that it is like an injection.* After the procedure the mother's response to the pain was a simple "*it will get better.*" The pain during the procedure, however, was only '*the memory*'; after marriage most women's first sexual intercourse was reported to be excruciatingly painful. Both the wife and the husband feel the impact, their sex life is not enjoyable, and this spills over to all aspects of their marital wellbeing. She expresses surprise that despite this, she got pregnant. After the birth of her child, she started researching on FGM/C and discovered that a neurological trigger follows *khatna*, while her mother thought of this as a 'simple ritual'. The feeling of betrayal is common among all survivors. The reasoning given by the mothers is that this is done to keep a girl *pure*. The woman question: *what is purity?* She and her husband are both suffering and struggling to work it out between them till this day.

---

[16] In India, it is believed that this is not only a Bohra issue, it is happening all over India and there is evidence of the practice in Kerala. In India it mostly prevalent in Dawoodi Bohra, Alvi Bohra, Suleimani Bohra and a few other Sunni sub-sects of Kerala where the practice is referred to as 'Khatna' or 'Khafz/Khafd'.

[17] This ties in and exemplifies the context that all gender-based violence emanates from patriarchal structures and is not based on parameters such as education or prosperity. Patriarchy as a force shadows every parameter of progress made by women in all communities everywhere. '*all communities have their dark secrets*'.

[18] *We the Women, Horror of female genital cutting*.2017. https://youtu.be/WKS_R_-zBLE?si=praHDPwK09fGd8JD. Accessed 27 Nov 2023. The interview referenced was conducted for *We the Women*, in collaboration with UN Women.

[19] *Ibid.*

One of the expert panelists in the show, Insia Dariwala is a founding member of Sahiyo.[20] She says that during their work with FGM/C survivors they discovered that "*some survivors had intimacy issues and others had trust issues*." She stated, "*If there is one thing I could talk about, it is the loss of trust in the people who you have trusted the most, your mother, your grandmother, your aunts, these are women you have grown up with, so betrayal of trust is number one on the list [of traumas]*."[21] Her sister had a botched FGM/C following which her mother refused to let the second daughter go through *khatna*. Insia is the second daughter who is 'the uncut'[22]sister. She shares her trauma with 'survivor's guilt', borne out of the fact that her sister went through it and she did not have to. She says, "*you are damned if you do, damned if you don't*" and that being 'uncut' has its own associated trauma within the community. "*Since khatna is performed in India and in most parts of the world on minor girls, what we are dealing with here is a child's body*." Insia states that FGM/C is therefore a child's right issue and must be addressed as child sexual abuse. It is critical that religion[23] be kept out of this serious violation.

The 2017 Sahiyo report on online survey conducted worldwide, shows that 80% of the responders were subjected to *khatna* as children.[24] Among the survey respondents, 74% were 'cut' by an untrained traditional cutter (a Dawoodi Bohra woman from low-income family) and only 15% were 'cut' by a health professional. The decision to 'cut' daughters was made by mothers. Religious leaders heavily influenced this decision.[25] Among reasons used to justify this conduct by community members, the most common was *religious purposes, maintaining traditions, dampening sexual desire, and feminine hygiene*.[26]

The stories on the show are different from stories that emerged in the United States (US) around the same time. In 2017, an emergency doctor was arrested for charges under *18 U.S.C. 116*[27] in Detroit for conducting FGM/C on 6- to 8-year-old girls.[28] In these cases, the parents of the survivors travelled interstate, and the children believed that they were seeing the doctor because *their tummies hurt*.[29] The commonality is the role played by close family members in perpetuating the act of violence, the one glaring difference is the *space*—doctor's clinic in the US as against the community cutter's home in India. In a study conducted in Pakistan, a survivor from the Pakistani Bohra community who also continued the practice on her daughter, described the procedure as a religious obligation performed to keep *young girls on the right path* and to restrict their desires.[30] This highly educated Pakistani woman candidly discusses the practice of Khafd,[31] and adds, "*It is recommended to us by those who have our best interests at heart....it is a very minimal procedure which doesn't harm anyone, so why not?*".[32]

[20] 'Sahiyo is an organized, informed forum within the community [to] drive a movement to bring an end to khatna'. The reports from this organization has been utilized throughout this chapter. They can be accessed on www.sahiyo.org. Accessed 27 Nov 2023.

[21] *Insia Dariwala on the show.*

[22] The Un-Cut, Insia Dariwala, www.Sahiyo.com/2016/08/29/the-un-cut/.

[23] *Insia Dariwala on the show.*

[24] Taher (2017).

[25] *Ibid* at 57.

[26] *Ibid.*

[27] US federal law that criminalises FGM/C.

[28] *U.S. v. Jumana Nagarwala*, Criminal No. 17-CR-20274.

[29] Sahiyo, Detroit Arrest: It is time for the Bohras to get serious about ending Female Genital Cutting, https://sahiyo.com/2017/04/14/detroit-arrest-it-is-time-for-bohras-to-get-serious-about-ending-female-genital-cutting/. Accessed 27 Nov 2023. *US v. Jumana Nagarwala*, Criminal No. 17-CR-20274.

[30] Demystifying the practice of khafd in the Dawoodi Bohra community: A commentary on the WeSpeakOut report from India, ANIKA KHAN, SUALEHA SIDDIQ SHEKHANI, AAMIR JAFAREY, Indian Journal of Medical Ethics Vol IV No 1 January–March 2019, p. 66.

[31] Used interchangeably with Khatna and FGM/C.

[32] *Ibid.*

Loss of trust and a deep sense of betrayal is the fundamental harm common to all stories shared on the show *Spotlight*. The practice and the reasoning make *sexuality a bad thing*. The practice spoils relationships especially between mother, daughter and other female relatives. "*Why do women who have gone through this, an experience that could never have been pleasant, enforce it on their daughters*?" The women on '*Spotlight*' say that their mothers and other relatives are brainwashed by the community and its leaders. Another glaring feature of FGM/C is that the men are never involved, they do not even speak about it, while some women share that they feel that the men in their family do not even know about it. This practice is entirely perpetuated *from women to women*. Internalized patriarchy could explain this.[33] Additionally, there is *internalized peer pressure*. Women share that there is a code name (highlighting the secrecy about it), when women ask mothers of girls, "*are her ears pierced*?" The non-performance of this ritual is met with ostracization. This is also believed to be a necessary condition for getting married, 'not cut' is a disqualification. The practice of FGM/C is deeply rooted in the psyche of people, if a young girl '*runs away*', people will say it was because she was not 'cut'. While there are mothers who do not want to inflict *khatna* on their daughters, to escape disapproval they often lie to others that their girls are 'cut'. Male circumcision in Muslim communities was also discussed during the show. It was noted that while it is not good for either *because no ones' genitals should be touched*,[34] the two are very different.

A study conducted in United Kingdom (UK) with a small group of participants aimed at identifying: '*who to blame*',[35] revealed that the blame shifted between the known figures—parents, grandparents and the unknown figures—'the cutters'. It was easier to direct anger and aggression towards 'cutters' rather than towards one's close family. In some cases, the blame was directed at oneself.[36] In countries where cutting is the norm, 'uncut' girls faced social ostracization, while in countries to which they migrated, FGM/C was treated as a well-guarded secret.[37] In some cases, women did not want to identify parents as abusers and instead found solace in the fact that it was culture that was responsible. The pressure from extended family networks and communities is also a defining element of this practice. Where parents disapproved of the practice, extended families coerce them into following the *group law* so they could be part of the intimate social structure.[38] Some of these experiences of FGM/C are from the African context.

That this trauma continues[39] needs to be highlighted, also that *the practice is continuing in this day and age and that this is not about what happened twenty years back*.[40] It is an issue of harm to children.[41] Sahiyo believes in the power of storytelling in the hope that mothers' who are listening to the stories of trauma might empathize.[42] Mothers have referred to the clitoris as the '*lump of flesh*'—'*haram ki boti*' and they treat it like it is not supposed to be inside you.[43]

33 A woman in the audience said there are enough women who live healthy sexual lives. It is not sexual control—If it was harmful, we would not do it! If it's health, WHY HIDE? One of the girls responded by asking, why sexualize a child at the age of 7?

34 Insia Dariwala.

35 Newton and Glover (2022).

36 Ibid at 12.

37 Ibid at 13.

38 Koukoui et al. (2017).

39 Case of a girl child of a botched circumcision where she bled all night, she received 7 stiches to stop the bleeding. The child suffers from trauma even today. She checks bags of people who visit her home just to check if they are carrying blades or syringes.

40 Insia Dariwala.

41 *The argument that it is not mutilation, it's a nick. Even a nick could go wrong*.

42 Insia Dariwala.

43 See: Waris Dirie, n. 3.

The community where violence resides can be best understood through women's compelling stories. In the case of Bohra Muslims in India, religion is the thread that holds families together; '*relationships*' are thus built on religion. Mothers have an obligation towards the religion, as do other conservative practitioners. As Durkheim outlined in the *Sociology of Religions,*[44] religion often acts as a source of solidarity and identification for individuals in a society. As a minority community in India, religion builds this organic solidarity network for Bohra families. Being ostracized from this community could be a heavy price to pay. This explains to an extent, the pressure felt by Bohra families to adhere to the religious norm of cutting their daughters. These sentiments were shared by women on the show. Some women talk about avoiding geographical spaces altogether to avoid the violence.[45] In cases among African opponents of this practice, several parents had decided to not take their children to Africa on vacation, fearing interference from their community. One of the interviewees reported that 'uncut daughters' are forcefully taken and 'cut' if they were to visit their native country.[46]

A space that removes from within itself the sexuality of a woman, by nipping it in the bud at the age of 7 is a space that denies representation to such desires. The space that is defined by such ideas is therefore likely to create beliefs around sexuality and desire that potentially infringe on individual autonomy.[47] The discourse of FGM/C as violence in intimate spaces brings together culture, tradition within the context of community. Women in these setups play the role of conformists and reformists—obligers and resisters. The resisters face pressure not just from their immediate family, but also from this society created by religious institutions. The obligers live in a world of physical and emotional pain due to the act of 'cutting', which is the price to pay for being ideal representatives of their religion. The elements of 'individual autonomy' and 'bodily integrity' will be explored in the next section in analysing laws on FGM/C.

8.3 Legal Spaces Across Nations: Addressing FGM/C Under Domestic Laws

In the previous section, the chapter explores intimate spaces and relationships of the 'cut child' with the mother, familial relatives, the community and related trauma. This section examines *legal approaches* in responding and addressing FGM/C from several jurisdictions that have legal provisions aimed at eradicating the practice of FGM/C and protect victims. By 2020, 28 countries in Africa had enacted specific laws or added provisions on FGM/C under existing penal laws. 16 European countries, the UK, US, Canada, Australia, New Zealand; in the Middle- East- Iraqi Kurdistan and Oman had laws addressing FGM/C.[48] Migration is known to change attitudes towards social and cultural norms.[49] It can significantly alter the dynamic of politics and compel society to change its views and beliefs. Most States in Africa associate FGM/C with tradition and culture and not just with religion.

Not a single State in Asia or Latin America has legal provisions directly addressing FGM/C, this includes India. In 2018, the Supreme Court of India (SC) began hearing a petition[50] seeking the enactment of law for eradication of the practice of FGM/C in India. The petition filed

[44] *See generally* Pickering, W.S.F.1984. Durkheim's Sociology of Religion: Themes and Theories, The Lutterworth Press, James Clarke & Co Ltd, https://doi.org/10.2307/j.ctt1cgf6sv.

[45] Koukoui et al. (2017).

[46] Ibid.

[47] Colomina (1996). "But as the dictionary argues, admission is also a question of acknowledging, recognizing, accepting as valid. To be admitted is to be represented. And space is, after all, a form of representation.".

[48] Equality Now Report, FGM A Global Picture, 2020. www.equalitynow.org/fgm-a-global-picture/.

[49] Mesplé-Somps (2016).

[50] *Sunita Tiwari v. Union of India*, Civil Writ No. 286 of 2017. The matter has been referred to a larger bench.

by child rights advocate Sunita Tiwari invokes questions surrounding the violation of Dawoodi Bohra women's *right to equality, privacy, and personal liberty* under the Constitution of India and under the International Human Rights law framework. The petitioner prays that FGM/C should be included as an offence under the Indian Penal Code, 1860 (IPC) and until such time, appropriate directions should be issued to the police to undertake immediate investigation when complaints relating to this inhuman act are filed. The Indian State has consistently refused to acknowledge the prevalence of this practice in India.[51] The written affidavit filed by the Union of India (UOI) in this case, proclaimed that no official data or study supports the existence of FGM/C in India.[52] The *Dawoodi Bohra Women's Association for Religious Freedom* (DBWRF) opposed this petition[53] for criminalizing FGM/C by claiming it as an *essential religious practice*[54] that courts cannot interfere with[55] under the Constitutional Right to Freedom of Religion.[56] The lawyer representing the community members, also opposing the petition stated that in India, the Bohra community practices type 1 FGM/C procedure of the WHO categorization, arguing that this was a *de minimis procedure* and thus cannot be characterized as a human rights violation.[57] Additionally, arguments against the use of the word 'mutilation' to describe the practice by Bohra community in India were presented, stating that the act was only a *nick on the prepuce* and must therefore be differentiated from *extreme forms* of FGM/C practiced in African countries.[58] It must be noted that India is not included under the UN list of countries affected by FGM/C since the prevalence of this practice received little to no attention, until 2012 when, cases against the Bohra community members began to surface in the US[59] and Australia.[60] In India, there is an opinion, though it is contested, that a complaint of FGM/C can be filed under the IPC under Sections 319–326 as varying degrees of hurt and grievous hurt.[61] Additionally, Section 3[62] of the

[51] "The Minister for Women and Child Development, Maneka Gandhi in May 2017, publicly announced the government's intention to pass a law banning FGM/C if the community did not voluntarily abandon the practice. No headway has been made since nor is there any political interest in pursuing such a law. On the contrary, on December 29, 2017, the Ministry of Women and Child Development responded to an inquiry by the Supreme Court (in a Public Interest Litigation case on FGM/C in India) stating that "there is no official data or study which supports the existence of FGM/C in India." *See also*, Lawyer's Collective (2017)

[52] Anantarayan et al. (2018).

[53] Written submissions by senior advocate Abishek Manu Singhvi in Sunita Tiwari v. Union of India.

[54] The essential practices test is used to establish judicially if a practice or ritual is 'essential' or critical to the survival and practice of the religion.

[55] Rina Chandran, No evidence of FGM, India government tells court, appalling activists, Thomas Reuters (November 20, 2018) available at https://www.reuters.com/article/us-india-women-religion/no-evidence-of-fgm-india-government-tells-court-appalling-activists-idUSKBN1EN0QB.

[56] Article 25 Freedom of Religion, Constitution of India: Article 25(1) *Subject to public order, morality and health and to the other provisions of this Part, all persons are equally entitled to freedom of conscience and the right freely to profess, practice and propagate religion. (2) Nothing in this article shall affect the operation of any existing law or prevent the State from making any law(a) regulating or restricting any economic, financial, political or other secular activity which may be associated with religious practice; (b) providing for social welfare and reform or the throwing open of Hindu religious institutions of a public character to all classes sections of Hindus.*

[57] Written submissions by senior advocate Abishek Manu Singhvi in Sunita Tiwari v. Union of India.

[58] *Ibid.*

[59] *U.S. v. Jumana Nagarwala*, Criminal No. 17-CR-20274.

[60] *The Queen v. A2, Kubra, and Vaziri,* [2019] HCA 35.

[61] The former Central Bureau of Investigation (CBI) noted that while FGM/C is not included as a specific offence under IPC the police are obligated to register a case under Section 326 of IPC.

[62] Section 3 POCSO: *person is said to commit "penetrative sexual assault" if—(a) he penetrates his penis, to any extent, into the vagina, mouth, urethra or anus of a child or makes the child to do so with him or any other person; or (b) he inserts, to any extent, any object or a part of the body, not being the penis, into the vagina, the urethra or anus of the child or makes the child to do so*

Protection of Children from Sexual Offences Act 2012 (POCSO)[63] could be extended to cover cases of FGM/C since the provision under this section states a "*sharp object inserted into the vagina of a child*."[64] These arguments are not adequate, since they do not completely capture the harm caused by violence committed behind doors by parents or relatives, in addressing this serious violation against women and children in India, hence the demand for a special law addressing FGM/C in India.

The petitioners' position is that FGM/C is not a part of Islam since it finds no mention anywhere in the Holy Quran and even if it did, FGM/C is against *public order, morality and health* and hence can never be protected under the right to practice religion.[65] It constitutes an invasion of the body of a minor girl and violates Article 21 Right to Life,[66] a life with dignity and the right to enjoyment of all faculties including the right to family life, right to sexuality. Invasion of the body without consent violates provisions of IPC and cannot be claimed as protected under Freedom of Religion. The practice therefore cannot qualify as an 'essential practice'[67] which is the hallmark of the test for the constitutional right to religion. Critically, religious leaders of the Dawoodi Bohra community have advised Bohras living in Western countries in the strictest terms, to not practice *Khafz*[68] in States where FGM/C attracts criminality under the laws of these States. The declaration of the Anjuman-e-Burhani in Sydney received much attention.[69] Additionally, United Nations Population Fund (UNFPA) and WHO have noted that though there is evidence of the practice of FGM/C among Christians, Jews and Muslims; none of the holy texts of any of these religions prescribe FGM/C and that the practice pre-dates both Christianity and Islam. This clearly establishes that the religious leaders of the Bohra community themselves do not view this as an 'essential practice'.[70]

In Australia, FGM/C is criminalized through state and territory laws. All the states in Australia have passed criminal laws prohibiting FGM/C.[71] These laws can be applied in an

with him or any other person; or(c) he manipulates any part of the body of the child so as to cause penetration into the vagina, urethra, anus or any part of the body of the child or makes the child to do so with him or any other person; or (d) he applies his mouth to the penis, vagina, anus, urethra of the child or makes the child to do so to such person or any other person.

[63] POCSO, 2012, *The Act protect children from offences of sexual assault, sexual harassment and pornography and provide for establishment of Special Courts for trial of such offences and for matters connected therewith or incidental thereto.* https://wcd.nic.in/sites/default/files/POCSO%20Act%2C%202012.pdf.

[64] Ibid.

[65] Article 25(1): *Subject to public order, morality and health and to the other provisions of this Part, all persons are equally entitled to freedom of conscience and the right freely to profess, practice and propagate religion.*

[66] *Constitution of India.*

[67] *The essential practices test is used to establish judicially if a practice or ritual is 'essential' or critical to the survival and practice of the religion.*

[68] In countries such as Sydney, Washington, Tampa, New York, Bakersfield, London, Melbourne, Toronto, San Jose, Mississauga, Canada, Orange County, San Diego, Vancouver, Los Angeles, Boston, Miami and Detroit.

[69] Sahiyo (2016). Notices by Sydney, Melbourne and London's Anjuman-e-Burhani Trusts on 'Khafd' (Khatna) or Female Genital Cutting, https://sahiyo.com/2016/03/08/notices-by-sydney-melbourne-and-londons-anjuman-e-burhani-trusts-on-khafd-khatna-or-female-genital-cutting/. Accessed: 6 December 2023.

[70] New South Wales Supreme Court in the R v. A2; R v. KM; R v. Vaziri (No. 2) ([2015] NSWSC 1221): *The report of the Family Law Council notes that—[t]here is little doubt that female genital mutilation preceded Islam in Africa and it is likely that when Islam entered Africa the practice became linked with the new religion. It is also interesting to note that when Islam entered Asian countries through Arabia or Iran, it did not bring female genital mutilation with it, but when it was imported to Asia through Nile Valley cultures, female genital mutilation was a part of it. An example is the Daudi Bohra of India, a group which practises female genital mutilation and which was established by an Egyptian-based sect of Islam.*

[71] Crimes Act 1900 (ACT) s73-77; Crimes Act 1900 (NSW) s45; Criminal Code Act (NT) s186A-186D; Criminal Code 1899 (Qld) s323A-323B; Criminal Law Consolidation Act 1935 (SA) s33-33B; Crimes Act 1958 (Vic) s32-34A; Criminal Code Act 1924 (Tas) s178A, 178B, s389; The Criminal Code (WA) s306.

extraterritorial manner, with the intent to protect Australian citizens[72] abroad from being subjected to FGM/C in States where the practice is not 'illegal'.[73] A 1994 report[74] of the Victorian state government[75] noted the need for FGM/C laws after its meetings with women victims. The report quotes studies that indicate that criminalization can often lead to an increased risk of racist attacks on migrant women victims of FGM/C and this results in their children being denied medical care for fear of law enforcement authorities taking adverse action against the migrant women and their families. This fear discourages these women from approaching medical services for themselves and their families. The report amplifies voices and concerns of the migrant women victims who support the criminalization of FGM/C despite fear of repercussions under the law.[76] It further notes how authorities working on the criminalization of FGM/C must also focus on building *child protective services* to ensure protection of minor girls who are vulnerable. FGM/C is now recognized as physical abuse under child protection laws in Australia and any child who has undergone FGM/C or is at risk, can seek protection.[77] Medical professionals must report mandatorily if they suspect that a child is in danger. A survey conducted in Australia reported that at least 13 children were under child protection services related to FGM/C.[78] These reports highlight the significance of criminalization of FGM/C in Australia due to the high influx of migrant communities that practice FGM/C.

Despite criminalization of FGM/C in Australia since several years, it was only in 2015 that a court in Australia prosecuted three people from the Dawoodi Bohra community for practising FGM/C.[79] The case, commonly referred to as *Vaziri and Magennis* changed the landscape of the practice of FGM/C or *Khafz* in Australia and was the first case of its kind. The parties were a former midwife (Magennis), the imam (Vaziri) and the mother of two girls.[80] The question in this case was whether the act of *Khatna* involved any damage or cutting that could constitute mutilation as per the law.[81] Initially, the medical examiners and the independent forensic experts engaged by the prosecution could not provide any evidence of injury as the *nick to the clitoral hood* was not visibly damaged.[82] However, the jury accepted that the injury had occurred. The Supreme Court of New South Wales (NSW) found the three accused guilty of

[72] Irrespective of their countries of origin, they come under the preview of the law of the nation of their nationality.

[73] Attorney general's department (2013).

[74] Queensland Law Reform Commission, 1994, Female Genital Mutilation Draft No. 42,

[75] The state of Victoria in Australia.

[76] Ibid at 8.

[77] *See generally* Zurynski et al. (2017).

[78] Ibid at 513.

[79] *R v A2; R v KM; R v Vaziri* (No. 2) (2015) NSWSC 1221.

[80] The father was a doctor, he was not convicted, even though the evidence gathered by tapping his phone helped the police; Awford (2016).

[81] Crimes (Female Genital Mutilation) Amendment Act 1994 (NSW) *"45. (1) A person who: (a) excises, infibulates or otherwise mutilates the whole or any part of the labia majora or labia minora or clitoris of another person; or (b) aids, abets, counsels or procures a person to perform any of those acts on another person, is liable to penal servitude for 7 years. (2) An offence is committed against this section even if one or more of the acts constituting the offence occurred outside New South Wales if the person mutilated by or because of the acts is ordinarily resident in the State*".

[82] Dr. Susan Marks from the Child Protection Unit at Westmead Children's Hospital. Dr. Marks was unable to confirm or deny whether the girls had been circumcised. She has reported that she cannot exclude that a Type 1a or Type 4 FGM procedure (under the World Health Organisation ("WHO") guidelines) had been conducted, as she could not visualise the head of the clitoris on either child. Dr. Marks asserts that if there had been a small cut to the head of the clitoris, it would have been painful at the time, but would have healed in 3–5 days. She also confirmed that any cut or nick to the clitoris would include, at the very minimum, the removal of skin cells. Dr. Marks said that the procedures said to have been carried out on C1 and C2 could have included: (a) a cut or nick to any part of the clitoris, including the clitoral hood (prepuce), clitoral head (glans), including pricking or piercing, and/or (b) the removal of part of the clitoral head (glans).

mutilation. This was overturned in 2018 by the NSW Criminal Court of Appeal. It was observed that the injury was not severe, the judgment stated that the body part in question should *be irreparably damaged* for it to constitute *mutilation*.[83] In 2019, the prosecution appealed this judgement to the High Court (HC) of Australia. The Court deemed the nick as mutilation after taking into consideration the categorization of 'nicking' as type IV FGM/C by WHO and the Family Law Council's Female Genital Mutilation: A Report to the Attorney General (which references Walker's novel).[84] The HC charged the mother of the girls and Magennis for *mutilating the clitoris* of each of the complainants. The Imam was found guilty on two counts for acting as an accessory to the offence. The HC found that both accused were a *party to a joint criminal enterprise to perform a ceremony called Khatna*. The HC stated that contrary to what the defence was trying to establish as *merely ritualistic*, [t] *he word 'mutilate' in the context of female genital mutilation means to injure to any extent…., and that the term 'clitoris … includes the clitoral hood or prepuce*.[85]

The evidence gathering in this case showcased methods used by the authorities to penetrate the spaces occupied by the minority community. The two cut girls provided precise details of the FGM performed on them and their mental state during the entire procedure. Some scholars have remarked how the entire exercise bordered on extreme, where cars, phones, and the houses of the accused were tapped, conversations were recorded, and community members were interviewed.[86] The HC was strict in disallowing 'medically accepted' exceptions that permit nicking/cutting. Medical professionals are inevitably involved in practice of FGM/C. In the *Vaziri-Magennis* case, the father who is a doctor, created the environment for the FGM/C to take place. Even though his direct involvement was later questioned, it showed that the midwife and mother were confident to 'cut' because of the father's presence. This case shows that criminal law can enter private spaces where required. This is also true for domestic violence and other forms of intimate violence in most parts of the world. There are certain medical exceptions to performing surgery on a woman which are sometimes cosmetic, like Labiaplasty, but there are clear differentiations between medically necessary surgeries and FGM/C.

In an interview conducted in Australia with 11 midwives,[87] most of them expressed a lack of knowledge about the conduct of the practice of FGM/C. They were unaware of the care necessary for patients who had been infibulated, especially during the process of birthing. With increased migration into Australia, healthcare providers might be the first responders if complications during FGM/C arise. Some doctors also sutured infibulated vulva after the women give birth, which is also illegal in the country.[88] Midwives also usually discover or witness the

[83] *A2 v R; Magennis v R; Vaziri v R* [2018] NSWCCA 174.

[84] Rogers (2022); Alice Walkers book 'Possessing the Secret of Joy' and subsequent documentary' Warrior Marks' is about a woman's struggle recuperating from the emotional and physical trauma caused by circumcision, https://www.si.edu/object/siris_sil_1107575.

[85] R v A2; R v Magennis; R v Vaziri (2019) HCA 35.

[86] Rogers (2016).

[87] Ogunsiji (2015).

[88] This is also practised outside the norm of FGM/C and is called a 'husband stitch' where doctors, mostly without consent from the woman after childbirth, unnecessarily suture her vaginal tear to make it tighter for the husband's pleasure. It is ethically (for the lack of consent) and legally dubious, this practice is also a gross violation of bodily autonomy that objectifies women's bodies solely for male sexual pleasure and for procreation. The practice is deeply patriarchal as it invisiblizes the woman's sexuality and bodily autonomy. A very intact, terrifying description can be found in Carmen Machado's short story by the same name '*The Husband Stitch*'. https://granta.com/the-husband-stitch/ Husband stitches can easily be categorized under type 3 FGM as it includes infibulation but there is no clear definition for infibulation and health care professionals who unethically give the 'extra stitch' and can use this to defend themselves by arguing that the extra stitch was necessary due to significant vaginal tearing at childbirth, https://www.sydney.edu.au/news-opinion/news/2016/03/18/health-professionals-lack-knowledge-about-female-genital-mutilat0.html.

extent of these practices because of the nature of their jobs. This Australian FGM/C case treated the practice as 'cultural' and not 'religious'. The decision in this case was based on the Family Law Council's report that stated, *It has been estimated that FGM occurs in more than forty countries, and tradition is the major factor which contributes to its continuation. While the practice is often linked to certain religious communities, this view is, in fact, mistaken. The origins of the practice predate most major religions.*[89] Such a characterization of FGM/C is helpful in curbing the practice effectively. Australia follows a strict criminalization regime that does not allow for exceptions on claims of tradition or religion.

FGM/C has been a *severe criminal offence*[90] in the UK since 1985 under the *Prohibition of Female Circumcision Act*[91] (PFCA). This law was amended in 2003 to allow for extraterritorial application. The PFCA is now applicable to all UK nationals or permanent residents who conduct FGM/C overseas.[92] The extraterritorial jurisdiction of laws criminalizing FGM/C is critical, since there is a propensity for citizens of a nation where FGM/C is a crime to travel to a country to perform FMG/C in a State where it has not yet been criminalized. Additionally, the *Serious Crimes Act, 2015* under sections 3 and 5 addresses FGM/C, these sections were amended to make it mandatory for teachers, social care, and healthcare workers to report any cases of FGM/C to the police directly. The courts can issue FGM/C protection orders under the amendment to PFCA in 2003.[93] It was estimated that in 2011 there were at least 1,03,000 women aged 15–49 in UK who are survivors of FGM/C,[94] however, no data is available if anyone has utilized the mandatory reporting procedure under the law.

UK clinics freely advertise hymen repair after childbirth, and this is considered a cosmetic surgical procedure.[95] This could be one of the reasons why several FGM/C cases go underreported as many mutilations are conducted under the façade of cosmetic surgery in UK.[96] This was also a point of debate during the passing of the 1985 PFCA. The Bill allowed female circumcision to take place only if it was medically necessitated in the form of genital surgery for cancer.[97] The Conservative Party in power at that time agreed to pass the Bill if it allowed for surgery, especially if there was a *threat to physical or mental health*, without considering the prevalence of FGM/C.[98] No prosecutions were initiated under the 1985 PFCA or the amended 2003 PFCA until 2012. Four complaints were reported to have been filed and several arrests were made. However, the cases did not go to trial *for reasons of safeguarding unknown number of girls being taken into care and people being stopped from travelling with girl children to visit their families in FGM practising countries.*[99] In a 2014 civil case before the Leeds Family Court, the medical evidence presented was inconclusive because the medical experts had no expertise in the area

[89] Family Law Council, *Female Genital Mutilation: A Report to the AttorneyGeneral prepared by the Family Law Council* (June 1994) at 9 [2.1] as cited in *The Queen v. A2, Kubra, and Vaziri,* [2019] HCA 35 ¶ 23; New South Wales, Legislative Council, Parliamentary Debates (Hansard), 4 May 1994 at 1859 as cited in *The Queen v. A2, Kubra, and Vaziri,* [2019] HCA 35 ¶ 166.

[90] Amended to reflect FGM as a severe crime.

[91] Plugge et al. (2018).

[92] Ibid.

[93] Ibid, see Sections 3A and 5A of FGM Act 2003 (amended). Section 3 Offence of Assisting a non-UK person to Mutilate Oversees a Girl's Genitalia.

[94] Plugge et al. (2018).

[95] Dustin (2010), p. 13.

[96] Ibid at 14.

[97] Ibid.

[98] The 1985 Act therefore gave an exception to FGM/C on mental health grounds—2(1)(a) stated '*it is necessary for the physical or mental health of the person on whom it is performed and is performed by a registered medical practitioner.*' 2(2) states that "In determining for the purposes of this section whether an action is necessary for the mental health of a person, no account shall be taken of the effect on that person of any belief on the part of that or any other person that the operation is required as a matter of custom or ritual".

[99] Marge (2019).

of FGM; therefore, they could only recognize *irregular genitalia* without understanding if it was *mutilated*.[100] In a Bristol case in 2018, where the accused was acquitted, the father took the defence that as a practising Catholic, he does not believe in this practice.[101] While very little is known about this case, it is interesting that in UK where FGM/C is considered a *cultural practice*, communities are practising FGM/C unrelated to their religion. Also, religion does not form a part of the arguments, either in support or against this practice in the courts in UK.

The first prosecution of FGM/C in UK occurred only in February 2019 when a mother performed FGM/C on her daughter and she was forced to call an ambulance due to excessive bleeding of the 'cut child'.[102] She explained to the doctors that the child had fallen on a metal object from the cupboard during playtime. The judge, however, confirmed that this was a case of *witch doctor* as the defendant did not come from a State that practiced FGM/C. She was convicted for one count of FGM/C. Since UK does not have specific sentencing guidelines for FGM/C, the judge had to consult guidelines on child abuse, domestic violence sentencing, and other assault guidelines.[103] There were many inconsistencies in this case, especially with respect to evidence taking. The children (the cut girl and her brother) were questioned multiple times with pointed, leading questions.

A community advocate (who educates on FGM/C) commented on the above case:

> One of the key things I felt was left out of the trial was that the jury was not told it's impossible to cut a girl without a team to hold her down. Any of my women who share their stories of being cut will tell you that many people are involved in doing FGM on a young girl. Every part of her body must be held down, and every limb has to be put into a state that means the child has no power to move. There would be blood everywhere – on her thighs, on the floor, and bruising from being held down. She would also be traumatized. I know from my personal experience that it's the most painful thing and that you would hate anyone who was involved or around you when the cutting happens. Normally, all cutters are experienced women. In any community, it's never been known that a mother would cut her daughter unless she were a traditional, experienced cutter.[104]

No cutting equipment was found in this case and all testimony provided matched until the last stage. In most cases, law enforcement officers did not know of this practice, and the courts and jury struggled to understand whether the evidence was accurate, faultless, and fair. This could lead to low conviction rates and also *ethnic profiling*.[105] There are also concerns about issuing multiple protection orders by the court to take children into custody just because parents took the children to their FGM/C practicing home country, or the mother was cut in her childhood. In this case, the mother was taken into custody and sentenced to 14 years of imprisonment. The judge categorically stated that *the practice of FGM/C was comparable not only to child abuse but analogous to domestic violence, assault, grievous body harm and child cruelty, all of which are crimes which could attract a life sentence*.[106]

A targeted study on the perception of FGM/C conducted by the University of Oxford showed that participants were sceptical about the laws surrounding FGM/C in the UK.[107] They believed that stringent laws would drive the practice of FGM/C underground.[108] This could also be a

[100] *In the Matter of B and G (Children) between Leeds City Council and MFBG*, [2015]EWFC 3, Case No. LJ13C00295.

[101] Ibid at 264.

[102] "United Kingdom: First Successful Prosecution for Female Genital Mutilation," Library of Congress, 2023. https://www.loc.gov/item/global-legal-monitor/2019-07-31/united-kingdom-first-successful-prosecution-for-female-genital-mutilation/.

[103] Ibid.

[104] Marge (2019).

[105] Law enforcement officers engage in actions which target the ethnicity, race, origin, nationality, etc. of an individual rather than their conduct and other evidence.

[106] Marge (2019).

[107] Plugge et al. (2018).

[108] Ibid at 263.

reason that the UK does not have many cases of conviction under the FGM/C law, despite a large number of residents from practising regions such as Africa, Arab, and South Asian countries. Some women explained how mandatory reporting prevents them from seeking medical help and finding a safe space. Participants also believed that the law was yet another method to '*beat them up with*'.[109] According to some, law enforcement agencies in the UK have been using FGM/C laws to mistreat them and alienate specific communities.[110] This adds to the alienation experienced by them due to counter-terrorism measures employed by the State.[111]

Approximately 20,000 women and girls seek asylum in the European Union (EU) to escape cutting. According to the United Nations High Commissioner for Refugees (UNHCR) Report in 2011,[112] 4,210 women and girls were seeking asylum in France to escape FGM/C practicing countries.[113] There is difficulty in tracing 'cut girls' and women who are at risk as they usually do not speak the official language of the receiving country, additionally women are fearful in disclosing that they are victims of FGM/C because their families control such disclosure.[114] Though FGM/C has an overarching effect on sexual health, reproductive health, pregnancy, birth, family, and marriage, most women and girls are discouraged from speaking up, as it is considered a taboo in their country of origin.[115]

The concept of *Laïcité* in the French multicultural society makes it interesting to study FGM/C in France.[116] FGM/C is a crime according to the provisions of the French Penal Code dealing with acts of *torture and barbarity*.[117] Articles 222-9 and 222-10 also criminalize *intended bodily harm causing permanent infirmity or mutilation*.[118] The penalty for these crimes is increased if it is committed against a minor. Until 2006, there was no extraterritorial application of these provisions, therefore, if a child was taken abroad (often to their home country in the case of migrants), non-French nationals could not be prosecuted.[119] Like in Australia and UK, the laws in France are now extraterritorial, which makes the practice punishable even when committed outside the country.[120] The '*cut*' child under

[109] Indicating behaviour akin to ethnic profiling.

[110] Ibid.

[111] Ibid at 264.

[112] UNHCR (2011).

[113] Ibid.

[114] Green (2018).

[115] Ibid at 136.

[116] Laïcité in the French Constitution guarantees *Freedom from Religion* in the public sphere.

[117] French penal Code provision 212-1 states Deportation, enslavement or the massive and systematic practice of summary executions, abduction of persons followed by their disappearance, of torture or inhuman acts, inspired by political, philosophical, racial or religious motives, and organised in pursuit of a concerted plan against a section of a civil population are punished by criminal imprisonment for life. 222-1 states that the subjection of a person to torture or to acts of barbarity is punished by fifteen years' criminal imprisonment. 222-3 states the penalty incurred is increased to 30 years' criminal imprisonment where the offence defined under article 222-1 is committed against a minor under the age of fifteen years by a legitimate, natural or adoptive ascendant or by any other person having authority over the minor. 222-5 states that the offence defined under article 222-1 is punished by 30 years' criminal imprisonment where it entailed mutilation or permanent disability.222-6 states that the offence defined under article 222–1 is punished by criminal imprisonment for life where it brought about the death of the victim without intent to cause it.

[118] 222-9 states that FGM acts that result in a mutilation or in a permanent disability will be punished with 10 years of imprisonment and a fine of 150, 000 Euros. 222-10 states FGM acts are punished with 15 years of imprisonment when the person is under 15 years of age and If the person who is subjected to FGM is under 15 years of age and if the act results in the death of the latter, the offender is to be punished with 20 years of Imprisonment. These provisions were a result of a penal code reform in 2006.

[119] European Institute of Gender Equality, Current Situation of Female Genital Mutilation in France, https://eige.europa.eu/sites/default/files/documents/current_situation_and_trends_of_female_genital_mutilation_in_france_en.pdf.

[120] 222-16-2 of French penal code reads that If the acts described in Article 222-8, 222-10 or 222-12 PC were committed abroad and on a person under 18 years of age who has their habitual residence in France, French criminal law is applicable.

18 can also seek protection under Article 375 of the civil code to be placed in public institutions, family shelters, or any authorized associations.[121] France has been systematically dealing with criminal and tortious cases on FGM/C since 1979 and has the most criminal cases concerning FGM/C; at least 37 cases have been tried in the country's highest court[122] under its general criminal law (mostly 222-9 and 222-10).[123]

Earlier, when French penal provisions did not recognize 'mutilation', the cases were tried by the correctional chamber.[124] In tortious claims, FGM/C was considered 'damage' and attracted compensation for the victim, anyone who called for a specific law for FGM/C was met with dismay. It was said that *the introduction of a specific penal provision would differentiate between citizens and thus might lead to discrimination and stigmatization of minority groups*.[125] The case of *Bobo Traore* in France was a watershed moment on FGM/C prosecution in French criminal law.[126] A 3-month-old girl bled to death after being cut and the judges did not know how to apply the criminal law to such FGM/C cases. This led to feminist organizations lobbying for criminal law to include FGM/C. A few months later, a Malian man admitted to cutting his daughter, which was a rare case as fathers are rarely seen performing FGM/C on their daughters. Even then, he was convicted in the correctional chamber as the act could not qualify as *mutilation*.[127] Another case involving a French mother, with no African roots sadistically cut off her daughter's clitoris and labia minora.[128] It was established in this case that white children and African/ South Asian children should not be discriminated (indicating any difference between origin and nationality) as the act was the same for all children—mutilating the clitoris.[129] This case allowed French judges to shed their qualms about criminalizing a *cultural norm*.[130] It gave them a chance to talk about FGM/C without *racializing* or *stigmatizing* its perpetrators.[131] Cutting off a body part is a violent act that causes serious bodily injury irrespective of any other consideration.

These cases demonstrate the medical complications that can arise from performing FGM/C at home. In one of the cases, the mutilated child bled to death. Upholding a practice in the name of religion or culture in fear that it will be perceived as racist, will thus continue to put the 'cut' children at risk. Suggestions for compulsory medical examinations and gynaecological screenings for at-risk girls have been viewed as debatable. Picking out only children of African or South Asian descent would be discriminatory. Medical professionals like doctors, nurses, and midwives can be given appropriate training for reporting any cases of FGM/C when they encounter at-risk patients. Moreover, social workers who work with 'cut women' explain how many in France are cut when they are still in the cradle and have no recollection until they

[121] Article 375 of French Civil Code states: If the health, safety or morals of an unemancipated minor are in danger, or if the conditions of his education or his physical, emotional, intellectual and social development are seriously compromised, educational assistance measures may be ordered. by justice at the request of the father and mother jointly, or one of them, the person or service to whom the child has been entrusted or the guardian, the minor himself or the public prosecutor. In cases where the public prosecutor has been notified by the president of the departmental council, he ensures that the situation of the minor falls within the scope of article L. 226-4 of the code of social action and families. The judge can take action ex officio in exceptional circumstances.

[122] The Court of Cassation is the highest court in the French judicial system.

[123] Els Leye and Alexia Saab, overview of legislation in the European Union To address female genital mutilation: Challenges and recommendations for the Implementation of laws https://www.un.org/womenwatch/daw/egm/vaw_legislation_2009/Expert%20Paper%20EGMGPLHP%20_Els%20Leye_.pdf.

[124] French Correctional Cambers are courts of first instance for trying misdemeanour.

[125] Le Bris (2019).

[126] Titze (2014).

[127] Ibid at 202.

[128] Ibid at 203.

[129] Ibid.

[130] Le Bris (2019).

[131] Ibid at 150.

come for a medical examination or during childbirth.[132] Women who have been cut also express how it is more damaging when medical professionals talk to them about 'normal vulvas'. Those who work with the women add how *it is a form of aggression against mutilated women who already tend to beat themselves up because they tell themselves that they are not normal.*[133] In France, medical professionals and social workers are mandated to report any physical or mental abuse perpetrated on children, since they do not have the capacity due to their age.[134]

The French laws concerning FGM/C are well established and are being implemented regularly. If convicted for FGM/C a French national who has acquired citizenship through naturalization could lose their citizenship.[135] The limitation period is 20 years, enabling children who were probably not aware of the long-term consequences of FGM/C to institute a case after they become adults.[136] Jurisprudence on FGM/C indicates that in France, mutilation is considered a *violent act* without attaching cultural or religious aspects to it. This makes it easier for the State to find methods to criminalize and accommodate 'cut' children. As soon as the cultural or religious essentiality of practices of FGM/C is questioned, it becomes difficult for the State to intervene, as has been observed in India.

In 1994, the *Fauziya Kassindja case*[137] in the US precipitated the recognition of FGM/C as *gender-based persecution* to be considered as a ground for granting asylum in the US.[138] Kassindja was initially denied asylum by an immigration judge. Soon after the *New York Times* published her story, she was granted asylum by the immigration appeal board. Her membership to the tribe that practised FGM/C was considered during the asylum hearing. As part of *Illegal Immigration Reform and Immigrant Responsibility Act of 1996*, US printed and distributed pamphlets in six languages to its embassies across countries to deter immigrants from practising FGM/C. This information stated that officers must explain to each immigrant *the potential legal consequences in the United States for: performing [FGM] or allowing a child under his or her care to be subjected to [FGM], under criminal or child protection statutes or as a form of child abuse.*[139]

In the US, a federal law was enacted in 2013 to prevent girls from being taken abroad for what was called 'Vacation Cutting' following the *Center for Disease Control and Prevention's Division of Reproductive Health* (CDC) estimate that as many as half a million girls and women in the US have either undergone or may be at risk for undergoing FGM/C.[140] The *US v. Nargarwala,*[141] a landmark US federal case judgement, involved a doctor (Dr Nagarwala) and seven others who were charged in the federal court in Michigan in connection with the *genital mutilation* of nine girls from Michigan, Minnesota and Illinois conducted between 2015 and 2017 at a clinic in Detroit. Authorities alleged mothers brought the girls to Dr. Nagarwala when they were around 7 years for the procedure. Dr. Nagarwala denied any crime was committed and that she had simply performed *a religious custom* on the girls belonging to the same Muslim sect as her, the India-based

[132] Article 44 of the Code of Medical Ethics, annexed to the Code of the Public Health; France 24, 2023, Female Genital Mutilation: Women Circumcise Little Girls For Men, https://www.france24.com/en/europe/20230206-female-genital-mutilation-women-circumcise-little-girls-for-men.

[133] Ibid.

[134] Leye and Saab (2009).

[135] Bris (2019).

[136] Ibid at 52.

[137] Matter of Kasinga (1996).

[138] Female Genital Mutilation in the United States, https://www.equalitynow.org/fgm_in_the_us_learn_more/.

[139] Center for Reproductive Rights, Legislation on Female Genital Mutilation in the United States, https://www.reproductiverights.org/sites/default/files/documents/pub_bp_fgmlawsusa.pdf.

[140] Smith and Whitcraft, https://abcnews.go.com/US/full-page/underground-america-female-genital-mutilation-undergroundfgm-31808869.

[141] *US v. Jumana Nagarwala,* Criminal No. 17-CR-20274.

Dawoodi Bohra community. Following an investigation after a tip-off was received by the authorities, nine cases of FGM/C were under investigation. Though the law banning FGM/C was passed by the US Congress in 1996, the *Nargawala Case* in 2017 was the first to be tried under this law. In 2018, six out of eight charges filed were dismissed by a federal judge in Detroit, because the law was deemed unconstitutional on grounds that the US Congress did not have the legislative powers to criminalize the act of FGM/C.[142] Nagarwala was, however, prosecuted under 18 US Code § 116[143] '*Female Genital Mutilation*' and was also charged for "*conspiracy to travel with intent to engage in illicit sexual conduct*" while others were charged for witness tampering.[144] *Strengthening the Opposition to Female Genital Mutilation Act of 2020* (STOP FGM Act 2020)[145] was passed by US Congress and an updated version of the law is now in force. It was noted by the US Congress that courts in Michigan had mistakenly declared the law unconstitutional.[146] This decision by the court created disbelief among those working on child rights and women rights.[147] It is interesting to note that the 1996 law in the US used 'circumcises' as against 'mutilates' to describe the offence of FGM/C,[148] unlike laws in all other jurisdictions on this practice. Though an analysis of the specific laws in each of the 41 states that have enacted laws on FGM/C in the US has not been undertaken in this section, it is clear that this implies that families desirous of conducting FGM/C can now drive across to states that are yet to legislate on FGM/C.

International law's focus on the practice of FGM/C is evident from the attention it has received under international refugee law. The UNHCR has, in 2011, estimated that around 2000 claims on FGM/C-related grounds were received throughout in Europe.[149] Noting that *this is not a negligible ground* since asylum systems in the EU received a few thousand applications every year relating directly to FGM. The countries to which girls and women fleeing FGM/C applied for asylum are Germany, Sweden, France, Switzerland, UK, Netherlands, Italy, Belgium, Norway and Denmark. Under international refugee law, FGM/C is now considered a ground for persecution. The asylum claims of FGM/C arise from specific risk profiles—female and male activists persecution for their opinion and commitment to end FGM/C in their home states and/or the perceived threats to their religious beliefs; women and unaccompanied separated girls who seek protection from being subjected to FGM/C. Parents who seek protection in order to protect their daughters from FGM/C, women who refuse to become cutters, women who have gone through reconstructive surgery in Europe and fear being cut again upon return to their country of origin are also included as risk profiles of those who can seek asylum.

142 Female Genital Mutilation in the United States, https://www.equalitynow.org/fgm_in_the_us_learn_more/.

143 The FGM Criminalization Statute provides that "whoever knowingly circumcises, excises, or infibulates the whole or any part of the labia majora or labia minora or clitoris of another person who has not attained the age of 18 years shall be fined under this title or imprisoned not more than 5 years, or both".

144 Galbraith (2020).

145 On January 5, 2021, the Strengthening the Opposition to Female Genital Mutilation Act 2020 (the STOP FGM Act, HR 6100) became law. The STOP FGM Act clarifies and amends provisions of the underlying 1996 and 2013 FGM laws, which prohibit female genital mutilation (FGM) of girls in the United States and the transportation of girls outside the United States for the purpose of having FGM performed. See 18 U.S.C. §116, https://www.justice.gov/criminal-hrsp/file/1356451/download#:~:text=The%20STOP%20FGM%20Act%20clarifies,%C2%A7116.

146 Ibid.

147 Baldas (2021).

148 The FGM Criminalization Statute provides that "whoever knowingly circumcises, excises, or infibulates the whole or any part of the labia majora or labia minora or clitoris of another person who has not attained the age of 18 years shall be fined under this title or imprisoned not more than 5 years, or both".

149 UNHCR (2011).

8.4 Conclusion

Since FGM/C is directly attributable to the actions primarily associated with women from the family or community, it is frequently claimed that this form of gender-based violence is not perpetrated by men, but rather by women. This view overlooks the fact that it is men who enforce religious, cultural domination on women and ensure patriarchal supremacy within these social institutions and that patriarchy serves men and not women. For all women, internalized patriarchy and fear of non-compliance operates at a sub-conscious level in ways that could manifest as control and dominance on less powerful women in the family and community. FGM/C is thus a form of male violence on women's bodies perpetrated through institutions and community. The practice of cutting was historically done to reduce the time spent on supervising the sexual activities of young girls, it fulfilled marriage market conditions,[150] and communicated to all women and young girls as a group that adherence to their expected social roles and regulations on their body are rewarded while non- compliance is punished. FGM/C is thus an *identity marker* that demarcates 'insiders' from 'outsiders'. Being a part of the community becomes even more critical as a migrant.[151] The community attachment in the form of adherence to religious norms drives practitioners deep into their culture.[152] FGM/C also poses a challenge to the healthcare situation in the areas of gynaecology and obstetrics. 'Cut' children and women are reported to be increasingly affected by urinary tract infections (UTI), sepsis, bleeding, anaemia, etc. According to several surveys, only 45 healthcare providers in the UK were aware of FGM/C, and many could not list the different types of FGM/C.[153] Nurse-midwives in the US, UK, and Australia are generally unaware of the legal and cultural consequences of the practice. Medicalization of FGM/C is an attempt to legitimize the practice by practitioners which sometimes hides the practice in plain sight.

According to the Dawoodi Bohra community,[154] there are one million members from the community residing worldwide.[155] The USA has the largest population of Dawoodi Bohra community with around 5,000 families living across the country. UK has around 2,000 Dawoodi Bohra families, while 600 Dawoodi Bohra families have migrated to Australia since 1980. The Bohra clergy continues to have a firm hold on the diaspora across these and other states.[156] This resulted in a UK-based charity with the imam as its corporate trustee, spending more than £800,000 on litigation costs to defend four members of the Dawoodi Bohra congregation in Australia in connection with the *Vaziri* and *Magennis* case.[157] The UK government came under fire after the leader of the Bohra clergy was granted a UK visa to meet followers and subsequently, it led to meetings with (the then) Prince Charles.[158] The prevalence of the diaspora in different parts of the world also highlights the necessity for enactment of laws to address FGM/C.

Legitimacy on grounds of culture and tradition must be challenged. Criminalization of FGM/C in countries that do not address this form of violence under their laws is a priority. FGM/C constitutes a grave breach of trust between family members, especially the mother and the 'cut' girl child. The immediate and

[150] Protection of virginity, endogamy, class.

[151] Sandrine Mesplé-Somps (2016), Migration and female genital mutilation. IZA World of Labor, https://wol.iza.org/articles/migration-and-female-genital-mutilation/long.

[152] *Ibid* at 6.

[153] Ogunsiji (2015)..

[154] The Dawoodi Bohra.com.

[155] The statistics are present on the website https://www.thedawoodibohras.com/.

[156] France, Germany, Sweden.

[157] Johnson (2022).

[158] The Syedna's visit to UK was questioned and creates concerns for *survivor-led organizations* and *excommunicated* members in UK of the community who feared that his meetings with followers might put young children at risk.

long-term health consequences are well documented throughout the world wherever the practice is prevalent. Survivors of FGM/C report feeling wounded and damaged in three primary ways: physical risk, the emotional trauma and the sexual damage.[159]

The discussion on legal avenues and jurisprudence discussed in the chapter reflects a wide variety of approaches within civil and criminal systems. The critical commonality is that States are indeed able to send out a clear message that FGM/C is a crime and will not be tolerated as a justification for tradition, culture or religion. This is in direct consonance with the vital provisions under CEDAW Article 5 that creates an obligation on state parties shall:

(a) *to modify the social and cultural patterns of conduct of men and women with a view to achieving the elimination of prejudices and customary and all other practices which are based on the idea of the inferiority or the superiority of ether of the sexes or on stereotyped roles for men and women.*
(b) *To ensure that family education includes a proper understanding of maternity as a social function and the recognition of the common responsibility of men and women in the upbringing and development of their children, it being understood that the interest of the children is the primordial consideration in all cases.*

General Recommendations 14 and 19 of the CEDAW Committee clearly articulate FGM/C as a form of gender-based violence and discrimination under international human rights law. The chapter provides an 'overview' of the practice of FGM/C and the legal field within which it has been addressed in several parts of the world. The private-intimate dimensions of violence that is perpetrated at the behest of the family elucidate this as a unique form of violence.

[159] As said by Mallika on the show Spotlight—*We the Women, Horror of Female Genital Cutting*.2017. https://youtu.be/WKS_R_-9th-10th2017,zBLE?si=praHDPwK09fGd8JD. Accessed 27 Nov 2023.

References

A2 v R; Magennis v R; Vaziri v R (2018) NSWCCA 174
Anantarayan L, Diler S, Menon N (2018) The clitoral hood: a contested site. WeSpeakOut and Naari Samta Manch
Article 25 Freedom of Religion, Constitution of India
Attorney General's Department (2013) Review of Australia's female genital mutilation legal framework. https://nla.gov.au/nla.obj-2817044791/view
Awford J (2016) Doctor 'who covered up the genital mutilation of his two daughters to protect his wife' is banned from seeing female patients alon. https://www.dailymail.co.uk/news/article-3436424/Doctor-covered-genital-mutilation-two-daughters-protect-wife-banned-seeing-female-patients-alone.html
Baldas T (2021) Judge throws out historic female genital mutilation case, calls feds 'vindictive', Detroit Free press. https://www.freep.com/story/news/local/michigan/detroit/2021/09/28/judges-tosses-detroits-historic-female-genital-mutilation-case/5902782001/
Blank J (2021) The Daudi Bohras in handbook of Islamic sects and movements. Bril Handbooks on Contemporary Religion, vol 21
Center for Reproductive Rights, Legislation on Female Genital Mutilation in the United States. https://www.reproductiverights.org/sites/default/files/documents/pub_bp_fgmlawsusa.pdf
Chandran R (2018) No evidence of FGM, India government tells court, appalling activists. Thomas Reuters available at https://www.reuters.com/article/us-india-women-religion/no-evidence-of-fgm-india-government-tells-court-appalling-activists-idUSKBN1EN0QB
Code of Medical Ethics, annexed to the Code of the Public Health
Colomina B (ed) (1996) Sexuality and space. Princeton Architectural Press
Crimes (Female Genital Mutilation) Amendment Act 1994 (NSW)
Crimes Act 1900 (ACT) (NSW)
Dirie W, Miller C (1998) Desert flower: the extraordinary journey of a desert Normad. Harper Collins
Dustin M (2010) Female genital mutilation/cutting in the UK: challenging the inconsistencies. Eur J Women's Stud 17(1):7–23
Dyfan I. Chief of the women and gender section, UN Human Rights Office. As a speaker on a panel discussion during the session of the Human Rights Council titled, 'Harmful Traditional Practices, Rhetoric or Reality.'
Equality Now Report (2020) FGM a global picture. www.equalitynow.org/fgm-a-global-picture/

European Institute of Gender Equality, Current Situation of Female Genital Mutilation in France. https://eige.europa.eu/sites/default/files/documents/current_situation_and_trends_of_female_genital_mutilation_in_france_en.pdf

Family Law Council (1994) Female genital mutilation: a report to the attorney general prepared by the family law council

Female Genital Mutilation in the United States. https://www.equalitynow.org/fgm_in_the_us_learn_more/

France 24 (2023) Female genital mutilation: women circumcise little girls for men. https://www.france24.com/en/europe/20230206-female-genital-mutilation-women-circumcise-little-girls-for-men

French Civil Code, 1804

French Penal Code,1791

Galbraith J (2020) Department of justice declines to defend the constitutionality of a statute criminalizing female genital mutilation. Am J Int Law 114(2)

Health professionals lack knowledge about female genital mutilation. https://www.sydney.edu.au/news-opinion/news/2016/03/18/health-professionals-lack-knowledge-about-female-genital-mutilat0.html

In the Matter of B and G (Children) between Leeds City Council and MFBG, [2015] EWFC 3, Case No. LJ13C00295

Johnson S (2022) Bohra Imam's visit puts British girls at risk of mutilation, warn FGM campaigners. The Guardian. https://www.theguardian.com/society/2022/jul/29/dawoodi-bohra-imam-mufaddal-saifuddin-visit-uk-british-girls-risk-mutilation-warn-fgm-campaigners

Khan A et al (2019) Demystifying the practice of Khafd in the Dawoodi Bohra community: a commentary on the WeSpeakOut report from India. Indian J Med Ethics 4(1):66

Koukoui S, Hassan G, Guzder J (2017) The mothering experience of women with FGM/C raising 'uncut' daughter, in Ivory Coast and in Canada. Reproductive Health

Lawyer's Collective (2017) A guide to eliminating FGM practice in India. WeSpeakOut

Le Bris C (2019) The legal framework for the fight against female circumcision: from cultural indulgence to human rights violations. The French example. Eur J Health Law 26(2):141–158

Leye E, Saab A (2009) Overview of legislation in the European union to address female genital mutilation: challenges and recommendations for the implementation of laws. https://www.un.org/womenwatch/daw/egm/vaw_legislation_2009/Expert%20Paper%20EGMGPLHP%20_Els%20Leye_.pdf

Machado C. The husband stitch. https://granta.com/the-husband-stitch

Marge B (2019) Prosecution of female genital mutilation in the United Kingdom: injustice at the intersection of good public health intentions and the criminal law. Med Law Int 19(4):258

Matter of Kasinga (1996). https://cgrs.uclawsf.edu/our-work/matter-kasinga-1996

Mesplé-Somps S (2016) Migration and female genital mutilation. IZA World of Labor. https://wol.iza.org/articles/migration-and-female-genital-mutilation/long

Newton RJ, Glover J (2022) "I Can't Blame Mom": a qualitative exploration of relational dynamics in women with female genital mutilation (FGM) in the United Kingdom. Violence Against Women 28(1):3–25

Ogunsiji O (2015) Female genital mutilation (FGM); Australian midwives' and attitudes. Health Care Women Int 36(11):1179–1193. https://doi.org/10.1080/07399332.2014.992521

OHCHR. Female genital mutilation: over 3 million women and girls are at risk. https://www.ohchr.org/en/stories/2012/09/female-genital-mutilation-over-3-million-women-and-girls-are-risk

The Indian Penal Code, 1860

Pickering WSF (1984) Durkheim's sociology of religion: themes and theories. The Lutterworth Press, James Clarke & Co Ltd. https://doi.org/10.2307/j.ctt1cgf6sv

Plugge E et al (2018) The prevention of female genital mutilation in England: what can be done? J Public Health 41(3):261–266

The Protection of Children from Sexual Offences Act, 2012

Queensland Law Reform Commission (1994) Female genital mutilation draft no. 42

R v A2; R v KM; R v Vaziri (No. 2) (2015) NSWSC 1221

Rogers J (2016) The first case addressing genital mutilation in Australia: Where is the Harm. AltLJ 41(4):235–238

Rogers J (2022) Remnants of mutilation in anti-FGM law in Australia: a reply to 'The prosecution of Dawoodi Bohra women' by Richard Shweder. Bristol University Press 12(1):145–157. https://doi.org/10.1332/204378921X16349692612474

Sahiyo (2017) Detroit arrest: it is time for the Bohras to get serious about ending female genital cutting. https://sahiyo.com/2017/04/14/detroit-arrest-it-is-time-for-bohras-to-get-serious-about-ending-female-genital-cutting/. Accessed 27 Nov 2023. US v. Jumana Nagarwala, Criminal No. 17-CR-20274

Sahiyo (2016) Notices by Sydney, Melbourne and London's Anjuman-e-Burhani Trusts on 'Khafd' (Khatna) or female genital cutting. https://sahiyo.com/2016/03/08/notices-by-sydney-melbourne-and-londons-anjuman-e-burhani-trusts-on-khafd-khatna-or-female-genital-cutting/

Green SO (2018) 'I have a story to tell': researching migrant women's experiences of female genital mutilation and gender-based violence in Ireland and Europe. Soc Work Soc Sci Rev 19(3):134–151

Smith O, Whitcraft T. Underground in America: female genital mutilation. https://abcnews.go.com/US/full-page/underground-america-female-genital-mutilation-undergroundfgm-31808869

Sunita Tiwari v. Union of India, Civil Writ No. 286 of 2017
Taher M (2017) Understanding female genital cutting in the Dawoodi Bohra community: an exploratory study. Sahiyo
The 2030 Agenda for Sustainable Development. https://sustainabledevelopment.un.org/content/documents/21252030%20Agenda%20for%20Sustainable%20Development%20web.pdf
The Commission on Status of Women, E/CN.6/2008/L.2/Rev. 1. https://www.un.org/womenwatch/daw/csw/csw52/AC_resolutions/Final%20L2%20ending%20female%20genital%20mutilation%20-%20advance%20unedited.pdf
The Official Website of Dawoodi Bohra Website. https://www.thedawoodibohras.com/
The Queen v. A2, Kubra, and Vaziri, [2019] HCA 35
The STOP FGM Act, 2020. https://www.justice.gov/criminal-hrsp/file/1356451/download#:~:text=The%20STOP%20FGM%20Act%20clarifies,%C2%A7116.
Titze (2014) Women's rights and cultural claims: female genital mutilation in Germany and France. Negotiating boundaries in multicultural societies (Dina Mansour et al.). Inter-Disciplinary Press,Oxford
To address female genital mutilation: Challenges and recommendations for the Implementation of laws. https://www.un.org/womenwatch/daw/egm/vaw_legislation_2009/Expert%20Paper%20EGMGPLHP%20_Els%20Leye_.pdf
Transforming Our World: The 2030 Agenda for Sustainable Development, A/RES/70/1 UN, sustainabledevelopment.un.org
U.S. v. Jumana Nagarwala, Criminal No. 17-CR-20274
UK Female Genital Mutilation Act, 2003
The Un-Cut, Insiya Dariwala. www.Sahiyo.com/2016/08/29/the-un-cut/
UNHCR (2011) Too much pain, female genital mutilation and Asylum in the European union. A statistical overview, https://www.unhcr.org/media/too-much-pain-female-genital-mutilation-and-asylum-european-union-statistical-overview
United Kingdom: First Successful Prosecution for Female Genital Mutilation (2023) Library of congress. https://www.loc.gov/item/global-legal-monitor/2019-07-31/united-kingdom-first-successful-prosecution-for-female-genital-mutilation/
We the Women, Horror of Female Genital Cutting (2017). https://youtu.be/WKS_R_-9th-10th2017,zBLE?si=praHDPwK09fGd8JD. Accessed 27 Nov 2023. The interview referenced was conducted for *We the Women*, in collaboration with UN Women
WHO. https://www.who.int/news-room/fact-sheets/detail/female-genital-mutilation. Accessed 28 Sept 2023
Zurynski Y, Phu A, Sureshkumar P et al (2017) Female Genital Mutilation in children presenting to Paediatricians. Arch Dis Child 102(6):509–515

9 'Family Disruption' as 'Family Violence': Immigrant Sikh Families in the United States

Diditi Mitra

Abstract

In the context of dominant patriarchal gender roles, the discourse on domestic violence in (heterosexual) families directs attention to women's experience of abuse from their male partners. Introducing international migration in this equation, however, complicates the discourse. Focusing on immigrants who live with a degree of precarity (undocumented immigrant families, dependents, and immigrant families on temporary legal statuses), I argue that a more expansive and nuanced meaning of violence should be applied to immigrant domestic strife because the contexts in which international migration occurs has the potential to inflict harm on all members of the family, including men. The central argument is supported with ethnographic material and semi-structured interviews conducted with immigrant Sikh families in the United States and Punjab, India, analysis of news reports on abandoned Sikh husbands and wives as well as secondary literature. An integral part of the analysis involves reflection on the meaning of family violence in the context of international migration.

Keywords

Family disruption · Violence · Immigration · Domestic violence · Family · International migration · Employment · Relationships · Patriarchy · Gender roles · Forceful separation · Dependents · Legal violence · Deportation · Symbolic violence · Structural violence · Abandoned spouse · Dependent spouse · Emotional instability

9.1 Introduction

Ranjit's[1] story

> Leaving his wife and children in Jalandhar, Ranjit Singh decided to immigrate to the United States. It was not the first time Ranjit had stepped into the country. He had lived in the United States for about five years in the early 1980s. Upon advice from friends and relatives, Ranjit came on a tourist visa for "vacation." Like many others, he likely let his tourist status lapse and became "illegal" in the United States. He did make the decision to return to India, but only after about five years when his attempts at legalization of his status failed. After a three-year hiatus, however, he returned. That was in 1990. This time, too, he had entered with fraudulent documents. Since his arrival, Ranjit had unsuccessfully attempted to bring over his wife, son and daughter. The immigration plan, of course, had been to bring them over availing the services of an "agent." His wife

D. Mitra (✉)
Brookdale Community College, Middletown, NJ, USA
e-mail: diditimitra@gmail.com

[1] All names are pseudonyms.

P. M. Anurag and S. Dwivedy (eds.), *Violence in Intimate Spaces*, Sustainable Development Goals Series, https://doi.org/10.1007/978-981-97-2657-8_9

would pose as someone else's wife. Ranjit himself had entered disguised as a businessman on someone else's passport, adorned with gold jewelry. But his attempts at bringing over his wife and children were met with obstacles, just as his attempts to legalize his own status. His wife's maternal aunt and her husband lived in the United States, though. The uncle and his children drove taxis. While his uncle drove during the day, the children took on the night shifts. Ranjit lived with an elder woman and her granddaughter who was a year and a half old. The little girl's father was in prison and her mother had gone back to India. In India, Ranjit had worked for the Punjab Police. In New York City, he drove yellow taxis. Ranjit Singh showed me the neighborhood gurdwara. Ranjit is religious. He prays every day. I had interviewed him in 2000.

Ranjit Singh's story is emblematic of the *violence* that international migration can inflict upon (undocumented) immigrants and their families. This kind of *violence* experienced by Ranjit and his family is not physical in nature. It is at the level of the psyche, or as Galtung (1969) said, "violence that works on the soul" (p. 169). Given that he wanted his wife and children to immigrate, it can be reasonably assumed that physical separation from them was not something that he desired. He had not seen them in the three years prior to my interview of him. Effects of the separation were likely to have been felt by his wife and children too. Presumably, Ranjit's wife, being the sole parent living with the children after his emigration, had to perform the roles of both parents now. Ranjit's decision to emigrate was motivated by his perception of better opportunities abroad. It is the reason why people immigrate, he said. Among the participants of this study, obstacles to employment were cited as a key motivator for international migration. Various reports about Punjab's economy also point to its very tenuous state of employment.[2] Accordingly, Ranjit quit his decade long job with the Punjab Police and followed the advice of his friends and brother-in-law to emigrate. They were already present in the United States. Furthermore, they were the ones who advised him to come for a 'vacation'—an accepted strategy among the informants as a mode of entry—with the goal to remain in the United States and work, albeit without proper or any documentation. But of course, as an undocumented immigrant, Ranjit lived on the legal fringes of the society. Consequently, Ranjit's entire family lived in a general state of instability that meant physical separation from each other and accepting the absence of routine/mundane support of living together as well as accompanying changes in the roles played by members of the family. Despite Ranjit's undocumented status, he found work. After working at a convenience store and as a gas station attendant, Ranjit moved onto driving yellow taxis. Shunned by the native-born, particularly whites, for its declining and harsh conditions of work, according to the informants, the taxi industry was dominated by immigrant drivers. The drivers' analysis of race and the New York taxi industry is supported by Mitra's (2012) assertion of a white decline in general in low-wage jobs over time as the group experienced upward social mobility. Furthermore, analysis of the industry shows a decline in the proportion of native-born drivers and a corresponding increase in the proportion of foreign-born drivers from the early 1980s (Schaller 2004; Morris 1986). Additionally, the flexibility around requirements for obtaining and especially, renewing a hack license from the New York Taxi and Limousine Commission (TLC) even without 'papers' made it possible for the undocumented to work as cabbies; therefore, the group in question was kept vulnerable in the system. Thus, Ranjit Singh continued to live and work in New York as an undocumented immigrant, forcefully separated from his wife and children. Seemingly, he was embedded in a social network of co-ethnic 'disrupted families,' as documented in the above told story of the little girl and her grandmother whom I met at his residence in Queens, New York.

The discourse on international migration and domestic/family violence focuses its attention mainly on the vulnerability of immigrant

[2] https://timesofindia.indiatimes.com/city/chandigarh/pbs-employment-woes-get-graver-with-each-passing-year/articleshow/90088492.cms.

women, a position scholars argue is exacerbated by the conditions of immigration (Segrave et al. 2021; Tonsing 2016; Menjivar and Salcido 2002). Some of those conditions of immigration that intersect with patriarchal family arrangements and limit immigrant women's alternatives to leaving abusive family relationships can be poor language skills, ambiguous and/or dependent legal status, and limited access to adequate employment (Menjivar and Salcido 2002). This view of domestic violence is aligned with the literature on domestic violence as it occurs in the United States. The latter body of knowledge also directs attention towards violence on women by men and rightfully so, because research shows this kind to be the dominant pattern in instances of intimate partner violence in patriarchal societies (Ciabattari 2022).

In this chapter however, I assert the importance of expanding the definition of family/domestic violence when examining the phenomenon in the context of international migration. To do so, I invoke the literature on the meaning of violence itself. Galtung (1969) conceptualized violence as "present when human beings are being influenced so that their actual somatic and mental realizations are below their potential realizations" (p. 168). In other words, as Galtung goes onto explain, violence is "the cause of difference between potential and actual, between what could have been and what is" (p. 168). Later, Farmer (1996) built on this definition of violence to inform his concept of 'structural violence' and its (invisible) manifestation as diseases. Yet it is necessary to note that for the purposes of this chapter, family is defined as heterosexual marriages between men and women. Patriarchy is the context for such marital unions that hold within it clearly defined gender roles, whereby women are expected to primarily satisfy the role of the nurturer and the primary role of men is to satisfy the role of the breadwinner.

Drawing from the scholarship on international migration and violence (Menjivar and Abrego 2012; Solis 2003) as well as the discourse on the meaning of violence itself (Jackman 2002; Farmer 1996; Galtung 1969), I advance the argument that *'family disruption,'* as illustrated with the story of Ranjit Singh and his family, should be understood as family violence. '*Family disruption*' is defined as disturbing gender roles and relationships within families generating conflict within the unit and/or forcefully separating families resulting in harmful consequences for its members. It is not family violence that necessarily involves "violent acts between family members or between partners in intimate or dating relationships" (Cherlin 2013: 298). Within that dominant framework, analytical emphasis is on patriarchal family dynamics as the source of violence whereby powerful member(s) in the family abuse those who are perceived to be weaker than them. Instead, I argue that the social, legal, and economic contexts in which international migration occurs can inflict violence *on* the immigrant family, including men, of which violence by members within the unit motivated by patriarchy is only one form. Therefore, to grasp the breadth of injury caused to families in the course of international migration, an expansive definition of violence is imperative. An expansive view of violence and immigrant families would illuminate how the very parameters within which immigration occurs inflicts harm on the entire family unit, including men, while not disregarding more commonly identified forms of domestic violence in immigrant families. My focus is on immigrant Sikhs, mostly from Punjab in India, on various kinds of 'precarious' legal status (i.e. dependents, temporary immigrants, and those without proper documents).

9.2 International Migration and Family Violence

Thus far, the scholarship on international migration and domestic/family violence has focused on instances of abuse within the family unit. Primarily, this literature has documented the abuse of women by men in heterosexual family contexts. Although data documenting the frequency of family violence for immigrant women in the United States are lacking, the scholarship has established that immigrant women face a unique set of circumstances that predispose them to becoming victims of domestic violence (Narayan 1995; Park et al 2021; Sabri et al. 2019; Goncalves and Matos 2016; Tonsing 2016; Menjivar and Salcido 2002; Abraham and Tastsoglou 2016; Rhee 1997). Scholars do note that the occurrence of domestic/family violence for immigrant women is not greater in numbers than the native-born[3] (Menjivar and Salcido 2002). However, they argue that there are factors specific to the immigrant status which make immigrant women more vulnerable to it. Culture has been identified as an important variable in supporting domestic violence, particularly among immigrant families from South Asia (Sabri et al. 2019) or other Asian countries like Korea (Rhee 1997).[4] Values of collectivism and preservation of harmony in the family and, thus community, is viewed as the woman's responsibility (Park et al 2021)—an impediment to women's reporting of abuse (Park et al 2021). The dislocation experienced by immigrants, such as unfamiliarity with language, culture, support organizations of the receiving society, disconnect from personal networks, are other obstacles to reporting of domestic violence by immigrant women. Moreover, immigration laws themselves keep immigrant women locked in abusive relationships (Park et al. 2021; Cassidy 2018; Anitha 2008; Narayan 1995; Abraham and Tastsoglou 2016; Menjivar and Salcido 2002), particularly dependency on their primary immigrant husbands for obtaining legal permanency in the United States and prohibitions on gainful employment. Accordingly, Menjivar and Salcido (2002) have asserted that exploration of these factors regarding domestic violence and immigrant women is essential for the advancement of scholarship and for informing policy.

While the literature on domestic violence and immigrant women has shed light on immigration and the contexts it creates for immigrant communities resulting in abuse of women in families, few researchers have examined how those contexts of international migration can in fact inflict violence *on* the entire immigrant family. For that, attention should be directed to the body of work on international migration that has deliberated on a broader meaning of violence that speaks to its impact on the daily lives of immigrants. Solis (2003), for instance, has theorized the construction of the illegal immigrant identity that is produced at the societal level (through mass media, immigration laws, public opinion, and so on) to be infused with violence because it is injurious to the lives of those on whom the identity is thrust. Using undocumented Mexican youth as a case in point, Solis suggests that this kind of 'societal-institutional violence' is what leads to violent expressions by the youth to make sense of their lives. The societal violence and violence by immigrants, according to Solis, are therefore dialectically linked. Furthermore, scholars such as Menjivar and Abrego (2012) developed the concept of 'legal violence' to capture the harm caused to immigrants by immigration laws. Like Solis' conceptualization, this kind of systemic violence is not always physical in nature. Instead, Menjivar and Abrego propose that the gradual convergence of immigration and criminal laws over time and the various threats to immigrants' daily existence as a result constitute violence. More specifically, the constant threat of deportation combined with making immigrants criminally liable for their illegal status which leads to family separation, facilitation of abuse of immigrants in the workplace, and/or limitation on their educational opportunities is violence because it causes psychological harm and serves to marginalize the immigrants. Peter Benson's (2011) ethnography, '*El Campo: Faciality and Structural Violence in Farm Labor Camps*,' raises more questions regarding the meaning of violence in the lives of migrant farmworkers in particular. Focusing specifically on their living and labour

[3] 'Native-born' is a term used by American immigration scholars to differentiate those born in the United States versus those who are foreign born.

[4] I was unable to find any scholarship on domestic violence and families immigrating from Europe (read: white). If the research is lacking, then it is problematic to assert that only Asian cultures (read: nonwhite) ignore abuse experienced by women or have higher rates of domestic violence, as the extant research alludes.

conditions, Benson directs attention to violence as foundational to the history of farm work. Again, violence here is not physical. But, violence, suggested by Benson, is understood as normalization of the oppressive working conditions of farm work and squalid living conditions because the workers are seen as racially unworthy of belonging to the United States. Profit motives of capitalist agricultural production, working in tandem with the construction of migrant farmworkers as the 'other,' hold up this system of violence.

This discourse specific to the link between international migration and violence is informed by larger conversations on the very meaning of violence. Scholars in this tradition have theorized violence as wider and multi-layered than its commonly identified manifestation in physical form. Going beyond this narrow legal definition of the phenomenon, Jackman (2002) "provides a stripped-down template to identify all behaviours that inflict, threaten, or cause injury" (p. 405) as violence. The definition includes a range of actions and injuries that constitute violence, of which corporeal action and injury is only one. Moreover, and perhaps even more importantly, Jackman asserts that all, regardless of social location or internalization of social morality or investment in social status, commit violence. Violence, thus, from Jackman's framework is all encompassing and infused into the fabric of social life. Quite to the contrary, Farmer's (1996, 2004) concept of 'structural violence,' which "is violence exerted systematically—that is, indirectly—by everyone who belongs to a certain social order" (Farmer 2004: 307), is grounded on a moral position against oppression. It is "intended to inform the study of the social machinery of oppression" (Farmer 2004: 307). Farmer uses Haiti to illustrate this concept of 'structural violence.' Accordingly, Farmer posits that this "social machinery of oppression" must be located within Haiti's history of colonization and integration into transnational slavery in explaining its contemporary social struggles with poverty and diseases. For Farmer, violence is committed when the powerful subjugates for its own interests. In developing this theoretical framework, Farmer invokes the work of Johan Galtung. Akin to Farmer, Galtung (1969), who was a Norwegian sociologist, referred to "structural violence as *social injustice*" (p. 171). Galtung developed this concept basing it on an idea of violence whereby power is mobilized to limit the potential of individuals and/or groups of which somatic realizations are only one form. To that end, power imbalances were key in the definition of violence advanced by Galtung, including forms of violence that are normalized and find subdued or no expression in society or in individuals.

This discourse on international migration and violence lends support to expanding the extant frame of looking only within the family to reflect on the context of international migration and its impact *on* immigrant families. Afore discussed theoretical points concerning violence as infused in the very structures is necessary to keep in mind here. More specifically, it applies here because I explore how the framework of immigration laid out by receiving nations aim to serve its interests and destabilize family relationships as a form of violence. In other words, because international migration occurs within a context of power inequity whereby the flow of humans is mostly towards prosperous parts of the world, the violence inflicted on immigrant families is rooted in the very nature of (legal and illegal) crossing into the borders of the powerful nations that dictate its terms based on its 'national' interests. I use the term '*family disruption*' to capture this link between international migration and family violence. Undoubtedly, the research on domestic violence and immigrant women has been essential in understanding how international migration can create conditions ripe for either exacerbating or even sparking abuse of women in immigrant families. Contributions of this literature are important to the study of gender, family, and international migration. However, I advance the argument that the very structure of international migration lays the foundation for inflicting violence on all members of the family, men, and women, for which a broader understanding of violence is required.

9.3 Methodology

The analysis is based on both primary and secondary data. The primary data consists of ongoing research on immigrant families residing in the United States and Punjab, India as well as my prior work on immigrant Sikh yellow taxi drivers in the New York metropolitan area (Mitra 2012). For this article, 'immigrant families' is defined as families that have at least one immigrant member. The immigrant Sikhs, whether in the United States or in Punjab, were predominantly from the rural areas of Punjab. In Punjab, data were collected mostly from families who resided in the *Doaba*[5] region. All interviewees were accessed through personal networks and then snowballed from there onwards from multiple starting points.

For the research on taxi drivers in the United States, a total of fifty-nine immigrant Sikh men were interviewed. Forty of them were interviewed in 2000 and another nineteen were interviewed in 2008–9. The cabbies were approached where they stopped for rest in Manhattan, selected from a list of references for yellow cabbies obtained from New York Taxi Workers Alliance (NYTWA) which is an advocacy group for all taxi drivers in New York City and approached at the taxi garages that lease taxis.[6] Additional respondents were snowballed from the initial ones who were interviewed. To further diversify the source of the interviewees, drivers from both day and night shifts were included. Most of the interviews were conducted in the homes of the cabbies, with a very small number conducted at the Punjabi eateries in Manhattan where the cabbies stopped for rest. Over time, I also established rapport with the owners of the Punjabi eateries, commonly referred to as *dhaba* by the cabbies. This rapport was important in building trust with the owners who then gave me the space to spend time at the eateries and approach drivers for interviews. In fact, owners at two of the eateries introduced me to the drivers when they stopped for rest and encouraged them to speak with me. Only one interview was conducted at a popular fast-food restaurant.

It is also important to mention that I got my feet wet so-to-speak, as a novice researcher in 2000 when I initiated the research on immigrant Sikh yellow cabbies with the help of a Pakistani yellow cabbie, Bahadur Khan, who took me in his cab from Astoria, Queens (a suburb of New York City) to one of the *dhabas* in lower Manhattan (which no longer exists), paid for my lunch, and introduced me to the cabbies at the eatery. In fact, he did not charge me for the ride from Queens to Manhattan.

The relationship between gender roles in Sikh families and international migration was additionally assessed with interviewees sought from gurdwaras in the suburb of Queens in New York and primarily two gurdwaras in New Jersey. I established rapport with members of the *sangat*[7] by visiting the gurdwaras and spending time engaging in informal conversations at the prayer and *langar*[8] halls. Also, I introduced myself to the priests, or *gianijis* at the gurdwaras and key members of the board governing the gurdwaras who then took an interest in offering themselves as interviewees and/or made it comfortable for me to spend time at the gurdwaras. These relationships were crucial in making

[5] The state of Punjab in India is divided into three regions—*Malwa, Majha,* and *Doaba.*

[6] Individuals can lease taxis per shift or per week from what are called fleet garages. Fleet garages own several taxis that are leased to drivers. Or individuals can purchase taxis and/or medallions and drive as individual owner-drivers as well. The yellow cabbies of New York City are independent contractors who must pay a fee for leasing as well as for gas during their shift, in addition to being responsible for their own fringe benefits, such as health care. That is, the yellow cabbies are not employees of the fleet garages. For a detailed discussion on the system of leasing in the New York taxi industry and its impact on the cab drivers, please see *Punjabi Immigrant Mobility in the United States* (Mitra 2012, 2003).

[7] Congregation.

[8] Community cooking and eating area; for a basic knowledge on Sikhism, refer to https://www.britannica.com/topic/Sikhism/Guru-Angad.

me a familiar face in these places of worship. From the initial contacts at the gurdwaras, other informants were snowballed. Most interviews were conducted at the gurdwara.

Interviews were mostly conducted in Hindustani (i.e. Hindi-Urdu, commonly referred to as 'Hindi' in India) and Punjabi with a smattering of English. I transcribed and translated the interviews. Next, I looked for themes along which the informants converged or diverged as it related to the research questions. I identified the various larger patterns in their immigration experience which then informed the analysis.

The ongoing project is also a collaboration with filmmaker, Shashwati Talukdar. Included[9] in this discussion is one interview conducted by Talukdar of a Pakistani-Punjabi male immigrant in Hong Kong.[10]

9.4 *'Family Disruption'* and International Migration

To further the central argument of this paper—that the discourse on domestic violence in immigrant families should be expanded to include *'family disruption'* whereby disruption of gender roles within families generate friction within the unit to the detriment of its members because international migration creates the context for infliction of violence *on* immigrant families, including both men and women—I look at three types of "disrupted (immigrant) families" who are on immigration statuses with varying degrees of precarity. They are families that are forced to separate, immigrants on dependent spouse visas, and spouses abandoned in Punjab, India. To make it clear, I demarcate families that are forced to separate from spouses abandoned in Punjab. For the former, separation is a result of the immigration avenues availed to cross over into the destination country. Typically, these are families that utilize unauthorized means of immigration that bar spouses from immigrating with them, forcing separation among members of the family unit. In contrast, families where spouses are abandoned are those with whom all communication is severed by the immigrating spouse. Dependent spouses, for this chapter, are those spouses who immigrate with primary immigrants, upon whom the spouses' immigration status is dependent.

9.5 Family Separation

While separation of family members is the product of a choice at the individual level to emigrate, that individual level choice leading to this kind of *'family disruption'* must be located within broader contexts that influence these *choices*. Sukhwant's immigration story is instructive here because it speaks to the multi-dimensional factors that lead to *'family disruption'* and proved to be injurious to the family unit.

Sukhwant immigrated alone to the United States, leaving behind in Ludhiana his wife and two children. Sukhwant's separation from his family was a consequence of his *choice* to immigrate to the United States on a tourist visa. Notably, separation from family members is not an inevitable outcome of travelling on a tourist visa. Instead, the *'family disruption'* is a result of the socio-legal parameters that impacted Sukhwant's decision to emigrate and subsequent strategies of emigration that he adopted. While the legal parameters within which Sukhwant made his decision are set by United States' immigration laws, the social ones comprise the normative modes of immigration designed by Sukhwant's friends and family to bypass those legal restrictions. The immigration law to which I allude to here is specifically the 1965 Immigration and Nationality Act which lifted explicit prohibition on nonwhite immigration. Instead, the Act instituted several provisions via which individuals, regardless of race,

[9] For more information on Shashwati Talukdar's work, go to the website of Talukdar's film company, Four Nine and Half Pictures, https://fournineandahalf.com/.

[10] Do note that all names of informants mentioned in this article are pseudonyms to protect the anonymity of the informants.

could immigrate to the United States, including on the basis of employment. However, the quota for unskilled labour, for which immigrants like Sukhwant and his co-ethnics would qualify, was kept low. Typically then, the interview data suggest that immigrants of low socioeconomic status entered on tourist visas with the (unstated) intention to live and work in the United States. So, they would let their tourist status lapse, somehow secure work authorization, eventually become permanent residents and then sponsor their wives and children. Sukhwant followed the same path—one that was advised by his friend who had immigrated before him. It is also a path that led Sukhwant to driving yellow taxis as it did for his co-ethnics. Notably, vacancies in the New York City taxi industry were an outcome of a decline in its working conditions since its restructuring in 1979, along with a decline in the proportion of native-born white labour because the group moved up the social ladder and consequently, out of the industry (Mitra 2012). The vacancies were filled by immigrant workers like Sukhwant and his co-ethnics. Remarkably, the New York City industry is one that made it easy for those without proper work authorization to keep working. While it allowed the new (undocumented) immigrants to work, it also kept them legally vulnerable to the whims and fancies of the owners/employers in the business. Not only could they lose work if the employers decided to verify their documents, but they also risked deportation for their illegal presence in the country.

In such legally tenuous circumstances of immigration and employment, '*family disruption*' was inevitable. For Sukhwant, as the primary breadwinner for his family who migrated to look for better opportunities, that meant separation from his wife and children until he established himself in the United States. Otherwise, the entire family would become 'illegal.' The '*paper marriage*' he later contracted to get his legal permanent residency permitted him to reunite with his children because he could sponsor them through the family reunification provision of the aforementioned 1965 Immigration and Nationality Act. Since he had to officially divorce his wife in Ludhiana to remarry for the green card, he remained separated from his wife.[11] Notably, the 'family reunification' provision of the 1965 Act was intended to covertly encourage European (read: white) immigration in post-Civil Rights United States (Law 2002; Reimers 1996). Once put in place, however, it created avenues for those like Sukhwant to use it in their favour. Nevertheless, the mother of his children, now his 'former' wife, was 'stuck there,' as one of his children said when he walked me out after the interview. The '*family disruption*' experienced by Sukhwant was compounded by the financial stress of the '*paper marriage*' which was 25,000 dollars paid with credit cards and presumably, the expenditures for passage to the United States as well. In the United States, Sukhwant lived the life of a single parent of two children, presumably a disruption in the expectations of being the father and breadwinner for the family. One of his children was a teenager attending high school. The older one drove taxis with him. Both drove the day shift. Sukhwant decided against purchasing a medallion or a taxi and become an individual owner-driver, a common practice among the informant cabbies, partly because, as he said, "*...when will we meet if we drive at different times? So, we have dinner together every night. It's convenient.*" Inevitably, Sukhwant's wife role as a mother was also disrupted from the dominant expectation of motherhood.

The flip side of Sukhwant's story is of Maninder's. While Sukhwant's story speaks to the impact of '*family disruption*' from the perspective of the immigrant husband, Maninder's account brings to fore the harm inflicted on the family from the point of view of the wife left behind. Soon after Maninder and Sukhdev were

[11]Whether the wife consented to this separation is outside the purview of this research. But it seems that such decisions of family separation are a collective decision making within patriarchy whereby the roles and decision making follows dominant gender norms, whereby the man's role as the breadwinner is preserved as is the supportive role of the woman within the patriarchal heterosexual family.

married, Sukhdev left for Paris, leaving her with the responsibility of raising their two sons by herself. It was a decision that Maninder supported because emigration was perceived as financially beneficial for the family. The opportunities to earn a higher income were thought to be much greater overseas.

Maninder and Sukhdev's perception of poor job access in Punjab is not unfounded. Reports show the state's notably high unemployment rates (Gill 2004).[12] These contemporary figures on unemployment in Punjab, however, have a longer history. In '*Towards an Alternative Strategy of Economic Development in Punjab*,' Lakhwinder Singh's (2015) discussion suggests that Punjab's contemporary economic struggle should be contextualized within the Indian subcontinent's history of colonialism, making Punjab a border state that nurtured an antagonistic relationship between India and Pakistan, the government's focus on agricultural based economy versus development of industries in Punjab, strife among political parties, poor policy-making both at the level of the state and the Union government, as well as domestic political conflict that ravaged Punjab's economic stability in the 1980s (partly attributable to the historical backdrop of a gradual decline in Punjab's economic growth), while the rest of India moved ahead. Such factors combined with the rising cost of agricultural production and changing weather patterns have been detrimental to the economic returns of small farmers and agricultural labourers. Suicide, a form of violence, committed by both has been a fatal outcome of this decline in Punjab's economy. Certainly, such economic and political uncertainties have incentivized international migration—factors reported by the informants to have been influential in their decision to emigrate and endure '*family disruption*.'

For Sukhdev, poor access to work did not mean unemployment. But he did not earn enough to meet his expenses working as a scooter mechanic in a village shop. Sukhdev's less than high school education compounded those constraints on his employment options, at least Maninder seemed to think that to be the reason for limits on his opportunities to find work. Hence, Sukhdev decided to emigrate. It was a decision which Maninder supported, even though she expressly did not welcome the physical separation from him, conflict within the joint family and taking on the responsibility of raising the sons by herself. While her 'support' is not outside of patriarchy, I hesitate to characterize her as powerless. Maninder is an agent insofar as she acted in accordance with patriarchal gender roles and played a role in the subsequent immigration decisions as a member of the family. Nevertheless, my conversation with Maninder suggests though that Sukhdev's employment overseas did not significantly increase earnings for the family. His employment in the informal sector in Paris, the sector in which most of the Sikh immigrants from the *Doaba* region of Punjab likely work (Moliner 2011), tends to be marked by precarity and consequently, meant irregular remittances to the family. Maninder said,

> He does the same work as he did in the village here ...depends on how much work he gets. He works as labor. If he works continuously, then he sends money regularly. Otherwise, he can send money every two or three months.

That Sukhdev is undocumented in France, part of a globally increasing population of immigrants and particularly a notable proportion of immigrants from Punjab in France (Moliner 2011) only serves to increase his economic uncertainty and consequently his family's. Like the Chinese clandestine immigrants in Du's research (2020) who met the demand in sectors of the economy avoided by local labour, Sukhdev's illegality benefits France's economy as well, not to mention that illegality itself is an outcome of laws created by the state to control borders and justify implementing strategies to

[12] https://timesofindia.indiatimes.com/city/chandigarh/pbs-employment-woes-get-graver-with-each-passing-year/articleshow/90088492.cms. *See also* the lecture by Sucha Singh Gill entitled "Emigration from Punjab: Socio-economic implications" https://www.youtube.com/watch?v=Fa17kjRyP4o.

regulate the flow of individuals into a country (Franck Düvell, discussed by Moliner 2011). Here, the state holding power decides who crosses over the border and what kind of work they should get which, in turn, can lead to '*family disruption*.' For Maninder, this wielding of power by the French government meant uncertainty of employment for Sukhdev and consequently, financial precarity which ruptured relationships with members of the joint family with whom she and her sons lived.

> Fighting within the family [extended family members]. We [referring to extended family] used to live together before. We've been separated for four years. He didn't send money for two to four months. So, they [extended family members – mother-in-law and brother-in-law] were like how can we feed them? Too many difficulties when there was less money.

To resolve familial conflict, Maninder decided to live separately from the joint family, including her in-laws. Maninder and Sukhdev were also given a small share of the house and did not receive any money from sale of the family land. At the time of the interview, Maninder had been living separately from the joint family for about four years. The very patriarchal norms that influenced the decision for Sukhdev to emigrate for work are the same ones that proscribed Maninder from working outside the home. When I asked her the reasons for not working, she pointed to her lack of education and her joint pains as the reasons. In her words:

> What kind of work can I do? I am illiterate. I can only do housework. I can't do any work. What would I do? Plus, my knees and legs hurt. I can't work. I do some little work in the house.

Hence, the rules of border crossing determined by laws of the receiving nation (France, in this instance) partly based on its economic interests coincides with the economic precarity of Punjab resulting in disruption of Maninder and Sukhdev's family unit.

Every evening for the last fifteen years, Maninder, Sukhdev, and their boys 'met' on WhatsApp video calls. Sukhdev had attempted to sponsor Maninder and the two boys by paying an 'agent,' the avenue that he had availed to enter France. However, Maninder and the children's visas were rejected. Presumably, that further harmed the stability of the family. In addition to the emotional instability due to separation from each other, the family suffered financially too because they had paid about a lakh to the 'agent.' Although the sons were keen on emigrating, Maninder was reluctant. She would prefer that her sons "… enlist in the military, or get a bank job, or buy a store." Maninder advises them,

> Stay near your wife. You stay close and give them happiness. I have been unhappy all my life. I say that what happened with me shouldn't happen to my "nu" [daughter-in-law]. They stay well.

Evidently, for their family, immigration has meant separation and loneliness. She said:

> Because he [Maninder's husband] said he has to go for the happiness of the family… Now, he is alone there, and we are alone here. There's neither happiness, nor sadness. We can't take care of each other. We can't partake in each other's lives. When he gets sick, he doesn't have anybody to take care of him. At least I have my children here. He is more unhappy than me.

Maninder and Sukhdev had lived together for only about four years after she got married to him at age nineteen. Ever since, they have lived in two separate continents and have seen each other only on WhatsApp video calls. Maninder's husband calls.

> In the evenings at the end of his workday which is 10:30 Indian time. It's evening there. Then he calls… Yes, we do video call.

9.6 Dependent Spouses

Spousal dependent visas are another avenue through which immigration can occur. Both men and women can be dependents on the primary immigrants' visa. The legal process to acquire permanency for dependent spouses through sponsorship by the primary immigrant can be lengthy. Until the application process reaches a certain stage, the dependent spouse is also legally barred from working. More importantly, because the primary immigrant can withdraw sponsorship for permanent residency of the dependent spouse before the process is complete, it confers on the former a great degree of power in the marital relationship. This process allows the primary immigrant to exert control over the dependent spouse because of the latter's immigrant status and financial dependency on the former. It is this power imbalance in immigrant families created by the nonimmigrant visa system that can breed *'family disruption.'*

This link between the dependent visa program and *'family disruption'* is illustrated in Pallavi Banerjee's (2022) work on professional Indian immigrants on dependent visas living in the United States. In the book, *'The Opportunity Trap'*, Banerjee analyses how the racialized, gendered, and labour needs that structure the United States nonimmigrant visa category harm spousal relationships in (heterosexual) immigrant families that utilize it to avail work opportunities. Through ethnographic and semi-structured interviews, Banerjee looked at both husbands and wives on dependent visas and the subsequent disruption generated within families because of the legal framework, predicated on the United States interests of race, gender and capital, which create this dependency.[13] The analysis shows how financial dependency due to laws that prohibit dependent spouses from working and/or force upon them a professional non-identity (because the dependent spouse may have resigned from a thriving professional career prior to immigration) frustrate the relationship between the couples leading to divorce, dissatisfaction and/or abuse. While this structure of immigration laws suits the labour needs of the United States economy, it nurtures an environment conducive to *'family disruption.'* In families where men are the dependent spouses, albeit a much smaller number compared to families with women as dependent immigrants, legal prohibition on employment causes men to feel emasculated and, in turn, increases the potential for intimate partner violence in the home. Here, patriarchal values informing the dependency visa program which presumes all dependent immigrant spouses to be women intersect with patriarchal values of the immigrants, resulting in destabilization of immigrant families. Ester Gallo's (2006) work on dependent Syrian Christian husbands who accompany their wives from Kerala to Italy show a similar pattern in the intersection of immigration law and patriarchy leading to *'family disruption.'* Not only are the dependent men prohibited from working in Italy, compelled to reside with employers of their wives who work as domestic help, this severely curtails their autonomy within their 'own homes.' Because Italian immigration law permits employers to terminate domestic workers before the end of contracts, it disempowers immigrant husbands as well as entire family units. Termination by the employer also generates conflict between the men and their in-laws, the very source of the wives' employment. That these men are in a minority in Kerala whose job search failed and pushed them to become secondary to the women in the households can be particularly emasculating, a feeling that already existed prior to immigration, due to their unemployed status in Kerala.

For Italy, of course, the domestic workers, the majority of whom are immigrant women from Eastern Europe, Asia, Africa, and Latin America (Bonizzoni 2013), provide a 'vital and irreplaceable' service (Fondazione Ismu 2008, cited in Bonizonni 2013), a demand for which is created by poor investment in social welfare by the state (Bonizzoni 2013). Thus, vulnerability of the immigrant domestic workers allows Italian families "a flexible, personalized and intensive form of care at an affordable price; the State saves money and families gain more income as long as Italian women are relieved from care responsibilities to seek paid employment" (Bonizzoni 2013: 2). Therefore, the Italian state supports families by "leaning on a labour market which is, however, extensively characterized by informality and deregulation" (Bonizzoni 2013: 2), but it is this very system of labour immigration that establishes the context for *'family disruption'* of the immigrant workers' families.

[13] See Banerjee for a detailed discussion on American immigration laws, heterosexual immigrant family dynamic and its implications for immigrant family violence.

The phenomenon of 'slave grooms'[14] is illustrative of yet another link between immigration systems, dependent spouses, and '*family disruption.*' 'Slave grooms' is a term used to refer to married immigrant men who endure intimate partner violence as spouses who have immigrated on dependent visas. This is reflected in Afzal's immigration story where his trials and tribulations began when he immigrated to Hong Kong from Pakistan on a dependent spouse visa after getting married to Ayesha. According to Hasan (2010), an interconnected set of structural factors that go as far back as the colonial period that continue to define and restrain socioeconomic options for certain segments of the population are influential in making decisions of emigration from Pakistan. Relocation of population that destabilized community ties and created population pressure resulting from British policies of development of canal colonies as well as the Partition, Hasan argues, are two such examples of constricting socioeconomic options that incentivize migration. Later, implementation of structural adjustment programs in the early 1990s, a form of neo imperialism, is argued by Hasan to also be the foundation for poor social and economic outcomes contributing to emigration from the country. Afzal's life in Pakistan was confined within this set of structures from the past to the present. He experienced it as perceiving "...that countries like Pakistan, India, Nepal do not have strong 'economies.' Consequently, when his mother-in-law, coworkers and immigrant friends and family encouraged him to emigrate to improve his quality of life, including earning more to better support his parents, Afzal made the decision to marry Ayesha and leave for Hong Kong."

In Hong Kong, Afzal became a victim of what he defined as 'domestic abuse,' which he suffered at the hands of his wife. The abuse was both financial and physical, whereby his wife not only controlled his income, she also physically abused him for questioning her authority in the household. Afzal's accounts additionally suggest that the marriage was not consummated, and his living space was separate from his wife's. Ayesha, in fact, had a boyfriend. The boyfriend was of Chinese origin and a native of Hong Kong. Afzal's options as a spouse on dependent immigrant visa were limited. Since he hoped for long-term permanent stay in Hong Kong, leaving the marriage was undesirable. His wife could withdraw the application for permanency. The abusive situation was such that Afzal did not control his own salary. He was not even in possession of his passport and other related documents. It was his wife who collected his salary from the employer as well as kept his passport and other documents. Whereas Afzal had married Ayesha in search of a better life, Ayesha had married him due to pressure from her family to marry a Pakistani. Ayesha's marriage with Afzal was her second one. The first husband, according to Afzal, was from Pakistan and abused too. It is interesting to note the following—while patriarchal familial authority exerted on Ayesha influenced her to marry Afzal, immigration laws conferred power on Ayesha and her family who were all permanent immigrants of Hong Kong, power that Ayesha effectively mobilized in her favour.

After about a year of this ordeal, Afzal fled from his wife's home one night following a violent argument. Thereafter, he filed for divorce. But that did not mitigate the precarity of his living situation because his immigration status was tied to that of his wife's. Upon advice from his lawyer, Afzal applied for permanent stay as a 'refugee.' It was an immigration status of which he was ashamed. It was also one that legally barred him from working in Hong Kong. Until the final decision on his application was made by the government, Afzal continued to live in Hong Kong and worked illegally.

[14] See the documentary on "slave grooms:" https://www.youtube.com/watch?v=7GcyHONmS84. The documentary focuses on the South Asian men who are presumably trafficked to Hong Kong through arranged marriages subsequent to which they are forced to provide indentured labour for the wife and her family.

9.7 Abandoned Spouses

Domestic abuse inflicted on men is further evidenced in the phenomenon of husbands abandoned by their emigrant wives in Punjab.[15] A confluence of multiple factors facilitates this form of '*family disruption*.' As already mentioned, one factor is scarcity of employment for men in Punjab which incentivizes emigration. However, their lower human capital limit chances of emigration, in contrary to the women[16] who perform much better in education and thus, stand a better chance of emigrating. To overcome this obstacle to work, men marry women desirous of advancing their education and/or career abroad. Typically, it is the men who finance the women's passage and education abroad because the implicit marriage contract is this exchange, i.e. the wives will pursue education/employment abroad and the husbands will emigrate on spousal visa sponsorship to find employment abroad. The other piece of this puzzle is a demand for workers in health and personal care sectors in western countries (Walton-Roberts et al. 2017). This demand is met with labour migration from the Global South. It is a continuation of a migration of labour (forced or voluntary) starting with the expansion of western capitalism in the seventeenth century. 'Visa regimes'[17] continue the historical exploitative relationship between the Global North and South. It is here that the story of emigration of women nurses in Punjab fits, because it is Punjabi women who meet this demand in North America (Walton-Roberts et al. 2017). In so doing, the women use the 'visa regimes' in their favour and against the interests of the men they marry. That is, once they have emigrated, they decide against sponsoring their husbands for visas, effectively abandoning their husbands in Punjab. In such instances of spousal abandonment, which should be noted is far less than abandoned wives, reports have shown men to commit suicide.[18] Evidently, power that is conferred on women as the primary immigrant in this system of immigration is wielded by them in ways that harm men, albeit the contract for marriage was still within the boundaries of patriarchy. Paternalistic laws in India do not offer much legal recourse for abandoned husbands (compared to abandoned wives) because the patriarchal system assumes the former to be strong and not in need of protection and this facilitates abandonment of husbands.

9.8 Discussion

Emergent from the data is support for the concept of immigrant '*family disruption*' which I urge should be considered as family violence in the context of international migration. Galtung thought an expansive definition of violence was necessary to capture the range of behaviours and/or influences limiting human potential. Thus, it follows that violence can manifest as harmful actions of an actor, carrying adverse physical and/or psychological effects, and/or inhere in the very structures of a society with effects that are invisible. Galtung and Farmer's conceptualization of violence have been influential for scholars of international migration in exploring the meaning of harm, visible and invisible, as well as at the structural and individual levels, inflicted on immigrants as they

[15] https://www.vice.com/en/article/xgd547/whatsapp-group-abandoned-indian-punjab-men-wives-in-canada & https://theprint.in/features/punjabi-men-are-being-abandoned-by-nri-wives/815104/.

[16] https://theprint.in/features/punjabi-men-are-being-abandoned-by-nri-wives/815104/. The abandoned men have a WhatsApp support group called 'thugiya de peedit' (victims of fraud) where the men have created community by discussing this kind of abuse and violence faced from their wives. Refer to https://www.vice.com/en/article/xgd547/whatsapp-group-abandoned-indian-punjab-men-wives-in-canada. Also, a Ludhiana based organization, ABNHHI, is dedicated to addressing the concerns of both men and women abandoned by their immigrant spouses.

[17] See *The Opportunity Trap* by Pallavi Banerjee for a discussion of 'visa regimes'.

[18] https://theprint.in/features/punjabi-men-are-being-abandoned-by-nri-wives/815104/.

journey across international borders. In alignment with this expansive definition of violence, the data direct attention to three types of '*family disruption*'—separated families, dependent spouse families, and abandoned spouses. The violence inflicted on the families was in the form of a forced decision to live separately, unequal relationship of power among the couples which contributed to financial or physical abuse in immigrant families and abandonment of spouses in the country of origin—all a product of provisions of immigration laws that guided the entry and settlement of the immigrants. In other words, immigration laws prevented realization of the potential of the immigrants, whether it was as family units or as individuals. This, as Galtung theorized, is violence.

The distress of forced family separation was evidenced in the helplessness as well as material and emotional hardship experienced by the immigrants as they lived apart across continents. Menjivar and Abrego (2012) argue that immigrants in precarious legal statuses often make a 'choice' that involves "lengthy and uncertain family separations" (p. 1402) as a measure of safety for their families. Such separations become a normalized and routine part of what it means to be an immigrant. In the case of the Punjabi-Sikh men, the decision was for them to go ahead, leaving behind their children with their wives and extended family members until the men legalized their status. Like Menjivar and Abrego document for Central American immigrants, the periods of separation for the Punjabi-Sikh men were often lengthy, and in some cases union with the entire family seemed completely out of reach. This, Menjivar and Abrego assert, is legal violence. The violence is not visible. The violence is not direct. The violence is not inflicted by any member of the family. This violence is infused instead, into the laws that aim to preserve the 'sanctity' of national borders. The result of course is destabilization of immigrant families, a form of "legal violence that frames the everyday lives" (Menjivar and Abrego 2012: 1402) of the Punjabi-Sikh immigrants of this research, a phenomenon that should inform the discourse on immigrant family violence.

Additionally, the victimization and abandonment of men in immigrant (heterosexual) marital unions enabled by provisions in immigration laws reinforce the importance of going beyond dominant explanations of domestic violence in the context of international migration. That means, in these scenarios of immigrant domestic strife, a straightforward link between patriarchy and domestic violence is unworkable because the variable of immigration laws forms the overarching context for catalyzing domestic strife that breaks the expected rules of violence in patriarchy. In fact, it is the immigration laws, and not just dominant patriarchal expectations, that shaped the relationships of power within immigrant (heterosexual) households whereby men too could be subordinated and be subjected to violence. Certainly, this research recorded a pattern of violence experienced by men in immigrant families when they immigrated on the dependent visa category, even though heterosexual unions formed within the context of patriarchy. Here, the women, i.e. their wives, were the perpetrators of violence. Immigration laws trumped patriarchal authority of the men in the households by conferring power on the women, the primary immigrants, and/or the employers of the women. In the process, that patriarchal social relations are ultimately about uneven distribution of power is made clear. Moreover, the pressure of immigration laws on family relations is such that disruption occurred in the form of divorce or even return of the dependent spouse (men and women) to India, even if that meant prolonged or permanent separation from each other. Indeed, there is evidence of women being subjected to domestic violence, especially in instances where men on dependent visas attempted to forcefully assert their masculinity within families. But this commonly identified form of familial conflict does not capture the complete scope of domestic violence that marked the immigrant families.

Elements of structural and symbolic violence were also influential in shaping the larger context for '*family disruption*.' Structural violence resided in the creation of a system of labour supply for which immigrants on precarious legal statuses proved to be advantageous in sectors marked by declining conditions of work. The New York taxi industry is a prime example. It was the Sikh immigrants who satisfied vacancies in the New York taxi industry created by declining conditions of work resulting from restructuring of the industry in 1979 as well as due to a concurrent shift in traditional sources of labour for it.[19] That majority of the Sikh immigrants, at least based on the sample of my research, were undocumented was thus useful for the industry. Here, the pliability of undocumented immigrant labour is especially useful because the terms of employment set by employers are likely to be accepted without much resistance, including conditions for termination which can lead to deportation for those without adequate or any documentation. In fact, interviews with the immigrant Sikh cabbies showed that there were loopholes in renewal of taxi drivers' licenses that ensured work for the undocumented, with the tacit knowledge that they could be deported when/if deemed necessary. The violence here is embedded in the structure of an industry that thrives on vulnerability of its workers, specifically on their workers' undocumented immigrant statuses. The harm caused to them are manifest in the poor conditions of work and in the fear of deportation. This vulnerability translates into financial challenges to the families and keeps them separated. That the majority of the undocumented immigrant workers are drawn from the Global South speaks to a historical colonial relationship of power that explains contemporary immigration flows from the Global South to the Global North and immigration necessarily involves leaving 'home' and separation from families. For some, family separation is for a prolonged period. It is this deeply historical and exploitative relationship which continues through the present which Paul Farmer conceptualizes as "structural violence." The immigration policies that either create pathways of legal entry to fulfil labour needs of receiving nations or encourage undocumented immigration that lead to *'family disruption'* must be located within this historical-structural context.

Symbolic violence was present in the form of immigrants' submission to the immigration laws that reinforced their *'family disruption.'* One could assert that the choice made to submit to the law should not be seen within the purview of violence. But, as Jackman (2002) points out, "the compliance/noncompliance distinction is inherently ambiguous because people rarely act as free agents, but instead must usually make choices from a constrained set that has been predetermined by organizational or situational factors beyond their control" (p. 397). For the men and women of this research, the choices were made within the boundaries of a varying combination of immigration laws, gender expectations, employment opportunities in countries of origin versus destination and family well-being. A sense of powerlessness, therefore, was likely internalized by the immigrants considering such socio-economic-legal realities which circumscribed their lives. In the face of this experience of powerlessness, the immigrants 'chose' to separate from families, emigrate for better opportunities, escape patriarchy, and utilize extra legal avenues of immigration, thereby opting for submission, than resistance to the system. This is symbolic violence because these are actions that are detrimental to the immigrants, resulting from having internalized "social asymmetries, and to the legitimation of inequality and hierarchy, ranging from racism and sexism to expressions of class power" (Menjivar and Abrego 2012: 1386).

[19] See *Punjabi Immigrant Mobility* (Mitra 2012) for a detailed discussion on shifts in the racial stratification order along with changes in the New York taxi industry itself which Mitra argues impacted the source of labour for the New York taxi industry, leading eventually to a predominantly immigrant population becoming drivers of yellow taxis in the New York metropolitan area. For a discussion on broader changes experienced by the industry specifically, including its labour sources, see Anne Morris and Alan Foster's presentation at the Transportation Research Board in 1993 entitled "Changing Demographics of the Taxi Workforce: Implications for Taxi Driver Education." Bruce Schaller's work on the New York taxi industry provides additional sources on the structure, working conditions and labour sources in the industry (http://www.schallerconsult.com/).

To sum up, the data suggest a link between specific provisions of immigration laws, constructed based on the need for immigrants in the receiving nations, and the manifestation of the particular kind of '*family disruption*.' Those laws discourage immigration of entire family units and shape '*family disruption*' by forcing separation or creating conditions for domestic strife by conferring power on the immigrant desired in the receiving nation, subsequently increasing the chances of separation, abandonment or dependency. Acceptance of immigration provisions without resistance to them by the immigrants of course further leads to '*family disruption*.'

9.9 Conclusion

In this chapter, I have argued that '*family disruption*' is '*family violence*' in the context of international migration. The focus of this chapter has been on three types of immigrant '*family disruption*'—separated, dependent and abandoned. As discussed, this kind of violence in (heterosexual) immigrant families does not always manifest in commonly understood forms of physical force, including the dominant form of domestic abuse of women by men. But the violence lives in the structures of immigration laws of receiving societies that determine the avenue of entry, legal and illegal, and the subsequent position of those immigrants in the society. The violence of immigration laws coexists with the violence of limited job opportunities in sending societies, additionally pushing individual level choices to emigrate that are to the detriment of the families that choose to do so. This individual choice to emigrate and use of undocumented means of entry is further indicative of internalized oppression, or symbolic violence, that contributes to '*family disruption*.' While indirect, such forms of violence are injurious to the families. This injury should be considered within the range of violence that impacts immigrant households and analysed as '*family violence*.' By so arguing, I assert the importance of expanding the conversation to unseen/invisible forms of violence that inhere within structures and normalized with the support of power asymmetries exerted from the top as well as internalized by individuals at the bottom.

Acknowledgements I am indebted to the editors of this volume for their close reading and astute comments through the many stages of the draft that tremendously helped in improving it. Maggie Ussery deserves a special mention for sparing her valuable time to offer comments.

References

Abraham M, Tastsoglou E (2016) Interrogating gender, violence, and the state in national and transnational contexts: framing the issues. Current Soc Monograph 64:517–534

Anitha S (2008) Neither safety nor justice: the UK government response to domestic violence against women. J Soc Wlfre & Fam Law 30:189–202

Benson P (2011) El Campo: faciality and structural violence in farm labor camps. Cult Anthropol 23:589–629

Bonizzoni P (2013) Undocumented domestic workers in Italy: surviving and regularizing strategies. In: Trandafyllidou A (ed) Irregular migrant domestic workers in Europe. Routledge, London

Cassidy K (2018) Where can I get free? Everyday bordering, everyday incarceration. Trans Inst Brit Geogr 44:48–62

Cherlin A (2013) Public and private families. McGraw-Hill, New York

Ciabattari C (2022) Sociology of families: change, continuity, and diversity. Sage, Los Angeles

Du J (2020) Endurance, identity, and temporality: the ethnic labor market and labor process of Chinese migrant workers in France. J Chin Soc 7:1–22

Dủvell F (2008) Clandestine migration in Europe. Soc Sci Inform 47(4):479–497

Farmer P (1996) On suffering and structural violence: a view from below. Daedalus 125:261–283

Farmer P (2004) An anthropology of structural violence. Curr Anthropol 45:305–325

Gallo E (2006) Italy is not a good place for men: narratives of places, marriage, and masculinity among Malayali migrants. Glob Netw 6:357–372

Galtung J (1969) Violence, peace, and peace research. J Peace Res 6:167–191

Goncalves M, Matos M (2016) Prevalence of violence against immigrant women: a systematic review of the literature. J Family Violence 31:697–710

Hasan A (2010) Migration, small towns and social transformations in Pakistan. Environ Urban 22:33–50

Jackman M (2002) Violence in social life. Ann Rev Soc 28:387–415

Lum K (2016) Casted Masculinities in the Punjabi diaspora in Spain. South Asian Diaspora 8:31–48

Menjivar C, Abrego LJ (2012) Legal violence: immigration law and the lives of Central American immigrants. Am J Soc 117:1380–1421
Menjivar C, Salcido O (2002) Immigrant women and domestic violence: common experiences in different countries. Gend Soc 16:989–920
Mitra D (2012) Punjabi immigrant mobility in the United States: adaptation through race and class. Palgrave Macmillan, New York
Mitra D (2003) Rotating lives: indian cabbies in New York city. Dissertation, Temple University
Moliner C (2011) Sikh migration to France. In: Rajan SI, Percot M (eds) Dynamics of Indian Migration. Routledge, New Delhi, pp 49–63
Moliner C (2020) Vulnerable masculinities? Gender identity construction among young undocumented Sikh migrants in Paris. Religions 11:1–14
Morris A (1986) Taxi school: a first step in professionalizing taxi driving. Transpt Res Rec 1103:40–48
Narayan U (1995) "Male-Order" brides: immigrant women, domestic violence and immigration law. Hypatia 10:104–119
Park T, Mullins A, Zahir N et al (2021) Domestic violence and immigrant women: a glimpse behind a veiled door. Violence against Women 27:2910–2926
Reimers D (1996) Third World Immigration to the United States. In: Bean FD, Bell-Rose S (eds) Immigration and opportunity: race, ethnicity, and employment in the United States. Russell Sage Foundation, New York, pp 309–321
Rhee S (1997) Domestic violence in the Korean immigrant family. J Soc Soc Wlfre 24:63–77
Sabri B, Surendramal S et al (2019) Dangerous abusive relationships and source of resilience for South Asian immigrant women survivors of intimate partner violence. J Soc Work Glob Commu 4:1–18
Schaller B (2004) The changing face of taxi and limousine drivers. http://www.schallerconsult.com
Segrave M, Keel C, Wickes R (2021) One third of migrant and refugee women experience domestic violence, major survey reveals. The Conversation
Singh L (2015) Towards and alternative strategy of economic development in Punjab. Towards Alt Strat 2:249–265
Solis J (2003) Re-thinking illegality as a violence against, not by mexican immigrants, children, and youth. J Soc Issues 59:15–31
Sucha Singh Gill (2004) Emigration from Punjab: socio-economic implications. https://www.youtube.com/watch?v=Fa17kjRyP4o
Tonsing JC (2016) Complexity of domestic violence in a South Asian context in Hong Kong: cultural and structural impact. Soc Wrk Ed 35:18–30
Viddich C (1976) The New York cab driver and his fare. Schenkman Publishers, Massachussetts
Walton-Roberts M, Bhutani S, Kaur A (2017) Care and global migration in the nursing profession: a North-Indian perspective. Aust Geog 48:59–77
Zachariah KC, Mathew ET, Rajan IS (2001) Social, economic and demographic consequences of migration on Kerala. Int Migr 39:43–68

10 Violence on Naga Women in the Context of Illegal Liquor Trade: A Study in Kohima, Nagaland

Wungreithan Awungshi

Abstract

In 1989, the Government of Nagaland prohibited the sale, import, and consumption of bottled liquor. Illegal sale of liquor, however, continues to thrive throughout the state. A significant number of women, especially single mothers are involved in the illegal liquor trade. They conduct business mostly from their homes or from shops adjoining or close to their homes. The legal prohibition has created a space that allows several pressure groups to unofficially collect taxes from women liquor traders, thereby increasing their vulnerability to extortion, harassment, and violence. The chapter examines women's daily negotiations with violence within the context of illegal liquor trade in Kohima, Nagaland, to reorient the problem of violence in relation to labour vis-a-vis law and legality, as well as social norms and institutions. The findings and analysis in the chapter are based on primary research conducted by the author in Kohima, Nagaland, with the objective of understanding the social, legal, and historical contexts of the practice of liquor consumption within which violence in the form of mental harassment, physical altercations and threats endured by the Naga women liquor traders from intimate partners, customers, state authorities and the ostracization by the church operates.

Keywords

Liquor · Violence · Nagaland · Indo–Naga War · Kohima · Private · Public · Gendered work · Christianity · Single women · Prohibition · Labour · Immoral · Extortion · Threat · Social norms · Exclusion · Extortion · NLTP Act · Rice beer · *Zutho* · Dirty money · Illegal · Trade · Harassment · Bullying · Death threat · IMFL · Excise officers

10.1 Introduction

Historically Nagaland was an agrarian society largely dependent on forest and cultivated produce for its livelihood. Division of labour in Naga society was gendered, men would hunt and fish while women would collect firewood for domestic use, toil in the fields and tend to the work at home. This normative structure ensured that men remained engaged in work regarded as '*physically*' difficult or strenuous, while women were confined to tasks that qualified as '*lighter*'

W. Awungshi (✉)
Tata Institute of Social Sciences, Mumbai, India
e-mail: awungshijim@gmail.com

P. M. Anurag and S. Dwivedy (eds.), *Violence in Intimate Spaces*, Sustainable Development Goals Series, https://doi.org/10.1007/978-981-97-2657-8_10

work.[1] This clear demarcation of work based on gendered perceptions on who *could* and therefore *should* do *what* work while based on the physical strength required for the work, ensured at the same time that women remained confined to private spaces, namely, their home and surrounding cultivated fields; while men dominated all public spaces. The nature of work in Naga society was thus decided on patriarchal norms and sensibilities. The Indo-Naga war has seen a large number of men joining the '*national struggle'*, consequently, several men have moved out of the workforce to engage in the freedom struggle and many lives have been lost.[2] This period saw unprecedented number of women engage independently in food production, maintaining community affairs in addition to their household activities. With growing unemployment, Naga youth began migrating to metropolitan cities outside the state of Nagaland in search for work and employment opportunities. Since Naga women were always engaged in either agriculture or household activities, their passage from private to public spaces, specifically in areas traditionally dominated by men was viewed as unconventional and therefore unwarranted. Naga society is only gradually coming to terms with this transformation in traditional gender roles. In the context of Nagaland specifically and North-East India generally, there is a perception that Naga women are considered equal to men with regard to their social status. One reason for this perception is that the women have 25% reservation in the Village Development Board. Also the sex ratio of 943 against the average of 914 for all of India in 2001 indicates a favourable attitude towards women. Additionally, the female literacy levels stand at 76.11% which is 10% above the overall average for India. These numbers however, do not reflect the felt realities for women in Naga society. Despite the reservations for political participation of women, for the most part, women remained invisible in local and state level politics. No woman had ever been elected to the Nagaland State Assembly until the 2023 Nagaland Assembly elections.[3]

The gendered nature of public spaces, including work, provides a simplistic backdrop against which violence on Naga women engaged in the illegal liquor trade (women liquor traders) operates. The situation is complicated by the enactment of the *Nagaland Liquor Total Prohibition Act, 1989 (NLPT Act)*[4] that prohibits the sale, import and consumption of bottled liquor in the state of Nagaland. That the NLTP Act has failed in its objective is evidenced by the fact that illegal liquor from the neighbouring states of Assam and Meghalaya continues to flow *unregulated* into Nagaland. Though authorities patrol its borders with Assam, regularly seizing cases of liquor entering Nagaland, this does not appear to have acted as a deterrent.

Women traders interviewed during the course of fieldwork research reveal that customers pay as high as double or triple the original price of liquor at the black market that thrives in Nagaland and especially booms during the festive season. A beer can that costs approximately 120 Rs in Assam and Meghalaya, retails for 200 Rs in Kohima and other parts of Nagaland. The liquor bottles are clearly marked: "*For sale in*

[1] It was common to see women engaged in basket weaving and other crafts.

[2] The Government of India is in *conflict* with indigenous Naga Peoples who have inhabited the region for thousands of years. Estimates of the numbers killed in this civil war/struggle for independence vary—some claim it may be as high as 200,000. The *India-Naga conflict* is considered by India to be an internal civil war and by the Nagas to be the *self-defence of an independent people* against an external aggressor. Historically the Nagas were head-hunters, which may be the reason for their independence throughout the waves of colonialism. See: Phillips (2004).

[3] Ms. Jakhalu from the Dimapur-III constituency.

[4] The Nagaland Liquor Total Prohibition Act, 1989 (The Nagaland Act No. 4 OF 1990) https://www.indiacode.nic.in/bitstream/123456789/11850/1/the_nagaland_liquor_total_prohibition_act_1989.pdf. Accessed 3 June 2023. The Act came into force in 1990, it was amendment in 1994. The amendment brought about a change to the meaning of 'Para-Military forces' defined under Section 2(5) of the Act to accommodate the inclusion of other forces when posted in Nagaland.

Assam or Meghalaya only" yet it is freely available throughout Nagaland. Women engaged in the liquor trade have to pay several agencies including the police and the custom officers, to ensure that a regular supply of illegal liquor is smuggled into Nagaland. The truth is that the NLTP Act, far from deterring, has in fact enabled the proliferation of a framework within which pressure groups victimize women engaged in the liquor trade. The sale and consumption of liquor flourishes illegally, only now, women liquor traders are systemically exploitation by state entities such as the excise department, acting outside state authorization. In addition to state officials, women liquor traders face harassment from non-state-insurgent groups.[5] Evidently, those who enjoy the benefits derived from holding an official position per se, under the guise of this assumed authority, profit from the women liquor traders' intersectional marginalities[6] of gender, poverty and engagement in a trade deemed *illegal* and *immoral*. The power groups comprising state officials perform the role of violators of the very laws they are required in their official capacity to uphold. What remains a constant, is the presence of women in illegal liquor trade as one of the primary sufferers of the prohibition established under the NLTP Act and the recipients of depredation from state and non-state actors. In the district of Kohima[7], a significant number of women, particularly single mothers,[8] are involved in this trade. In patriarchal societies, the scrutiny on women engaged in the business of a product deemed not just illegal but also *immoral* goes up significantly. Majority of Nagaland's residents identify as Christians.[9] Among Christians in Nagaland, consumption of liquor contravenes their religious principles. It is therefore considered abominable in Naga society to consume or trade in liquor. Women traders as a result, fall far below the societal standards of *morality* marked out for Naga women and their earnings are regarded as '*unclean*' or "*dirty money*".[10]

This chapter examines the juxtaposition of '*violence*' and '*law*' within the context of illegal liquor trade in Nagaland and the engagement of Naga women in this trade. The findings and analysis presented are based on primary research[11] conducted between 2019 and 2020 by the author in Kohima, the capital city of the state of Nagaland in the North-Eastern part of India, with the objective of exploring the lives of

[5] *Supra* n. 2.

[6] Most women interviewed during the research and data collection process, stated that the liquor business was not their first choice of work since selling liquor is something that the society resents and the money that they earn is seen as *unclean* money. While in the initial years of the prohibition and engagement in the liquor trade, women felt a *shame* but over the period of time their presence in the trade has come to be normalised, yet most women also felt that given resources and other good opportunities they would leave the business.

[7] The town of Kohima was founded in 1878 when the British Empire established its headquarters in the Naga Hills. Kohima is the capital city of the state of Nagaland since 1963. The district of Kohima includes the capital city of Kohima and the adjoining areas that fall within the district.

[8] Most of the women traders are unmarried, divorced, separated, or widowed.

[9] Christians constitutes 87.93% of Nagaland population; https://www.census2011.co.in/data/religion/state/13-nagaland.html. Accessed 3 June 2023.

[10] Sharon (2007). Suggests how work is categorized into that which is considered dignified and that which is considered undignified and within the latter category, is also a sub-category of dirty work. Money earned from work considered 'dirty' is referred to as 'dirty money'.

[11] A qualitative approach and an individual case study method were adopted for data collection. The interviews were stretched over an extended time and semi-structured and open-ended questions provided a greater interactive space for the respondents to put forward their opinions. The objective of the study was to gain an insight from the stories narrated by the women. Open-ended questions were used during the interviews, to allow the women adequate space to speak their mind without any restraint that a structured interview may have presented. Nonverbal and emotional interchanges were noted, and a continuous exchange of multi-layered messages was therefore discernible. The chapter is carved out of primary data the secondary data on Naga society pre and post-prohibition. Secondary data used includes books, articles, record books, newspapers, pamphlets, and archive records.

the marginalized[12] women who sell liquor as a means of livelihood and are stigmatized by society. Empirical insights gained from first hand narratives by women liquor traders provide valuable insights into their life and their everyday struggles and negotiations with violence. The analysis presented in this chapter reorients the problem of gendered violence in relation to labour vis-a-vis law, social norms, and institutions, and is confined to understanding and exploring the nature and context of violence suffered by women liquor traders against the backdrop of the historical context of liquor consumption in Naga society, its subsequent prohibition[13] and most critically, its interaction with the *advent of Christianity in Nagaland.* The intimate and enclosed spaces from where women traders conduct their illegal liquor business remains the focus of this chapter. This has been examined under two broad categories—the first examines violence by intimate partners, customers, excise officers and other extortionists; the second is rooted in the idea of the *violence of exclusion* perpetrated by the Church in Nagaland, through its teachings on the *immorality* of liquor consumption that reinforces the vulnerable position of these women as *excluded* members of society.

10.2 *From Social to Immoral*—Nagas, Liquor, Christianity, and the Ban

> There are no smoky bars here where I can stroll in, order a shot of whisky and walk out like a brooding hero in an old Western. No, there are no smoky bars here, except for some scattered food joints we habitually label 'hotels', and, well... shady Zutho[14] shacks aren't meant for good girls now, are they?
>
> Emisenla Jamir[15]

Liquor has always played an important role in the socio-cultural life of the Naga people. It is integral to all rituals, ceremonies, festivals, marriages and death ceremonies. The consumption of Rice beer,[16] a fermented drink brewed and obtained from rice has always been a staple food. *Zutho* is the name given to Rice beer by *Angami Nagas* and has been in use for decades. The consumption of Rice beer is a practice among several tribal communities residing in North-Eastern India.[17] Rice beer has traditionally been preferred to tea. Though now tea has a strong presence in Naga society,[18] in the olden days when a guest arrived they would be served *Zutho*. While men and women both drink the Rice beer, consumption is largely concentrated among men. The popularity of Rice beer can also be discerned by the fact that it is consumed by both the young and the old. Interestingly, the ban on liquor in Nagaland is principally intended to stop the consumption of *Indian Made Foreign Liquor* (IMFL)[19] within the State and does not operate as an absolute ban on the sale or consumption of the local Rice beer which continues to be a popular beverage especially during the Hornbill Festival[20] in Kohima.

The NLTP Act is integrally connected to the conversion of Nagas into the Baptist denomination following the advent of Christianity as a religion and its impact in shaping Naga cultural identity. American Baptist missionaries arrived

[12] The women engaged in the illegal trade market are principally those who are at the margins because of poverty and lack of choice of alternate occupations, the involvement in this trade is at once the reason and the consequence of their involvement in such work.

[13] Imposed by the enactment of the NLTP Act.

[14] Zutho, an Angami term for local rice beer.

[15] Jamir (2018).

[16] Rice beer or *Zutho* has a fruity aroma and a sour taste, a whitish porridge like slurry consistency. It contains 5.0% (v/v) ethanol. *Zutho* in a stronger form is called *Okhe*. There are also other drinks such as *Ruhi* and *Dzutse* that are indigenously produced and consumed by the Nagas.

[17] Bendangnagshi (2004).

[18] Beer is Naga people's favorite drink. See: Elwin (1959).

[19] Indian-made foreign liquor (IMFL) is the official term used by governments, businesses and media in India to refer to all types of liquor manufactured in the country other than indigenous alcoholic beverages.

[20] https://www.hornbillfestival.com/about-hornbill-festival. Accessed 6 May 2023.

in the Naga Hills as early as the 1830s with their 'great civilizing mission' to tame and civilize the *hill people*. Their mission was incited by the constant raids at the colonial administered tea gardens by the people from the hills.[21] According to the missionaries, Nagas engaged in many 'wicked' practices, such as *drinking rice beer* and *having more than one wife*.[22] It is believed that their objective was not only to convert the Nagas to Christianity, but to completely *convert* their traditional way of life. Since Rice beer was used and consumed during Naga rituals and festivities, missionaries defined this as 'devil worship', advocating total abstinence from Rice beer, so the *Nagas could become true Christians*. They declared abstinence from Rice beer and from participation at all related festivals and rituals, a condition for baptism and for admission into the church.[23]

Tension between ethnic and Christian identities continues to this day, especially in relation to the open sale and consumption of Rice beer during the Hornbill festival in Nagaland. While Rice beer consumption during this festival is done with the consent of the state government, it has always drawn criticism from the church.[24] Athikho discusses that in the Naga cultural tradition, Rice beer was never treated as an intoxicating drink, but as one that provides energy and strength. A village elder, during the course of an informal conversation with the author, said that in the olden days Naga people would drink Rice beer in *exactly the same way as tea is consumed today, in the morning, in the evening while working in the fields, and sometimes at night after reaching home*. However, tea eventually replaced Rice beer in Naga society and the practice of drinking liquor has assumed a new meaning today, it is considered a symbol of modern lifestyle and is no longer attached to rituals, staple food or its medicinal properties. The nature of liquor consumption shifted further with the availability of IMFL which eventually led to alcohol consumption becoming a serious concern in Nagaland. The changing pattern of liquor consumption from Rice beer to IMFL is responsible for the enactment of the NLTP Act. The village elder ended the conversation with the lament that this has opened the way for liquor barons and bootleggers in the state.[25]

The experiences of colonial rule, Christianity as the dominant religion in the state and eventually the growth in the tourism industry in the state, have all contributed to introducing new forms of drinking patterns in Nagaland that had not existed previously. It is believed that the germination of the liquor business, from the earlier pattern of home produced Rice beer for personal and social consumption, also coincided with the Indian Army's entry and continued presence in Nagaland. The army introduced IMFL in the state that saw a steady rise in the consumption of liquor. Men in the village exchanged firewood, rice, and other raw materials with the army in exchange for liquor at the army camps, and sometimes, the military personnel would distribute free rum to the villagers.[26] It is believed that this is how the Naga people were introduced to IMFL. In any event, the church's disapproval of the traditional consumption of Rice beer meant that the social life of the Nagas changed drastically, which ultimately transformed their traditional way of life, institutions and practices.[27] Nagaland today is a Christian majority state with Baptist being

[21] Mepfhü-O (2016).

[22] *Ibid.*

[23] The first conversions are believed to have taken place in the latter part in the nineteenth century.

[24] Keditsu states how there is tension between ethnic and Christian identity in the context of the Hornbill festival in Nagaland. Such tension is particularly noted due to the open sale and consumption of rice beer. It is done so with the consent of the government however this had drawn criticism Keditsu (2014).

[25] Bootlegging is the illegal business of smuggling alcoholic beverages where such transportation is forbidden by law. Smuggling usually takes place to circumvent taxation or to prohibit laws within a particular jurisdiction.

[26] *Supra n. 19.*

[27] *Ibid.*

the predominant denomination. The Nagaland Baptist Church Council (NBCC) office is based in Kohima.

There are divergent opinions on the phenomenon of Naga conversions to Christianity. While one view holds that Christianity has destroyed traditional Naga cultural life, the other position is that 'Naga Christianity' is in fact a nativized form of Christianity, in which the Nagas have found elements of their own culture that had affinity with Christian teachings, leading to an individualized interpretation and application of Christianity in the way it was adopted by them into their lives. Whichever version be embraced, one thing is certain that the Naga people's conversion to Christianity marks a distinct line in the progression of Naga life. The presence of liquor is argued to be one of the most contentious issues and the consumption of liquor is now fixed in popular imagery as a sign of *sinful character* and this is reproduced and reinforced on a daily basis by the Church through its teachings. Today Nagaland Christian identity has become synonymous with a *civilized identity*, thus the *sinful drunkard* is not only morally debauched but is also assumed to be *uneducated* and *uncivilized,* placing him at the bottom of the social hierarchy.[28]

The Nagaland Church Baptist Council (NBCC), churches belonging to other denominations, the *Naga Scholar Society*, and most critically, the *Naga Mother Association* (NMA) exerted tremendous pressure on the state government to enact a law banning the sale and consumption of alcohol in the state. The NLTP Act was a result of this concerted effort and commitment. The influence, advocacy and pressure on the state government to ban liquor, especially by the NMA is significant. The principal reasons for their campaign against liquor was its adverse effect on the health and well-being of their own families. Deka's[29] analysis of women's involvement in socio-political issues in northeast India focuses on two prominent women's groups in Manipur and Nagaland. The *Meira Paibis* (the torch bearer) has a legacy of protest against the armed forces, the insurgency, and also, the anti-liquor campaigns in Manipur. In Nagaland, the NMA had performed the role of peacemakers during times of conflict. This is a voluntary organization open for membership to all adult Naga women. Their campaign against alcohol abuse, drug addiction and spread of HIV-AIDS was fuelled by their personal sufferings as mothers. They had experienced first-hand the damage that alcoholism and drug addiction could do to the individual, the family and society. Their convictions were therefore based on personal sufferings. The NLTP Act must be appreciated in light of the circumstances prevailing in society at the time of its enactment. The leadership provided by the NMA and the NBCC were significant in the Nagaland state government's decision to enact a law to control and address what was perceived by Naga society as a serious social crisis at that time.

10.3 *Violent Spaces*—Women in Illegal Liquor Trade in Kohima

The capital city of Kohima was founded in 1878 when the British Empire established its headquarters in the Naga Hills. Despite the NLTP Act, liquor shops are found in plenty in all districts of Kohima. Most of these operate as *modu ghors*[30] as they are locally called, they are located in residential colonies or along the roadside close to residential colonies. Also, local *paan shops*[31] conceal and sell liquor. These *modu ghors* and *paan shops* are typically run

[28] *Ibid.*

[29] Deka (2016).

[30] *Modu ghors* are the local drinking houses in Kohima, Nagaland.

[31] Paan shops are usually small in size shops that sell leaves of the betel plant wrapped around tobacco, fruits etc. and chewed especially because they have a pleasant effect like a drug. They also sell confectionery, biscuits, shampoo sachets, chips, noodles, and anything that is an impulse purchase.

by Naga women.[32] While a small number of women engaged in the illegal liquor trade are married, most are single mothers and the sole earning member of their family. The legal prohibition under the NLTP Act and the associated illegality does not operate in isolation. The church's disapproval of the sale and consumption of liquor permeates all social relationships in Nagaland. Christian religious moralities that provided impetus to the legal prohibition, direct and nourish the social perception of the women liquor traders as *immoral*. This social perception condones the harassment and violence inflicted on them and justifies their social exclusion from mainstream Naga society. While the NLTP Act makes the sale of liquor illegal, government agencies regularly collect 'illegal' taxes from the liquor sellers. The NLTP Act has articulated the duty of the authorities who oversee and report on any illicit activities related to the trading of liquor within the region, under the *Nagaland Excise Act, 1967*.[33] It is therefore ironic that while liquor is banned under the NLTP Act, excise officers from the state department collect unauthorized taxes from women liquor traders, effectively legalizing their businesses and allowing them to continue their operations. This paradoxical site is described well by a woman in the liquor trade:

> It's not an easy job, but nothing ever is. I worry about my shop getting raided and to have to pay taxes to underground groups, the police and the excise team. If alcohol wasn't banned in our State, things might have been different. But people don't seem to care. Those who want to drink will drink, those who want to sell will sell, and those who want to tax people will do so.—Keneinuo (30)

Women engaged in the illegal liquor trade face harassment and violence from several quarters. Several women alluded to violence from intimate partners. Though the dynamics of violence from intimate partners exhibit patterns similar to most atypical domestic violence situations, with the objective to understand the specific situation of women liquor traders, their response to questions such as: do the men work? What are the sources of altercations? Is the violence by intimate partners connected in any way to the illegal liquor trade followed by the women? becomes significant. The responses to these questions indicated that the inherent perception of '*immorality*' associated with the trade engaged in by the women, deeply impacted their personal life. Physical violence, emotional abuse, verbal threats, and controlling behaviour by the husband or live-in partner were reported by several women. Factors that contributed to, and impacted interpersonal dynamics and the associated violence included deeply ingrained patriarchal gendered norms, economic stress, alcohol abuse and the stigma associated with the illegal liquor trade, that predisposed the women liquor traders to a higher risk of intimate partner violence.

The second and the most critical form of violence suffered by women liquor traders is associated with the constant presence of customs and excise officers, the police and underground power groups within their work spaces, in the form of regular threats and extortions. Narratives by women traders recorded mental harassment, insults, demeaning comments and belittlement by these men, while their principal goal remains extortion of money. Geographically, the violence is located in the domestic or the private business space. The third category of violence suffered by women liquor traders is inflicted by their customers who exhibit aggressive behaviour and engage in altercations with the women liquor traders. Disputes regularly arise over the prices of liquor,

[32] The author travelled to several locations in Kohima town with a friend and a resident of Kohima as a local guide to help in identifying locations from where women traders conduct their biasness. While some were located in urban areas, the rest were in suburbs. The illegal liquor business operates from their home for some owing to financial constraints in setting up shop outside their home. Some establishments masquerade as a paan/grocery store on the roadside or inside residential colonies.

[33] *The Nagaland Liquor Total Prohibition Act*, 1989 Chapter 3 no 32. Investment of Powers of Officer-in-charge of Police Station: The State Government may invest any officer of the Excise Department not below the rank of Inspector with the Powers of an Officer-in-Charge of a Police Station for the investigation of offences under this Act.

or as a result of alcohol-fuelled anger. This operates within the dynamics of the latent *illegality* and *immorality* associated with the liquor trade and the complete absence of protections under a regulatory framework for their business and the associated vulnerability to exploitation and violence. Women liquor traders view this constant presence of violence in their work lives as a 'given' in their trade, they are often oblivious and sometimes carelessly unmindful of the trauma suffered by them from all three quarters. Further, it is worth noting that the closed, confined and secret nature of their *place of business* also renders these drinking spaces unsafe. 'Drinking spaces' refers to the physical locations from where the women liquor traders engage in selling and serving alcohol to their customers.[34] These drinking spaces are rife with a constant stream of derogatory remarks and hostile behaviour that is deeply gendered in nature. The latent hostility in the drinking spaces is rooted in deep-seated cultural norms and biases that stigmatize women associated with the liquor trade.

During business hours, women face disgruntled customers on a daily basis. Within these private spaces where liquor is surreptitiously sold and served there is a general atmosphere of indiscipline. Several customers resort to physical assault as a way of expressing their dissatisfaction with the services, or simply to assert their authority over them. The women recount being physically and emotionally traumatized in these situations. The fear and insecurity experienced by them within their own establishment is fuelled by the illegalization of their businesses and the resultant lack of recourse to legal mechanisms to ensure the safety of those engaged in this work. Above all, patriarchal configurations comprising power dynamics, societal norms, unequal gender relations render these spaces 'unsafe' for women liquor traders. Violence from all the three principal groups of perpetrators categorized in this section, ranges from direct physical assault, sexual harassment to subtle forms of manipulation, emotional abuse and extortion in the form of bribes and taxes. The normalization of this violence breeds a culture of silence and enables its perpetuation. Fear of losing their business, societal stigma, and lack of social and institutional support prevents women from reporting incidents of harassment and violence or seeking help.

10.4 *Everyday Negotiations with Violence*—Empirical Insights

This section presents women liquor traders' experiences, challenges, and perspectives on the nature of trade they engage in and its associated vulnerabilities, including harassment and violence—as narrated by them to the author.[35] Their personal narratives provide valuable insights into the several difficulties they face, including raids, heavy taxation, credit issues, societal stigma, disruptive customer behaviour, and intimate partner violence.

> People from different groups will come for checking and collecting taxes, some will be in uniforms, and the very same men will come again to buy alcohol. This time without their uniforms. A lot of these men create commotion in my shop, they get drunk right here in my shop when they come to purchase alcohol and get into fights. If I refuse to give them alcohol on credit, they start quarrelling and hurling insults at me. This is not an easy business to be in, and I have considered leaving it, but I can't just leave the business because of the difficulties and challenges it poses, the discomfort I have to endure, the constant threat of violence. I must think about so many things before I can leave......
>
> —Asie-ü (40)

The hypocrisy of demanding obedience to the law, while at the same time breaking the law by exploiting persons engaged in illegal trade of

[34] These spaces can vary from small roadside stalls to more established shops or establishments.

[35] For this research, due to the sensitivity of the issue and the request of a few participants desiring anonymity, all respondents have been given pseudonyms names. The statements below are given by Asie-ü, (40) Asenuo, (45) and Tunuo (47), Eli (37), Keneinuo (30), Dziese (48) who have been in this business for a long time and share similar experiences.

liquor has become normalized in Naga society. The system of harassment and extortion following the prohibition, especially directed at women liquor traders ensures that the law serves and benefits these men. It is pertinent to note, that if liquor trade was simply regulated and not prohibited by the law, valid licences could be issued for the business and only the state excise officials would be able to tax license holders and the revenue generated through taxes would contribute to state funds. The present situation, on the other hand, has opened the doors to multiple levels of exploitation by several actors in society. The illegality associated with the trade has submerged women traders into *invisible spaces* potent with violence and harassment at every level.

The sun sets early in Kohima. When I met Asenuo (45) at 5.30 pm, it was already dark outside and her shop had eight or nine male customers standing around placing orders for their drinks. Asenuo escorted me to the back of her shop that was separated from the front by a floor to ceiling shelf. There was another girl in the shop to attend to the customers, so Asenuo was able to sit with me for the interview without much distraction. She apologized that this was a busy time of the day for her and that she will not be able to spare much time for the interview. I told her it was completely fine and thanked her for taking the time to speak with me. While we were still exchanging these pleasantries, a man walked in. He was visibility drunk, he came and sat next to Asenuo and started talking to her, asking who I was and why I was there. My guide[36] explained the purpose of my visit to him and he soon got up and left without another word. Asenuo was however, uncomfortable with this intrusion in the space she considered private and separate from the shop. She offered the following explanation:

> Men like him always come to the shop and because they are regular customers, they feel they can come inside without permission and sit around treating my shop like it is their home. But even if I ask them to leave or check their behaviour in anyway, they will not listen to me, they will forget it by tomorrow. And there is no use arguing with drunks; they always think they are right.

This account of unruly customers is standard behaviour in liquor shops, where under the influence of alcohol or otherwise, customers who are regulars intrude on the women shop owner's personal space and display a sense of entitlement in the way they conduct themselves and occupy these private spaces. The back of the shop where we were seated was where most of the liquor was stored, Asenuo did not ordinarily allow customers here, this space was used by her as her office space. The discomfort experienced by Asenuo at this intrusion highlights the complete lack of respect and consideration for her boundaries. Customers regularly pass demeaning comments and make unwelcome gestures, often these acts of verbal abuse are disguised as harmless jokes or casual remarks, making it difficult for the women to articulate and respond to these as violence.

Tunuo (45) is the only woman trader I met during the course of field research who was engaged in the wholesaler business of liquor. I was informed by my guide that she is one of the largest wholesalers in Kohima. We sat in her kitchen. The kitchen door was guarded by a large hound dog, she told me that his presence 'scares away rude customers'. Through the course of the interview, customers kept coming into the kitchen, asking for whiskey and rum, which she did not have in stock. Sounding exasperated she offered:

> This is not a decorated profession, society will always point fingers and people will always talk ill about us, but this comes with the business. To be honest, I think this is one of the most stressful jobs. As a wholesaler, I deal with a lot of pressure, because I always have a large amount of alcohol inventory in my shop. I am constantly worried and anxious. From the moment the trucks are on their way to my shop, until the last bottle is sold. On one occasion, the army caught one of my trucks

[36] My guide was also my friend who is a resident of Kohima. He knew of a number of women traders personally. He had grown up with several of them. This eased the process of identifying and tracking down women traders for the interviews.

> and destroyed all the bottles, which was a huge loss for me. We don't have proper lunch timings and are always either selling alcohol or waiting for more inventory to arrive. I only get a few hours of sleep every day because I'm constantly afraid that something might go wrong, anything can happen to my business.

In Tunuo's case, the ordinary stress of the trade is compounded by the unpredictability and insecurity inherent in the wholesale business. Women who were in the liquor trade before the legal prohibition was enforced have continued to sell liquor post the enactment of NLTP Act. Evidently, the prohibition has simply multiplied the daily challenges and anxieties faced by them, from the secrecy involved in managing large quantities of alcohol to encountering unexpected losses, the law has disrupted their personal lives.

> Customers occasionally argue amongst themselves, and yes, sometimes they do use some harsh words that affect my feelings. From time to time, police and other authorities visit my shop to check. If I am caught selling illegal goods, they confiscate them. Additionally, I may be required to pay a fine, and could even be taken into custody temporarily, but after paying the designated amount, we are typically released.
> As someone who's in this business, my husband tends to drink excessively and unfortunately, I sometimes end up being physically abused by him as a result of his alcoholism. This usually happens when I express my frustration about his drinking or gambling too much. It's a tough situation to be in, and I often find myself questioning why I'm doing this. However, at the end of the day, I realize that if I don't continue working, who will take care of my family? Occasionally, I experience the strain of all this, especially when I am left with bruises from the physical beating and abuse from my husband. It can be quite distressing, and I often find myself crying when this happens. It's a scary experience, but my husband usually apologizes afterward. Since I'm the primary provider for our household, I have to push through the stress and fear that I feel and tend to my business responsibilities.
>
> —Eli (37)

Encounters with customers who are verbally abusive, hurl insults and derogatory comments at the women is a common thread in all women liquor traders' lives. Eli also shares with us her struggle with intimate partner violence. This points to the critical intersections of substance abuse, domestic violence, and economic empowerment that impacts women traders' experiences. Eli's determination to provide for her family, despite these challenges, emphasizes the multifaceted nature of women's experiences with violence and their resilience in navigating complex circumstances. Eli's account also demonstrates the cycle of abuse common in intimate relationships, where violent conduct by the abusive partner is followed up with reconciliatory behaviour by the abuser, only to find itself repeating.[37] In Eli's case, the patriarchal attitude of the husband collides with economic empowerment of the wife. There is a sense of pride and perhaps the attitude of forgiveness that comes not only from internalized patriarchal attitudes but also from the realization that she holds the economic power in the relationship. Yet, her attitude of forgiveness is also underlined by normalization of male violence under the influence of alcohol, which she encounters both in her business space and at home.

> Underground groups come and ask for taxes and I have to give it to them immediately or else they threaten me and say, "you are worth one capsule" and who isn't scared of bullets? What will happen to my children if I die? So, I take loans from people, usually, I don't have enough money to pay taxes. I have to think about my children who are studying outside Kohima and send them money for their fees and expenses. If I don't, who knows what would happen to them? All of these thoughts kept going inside me.—Dziese (48)

Dziese shared during the interview the starkness of the threats that women liquor traders receive from extortionists. "*You are worth one capsule*", there is fear in her voice when she speaks about the blackmail and death threats she has received from underground groups who visit her regularly to extract sums, she is not left with any option but to pay them. She is forced to borrow from money lenders and relatives, these loans add to her financial anxieties. Threats on

[37] The cycle of abuse is a social cycle theory developed in 1979 by Lenore E. Walker to explain patterns of behaviour in an abusive relationship.

non-payment of illegal taxes are direct. Dziese has sent her children out of Kohima not just for a good education, but also to protect them from exposure to violence and threat of violence that remains all pervasive in her life. She fears for her life and is forced to borrow money to pay the excise officers and non-state actors who demand payments by way of illegal taxes. As a mother, she must do as told, else she worries that if something was to happen to her, her children will have no one to care for them. Her story exposes the deep sense of vulnerability and paucity of options available to women liquor traders. Threat of violence and the fear and anxiety it generates undermines her well-being, yet she persists out of economic necessity, and in hope for a better future for her children. Her narrative exposes the violence perpetrated by state and non- state actors.

Certain types of labour are considered to be outside the moral purview of the state. Does illegal labour formulate within the state's notion of *unauthorized labour*? According to the Ministry of Labour & Employment, Government of India, the term *unorganized worker* has been defined under the *Unorganized Workers' Social Security Act, 2008*[38] as a home-based worker, self-employed worker or a wage worker in the unorganized sector and includes a worker in the organized sector who is not covered by any of the Acts mentioned in Schedule-II of Act. The unorganized labour of women traders in illegal liquor trade represents a form of *unorganized work* where women lack formal organization or representation. They face various challenges due to their employment status and the nature of their work. Unorganized labour often lacks collective bargaining power, making it difficult for women to negotiate for regular wages, benefits, or improved working conditions. In the absence of formal organization or union to represent them, they are vulnerable to exploitation. This translates to instability and economic insecurity. Additionally, benefits such as maternity leave, flexible work arrangements or protection against discrimination, hostile work environment, sexual harassment and violence are not available to them. As single mothers they juggle multiple responsibilities including childcare, household tasks with the tiresome risky work they are engaged in.

10.5 *The Violence of Social Exclusion*—Immorality, Illegality, Religion, and Gender

> Society is hard on us, especially the women who are in this business. I know that a lot of people think ill of me, and do not want to be in my company. We are separated from the society, they might not say it but we know how it is, that's why I live here in the outskirts. It used to bother me a lot, how my children would be treated by others, but it doesn't anymore because why should I be ashamed of what I do for a living?
>
> - Ale

Women traders shared feeling neglected and excluded from mainstream Naga society. Most women in the liquor trade are single mothers; widows, unmarried, divorcees or separated. They are also the sole earners in their family. Their professional engagement in the liquor trade adversely affects their social status. Women traders face prejudice, discrimination, marginalization and social exclusion. *Social Exclusion* refers to the process through which individuals and groups are prevented from becoming a part of the processes in the society, whether social, economic or political. Exclusion

[38] The term unorganized worker has been defined under the Unorganized Workers' Social Security Act, 2008, as a home-based worker, self-employed worker or a wage worker in the unorganized sector and includes a worker in the organized sector who is not covered by any of the Acts mentioned in Schedule-II of Act i.e. the Employee's Compensation Act, 1923 (3 of 1923), the Industrial Disputes Act, 1947 (14 of 1947), the Employees' State Insurance Act, 1948 (34 of 1948), the Employees Provident Funds and Miscellaneous Provision Act, 1952 (19 of 1952), the Maternity Benefit Act, 1961 (53 of 1961) and the Payment of Gratuity Act, 1972 (39 of 1972). https://labour.gov.in/unorganized-workers#:~:text=The%20term%20unorganized%20worker%20has,II%20of%20Act%20i.e.%20the. Accessed 11 June 2023.

is a social process which involves the *denial of fair and equal opportunities to certain social groups in multiple spheres in society, resulting in the inability of individuals from excluded groups to participate in the basic political, economic and social functioning of the society*.[39] The stigma faced by women liquor traders forces them to live outside the main towns or villages that they belong to,[40] this further reinforces their exclusion and sense of isolation from mainstream society and its institutions.

> For me I don't really think of society as treating me differently just because I joined the business. But I know how I am seen and how I am treated by some people. They see us as bad and immoral. I can tell you from the way some customers also treat us. They disrespect us and treat us badly because that's what they think of us. But I also have to remember that I am earning my livelihood through this, I am not doing it through immoral means so even I fight back.
>
> —Asenuo

Social exclusion of the women liquor traders has its roots in Christianity and its associated ideas of *illegality* and *immorality*. The church is principally responsible for the stigmatization that results in their isolation and exclusion. This in turn forces them to exist on the fringes of society. The attitude of *moral superiority* and the association of *immorality* towards women liquor traders can be evidenced by the fact that workers from the church regularly visit the homes of women liquor traders and provide them counselling and offer prayers. The counselling is focused on advising and encouraging them to leave the liquor business. The open contempt and judgement, disguised as concern for the women and society's welfare is misplaced and hinges on the *suspect* morals of women traders. While women are encouraged to leave the liquor trade, the church is unable to provide them with alternatives that represent '*good work*'.

They are excluded from the church and their participation in any church-related activities is very limited. This stigma is carried over to the children of women liquor traders. They sense an isolation from their own communities, this direct and indirect exclusion by others in the community has its genesis in the perception created by the church and its teachings. Their engagement in a profession rendered illegal, principally at the behest of the church, impacts their sense of self and their social and individual identity; most critically, in the way they are viewed as *easily available* or as *dirty women*. The image associated with women liquor traders in Nagaland is one where they are projected as *immoral prostitutes*.[41] This severely impedes their ability to forge healthy, meaningful personal and social relationships.

> It is hard to make everyone happy and I know that this business makes a lot of people dislike me and what I do but if I had a choice to do something else for a living this wouldn't have even been my second choice. When I first started in the business I was very conscious about what people thought about me, I would always say I am doing some side business and I plan to leave the business soon, but now after all these years I no longer worry about what I do. I am not involved in any other side business nor do I plan to leave the business any time soon, this is how I earn my livelihood, and that is the truth. I know people say the money I earn is black money and the business I do is illegal and unclean but it's time the society also accepts that some people are dependent on this kind of business.
>
> —Nganuo

Samaddar reports that there are around 50,000 bootleggers[42] in Nagaland. This is a quarter of the state population. It is therefore surprising he notes, that bootleggers' lives are not spoken or written about, that the question of lack of choice

[39] Thorat and Newman (2012).

[40] Surveillance on liquor trade is also relatively stricter inside the cities and villages as compared to the areas outside, while stigma and social exclusion were cited as the reason by women traders interviewed, this could be an additional reason for their geographical location.

[41] That they engage in sex work, the use of the term prostitute is simply to highlight that they are seen as prostituting their body for money, thereby assigning an undignified existence.

[42] A person who makes, distributes, or sells goods illegally.

as the driving force behind the women's choice of trade has not been explored at all. The author also states that in the context of the liquor prohibition in Nagaland, women traders are looked upon as immoral. The women traders, referred to in his book as bootleggers, were seen as persons who were *sexually available*, there was a fear that women bootleggers were *moonlighting* as prostitutes. They were looked down upon as persons contaminating society and marked as *deviants*.[43]

Silver's theory on *social exclusion*[44] based on the *solidarity*, *specialization,* and *monopoly* paradigms provides a better understanding of the way women liquor traders' exclusion operates in Naga society. The paradigm on which Silver's *solidarity model* is based, views the existence of a *social bond* between groups of individuals and society as one constructed on moral and cultural values prevalent in society at that time. Thus, exclusion would indicate the rupture of the social bond or solidarity between individuals and society as a result of unfulfillment of the prevalent moral and cultural values or the inability to do so. Under the *specialization paradigm*, exclusion occurs as a consequence of specialization or social differentiation, essentially a separation of spheres based on the assumption that individuals differ, giving rise to specializations in social groups. *Monopoly*, the third paradigm, views exclusion as a result of the formation of *group monopoly* where exclusion arises from the interplay of class, status and political power. The *solidarity* and *monopoly paradigms* proposed by Silver, best explain the dynamics of exclusion of women liquor traders in Nagaland. Silver also posits that the paradigms explain exclusion as a social relationship between the 'included' and the 'excluded'. Women liquor traders in Nagaland face a kind of institutionalized or structural exclusion in the form of social distancing[45] where differentiation and isolation of the excluded group appears at once to be responsible for, and also the very cause of their inability to collectively bargain or demand their inclusion. In this sense, asks Silver, can social exclusion also be a *condition*? If one was to answer in the affirmative, this condition could well be attributable to patriarchal manifestations of masculine cultures[46] where the presence of women in masculine spaces is seen as an aberration and sometimes classified as deviant behaviour. The exclusion of women traders from Naga society does not directly point to the illegality of the sale and consumption of liquor as the reason for their segregation, associated with immorality. It appears to operate more as a form of *gendered segregation* associated with *immorality*. The immorality while immediately relatable to the illegality of the liquor trade after the enactment of the NLTP Act, appears to align more with control on women's sexuality and intimate relationships. Additionally, the consumption of liquor according to Christian sensibilities in Nagaland as an immoral and forbidden practice reinforces the perceived spaces of *illegality* that are then complicated with the notion of *immorality*.

Does social exclusion qualify as a form of violence? In establishing the linkages between the two, most studies focus on the co-existence of social exclusion and violence within the same space and time, more specifically, in situations of systemic and structural violence. Where one community suffers violence and exclusion at the hands of the powerful or dominant group, social exclusion and inequalities or unequal access to socio-economic resources between two groups in society can lead to group mobilization that might eventually lead to violence.[47] This type of violence would be understood as a form of political violence. Social exclusion has

[43] Samaddar (2009). Samaddar's field work is based in Nagaland, the book does not, however, contain the opinions of the bootleggers themselves.

[44] Silver (1994).

[45] *Ibid* at 15.

[46] Murphy (1994).

[47] Treistam (2021).

also been studied as a cause and justification for violence.[48] The nature of social exclusion of women liquor traders in Kohima is directly linked to their marginalization as a group. This exclusion is deliberate, it prevents them from participating in the social life of the community. Deliberate isolation of a group either by excluding them or by directly or indirectly shunning them clearly qualifies as covert bullying. The constant interference from the church in their attempt to coerce women traders to give up their trade qualifies as bullying, or even blackmail since the underlying message from the church is - what you do is immoral and if you continue, you will be excluded and remain isolated from the 'good' society, thereby creating barriers that impede social inclusion and participation. This qualifies as a form of structural violence defined by Galtung[49]. When people from an excluded group suffer, for example, from preventable diseases or if they are denied education, employment; *even when no physical harm is caused, a kind of violence is committed*, asserts Galtung. Social exclusion in the form practised against Naga women liquor traders thus unambiguously qualifies as structural violence.

10.6 Conclusion

The experiences of women traders within the existing structure of illegal liquor trade in Nagaland undermine the core principles that define a *good society*[50]—equality, fairness, and justice. In an *ideal* society, women should have equal opportunities to engage in any field of work, including the liquor business. By embracing gender equality and breaking down societal biases, a *good society* fosters an environment where anyone can thrive and contribute to the betterment of the community as a whole. Women traders are not against the greater good of society, or in opposition of any religious principles, their engagement in the liquor trade is driven simply out of economic necessity. The Supreme Court of India has consistently read the right to work and livelihood as a fundamental right and an integral part of the Right to Life under Article 21 of the Constitution of India.[51] Economic necessity explains women liquor traders' continued presence in this business, despite the violence that surrounds them. While some are able to send their children to school and college and built houses, others continue to struggle to support and meet the basic needs of their families. There is thus, the possibility of a better life, but not the guarantee of one. The risk and harassment endured is far greater than the profits, this further underlines the necessity element integral to their choice of trade.

> I've been in this business my whole life. I know there are people who talk badly about us, since my mother was also an alcohol seller and now I am in the same business, and why won't they talk bad about us? But since my children are getting educated, they also say oh! now her children are educated, some will say, just because someone sells liquor we can't mistreat them.—Abinuo

Abinuo, a second-generation woman liquor trader speaks about a transformation in social image of a 'mother' whose children are educated. Irrespective, the fact of the matter is that the type of work or trade, the gender of the person engaged, the mode of spending their earnings; is scrutinized and judged. Her story exudes a sense of pride and self-respect, this is something that they do not receive from society and have to engineer for themselves.

Violence in the form of mental harassment, physical altercations and threats from partners, customers, and authorities alike, undermine the safety and well-being of women liquor traders in Nagaland. The NLTP Act is sought to be implemented through extortion and exploitation of women liquor traders. It has been over three decades since the NLTP Act came into force in the State of Nagaland, yet liquor can be

48 *Ibid* at 6.

49 Galtung (1969).

50 See, Etzioni (2002).

51 Olga Tellis & Ors vs Bombay Municipal Corporation & Ors. Etc, AIR 1986 SC 180; 1985 SCR Supl. (2) 51.

found in shops, hotels, and restaurants. There are vendors renting rooms out of which they sell liquor. During the process of fieldwork, the author encountered several new restaurants, bars and hotels that serve alcohol openly. These are places owned by young entrepreneurs, some by reputed politicians and some even by government officers. While such establishments are seen as elite places frequented by the upper class, these spaces rarely invite the scrutiny of the church, the excise officers or civil society in general. It almost appears as if these establishments do not fall under the purview of the NLPT Act, to be deemed illegal or immoral. Does the law intend to demonize and maintain control and surveillance only over women engaged in the liquor trade to intimidate, harass, and draw illegal taxes from them? Does gender displace the perception of good, bad, and immoral? Does the refusal to perform normative gender roles and duties invite allegations of immorality?

References

Bendangnagshi (2004) History of Christianity in Nagaland. Shalen Ministry Publication, Natural Publication Press, Bangkok, pp 1987–1972

Deka K (2016) Prohibitionist protest by women in India's Northeast. Sage Publication, India

Elwin V (1959) The hill people of North-East India. Oxford University Press, Bungay, p. 20

Etzioni A (2002) The good society. Seattle J Soc Justice 1(1):83–96. https://digitalcommons.law.seattleu.edu/sjsj/vol1/iss1/7

Galtung J (1969) Violence, peace, and peace research. J Peace Res 6(3):167–191

Jamir E (2018) Loneliness is an orange. Barkweaver, Nagaland

Keditsu T (2014) Prohibition and Naga cultural identity: cultural politics of hornbill festivals of Nagaland. J Remerg Res Media Cult Stud 2(2):22–34

Mepfhü-o K (2016) Conversion: perception of the Christian 'self' and the 'other'. Asian Ethnicity 17(3):370–383

Murphy M (1994) Bootlegging mothers and drinking daughters: gender and prohibition in butte, Montana. Am Quart 46(2):174–191

Olga Tellis & Ors vs Bombay Municipal Corporation & Ors. Etc, AIR 1986 SC 180; 1985 SCR Supl (2):51

Phillips K (2004) The Indian-Naga conflict: a long-standing war with few prospects of imminent solution. CHRI News. https://www.humanrightsinitiative.org/publications/nl/articles/india/summer2004.pdf

Samaddar R (2009) State of justice in India: issues of social justice. Sage Pub, India

Sharon BC (2007) Dimensions of dignity at work. Burlington, USA

Silver H (1994) Social exclusion and social solidarity: three paradigms. Int Labour Rev 133/5–6

The Nagaland Liquor Total Prohibition Act, 1989 Chapter 3 no 32

The Nagaland Liquor Total Prohibition Act, 1989 (The Nagaland Act No. 4 of 1990). https://www.indiacode.nic.in/bitstream/123456789/11850/1/the_nagaland_liquor_total_prohibition_act_1989.pdf

Thorat S, Newman KS (eds) (2012) Blocked by caste: economic discrimination in modern India. Oxford India Pub, India

Treistam J (2021) Social exclusion and political violence: multilevel analysis of the justification of terrorism. Stud Confl Terror. https://doi.org/10.1080/1057610X.2021.2007244

Unorganized Workers' Social Security Act, 2008. https://labour.gov.in/unorganized-workers#:~:text=The%20term%20unorganized%20worker%20has,II%20of%20Act%20i.e.%20the

Index

P. M. Anurag and S. Dwivedy (eds.), *Violence in Intimate Spaces*, Sustainable Development Goals Series, https://doi.org/10.1007/978-981-97-2657-8

GPSR Compliance

The European Union's (EU) General Product Safety Regulation (GPSR) is a set of rules that requires consumer products to be safe and our obligations to ensure this.

If you have any concerns about our products, you can contact us on ProductSafety@springernature.com

In case Publisher is established outside the EU, the EU authorized representative is:

Springer Nature Customer Service Center GmbH
Europaplatz 3
69115 Heidelberg, Germany

Batch number: 10731385

Printed by Printforce, the Netherlands